COLLEEN WOLSTENHOLME

COLLEEN WOLSTENHOLME

Hyperobjectivity

Edited by RAY CRONIN

Essays by
RAY CRONIN and LAURA J. RITCHIE

Goose Lane Editions | Beaverbrook Art Gallery | Art Gallery of Nova Scotia

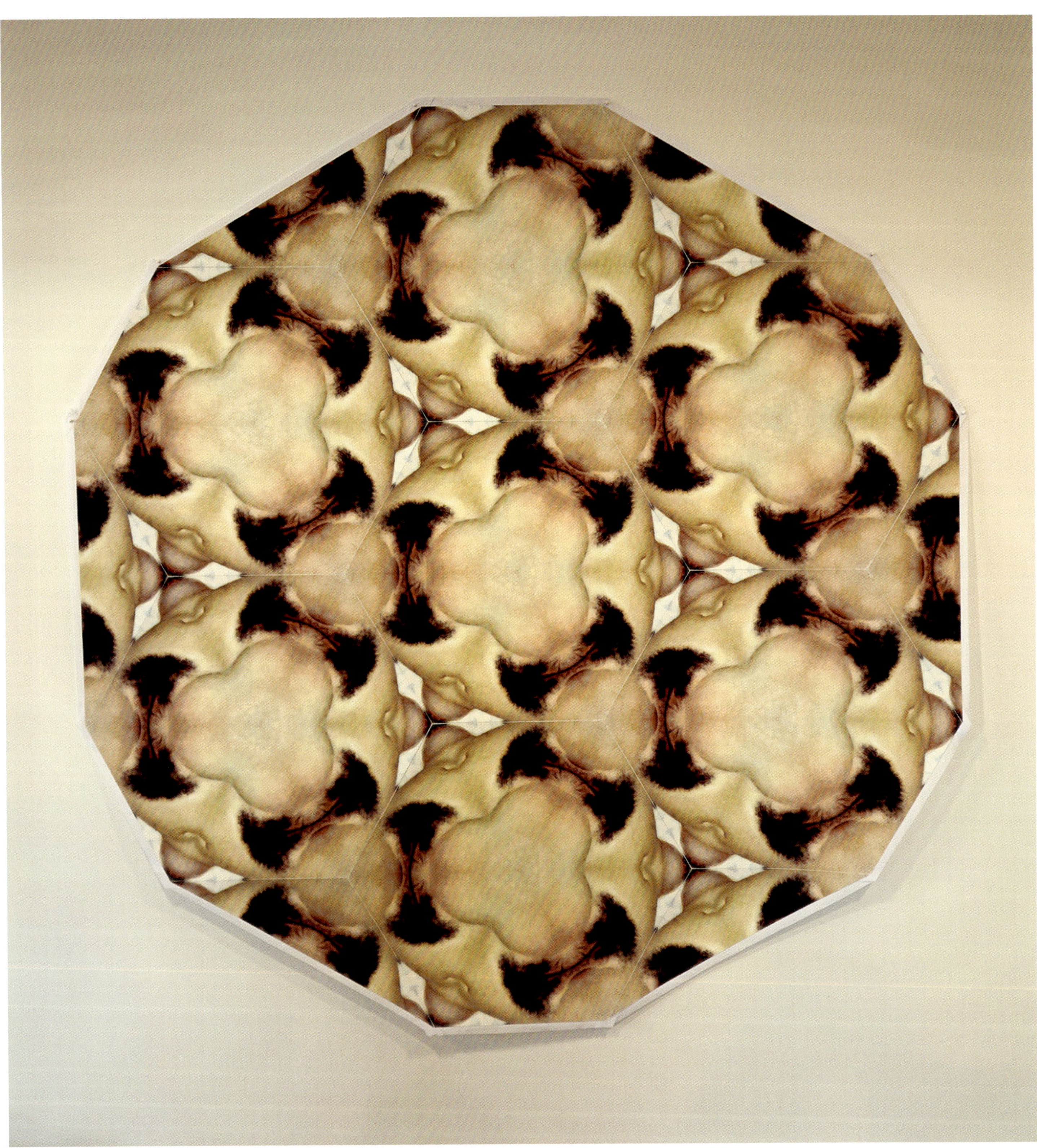

Original, 2005–06

Contents

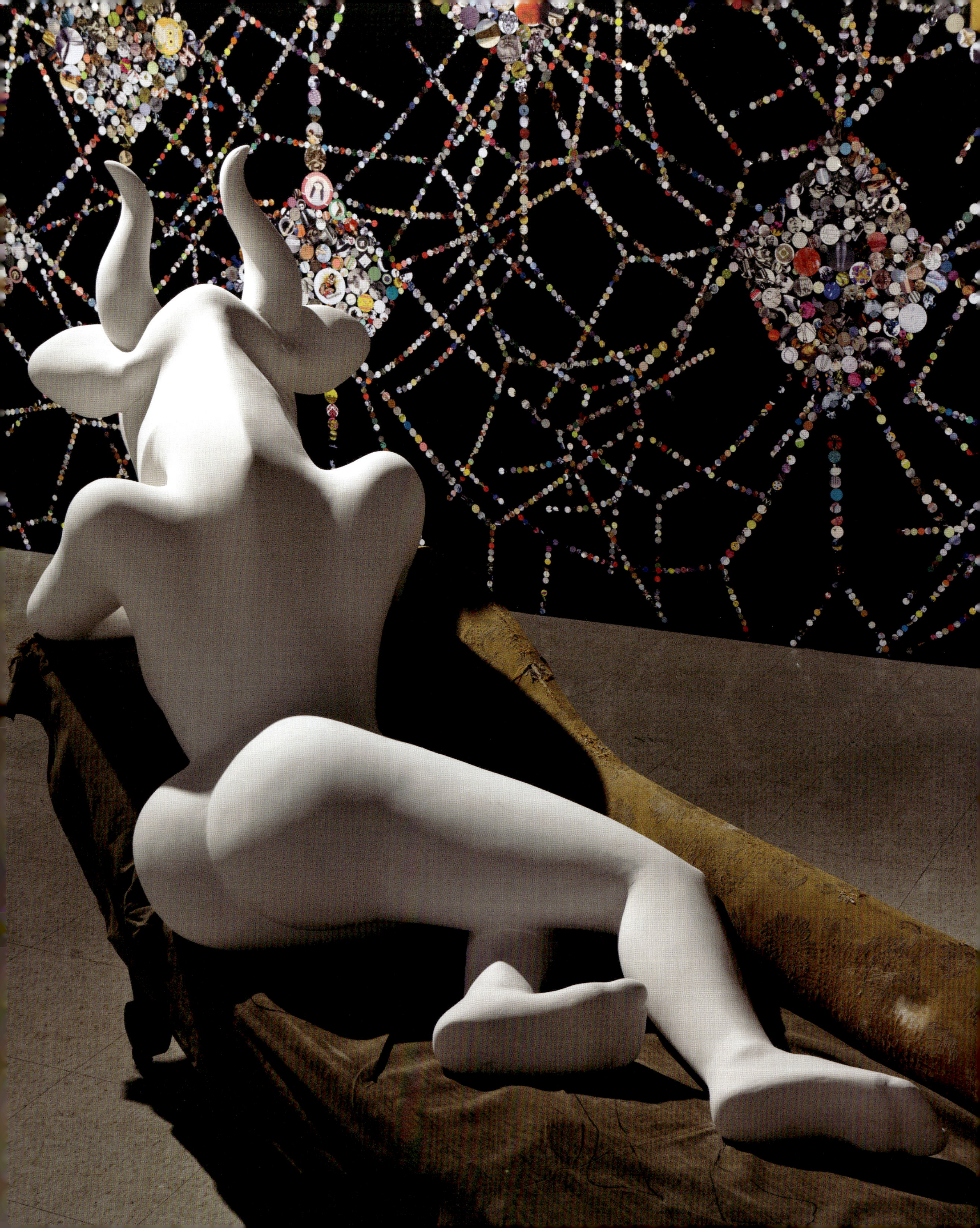

Foreword

Many who were paying attention to Canadian art in the 1990s will remember images of Colleen Wolstenholme's pill sculptures and jewellery. The work seemed to be everywhere: on the cover of *C Magazine* but also in the pages of *Psychology Today* and in *The Guardian*. Her work tapped into the zeitgeist, reaching beyond the borders of the art world.

Colleen Wolstenholme has lived across Canada and spent much time in New York; however, she remains an Atlantic Canadian artist, one whose career has been integral to the renaissance of contemporary art in this region since the 1990s. She was the Atlantic nominee for the inaugural Sobey Art Award organized by the Art Gallery of Nova Scotia (AGNS), and she represented Nova Scotia in a Marion McCain exhibition at the Beaverbrook Art Gallery. Wolstenholme's work has been collected by all three major Maritime art institutions – the Beaverbrook Art Gallery, the AGNS, and the Confederation Centre Art Gallery – where it is regularly on view in permanent collection exhibitions. She grew up in Nova Scotia and now lives in New Brunswick, so collaboration on this publication between the AGNS and the Beaverbrook is fitting.

Wolstenholme is an artist of national and international importance as well. Inclusion of her work in the public collections of the Montreal Museum of Fine Arts and the National Gallery of Canada attests to this. With the exhibition *Colleen Wolstenholme: Hyperobjectivity* and this accompanying book, it is our pleasure to present the full career of this important Canadian artist to audiences in Canada and beyond.

Exposé, 2010, with *Neuraesthezia*, 2011, as exhibited at Art Mûr, Montréal, in 2011

The AGNS and the Beaverbrook are lenders to the exhibition. We thank the other institutional lenders who have been integral to this project, with key loans provided by the National Gallery of Canada, the Confederation Centre Art Gallery, and the Cambridge Art Galleries. We would also like to thank the private lenders who have graciously made their work available for this project.

The team at Goose Lane Editions has once again produced a beautiful book. We thank the exhibition's curator, Ray Cronin, and art writer, Laura J. Ritchie, both of whom have contributed insightful essays to the publication.

We also wish to acknowledge the ongoing support of the institutional funders to our galleries: the Provinces of New Brunswick and Nova Scotia, the Cities of Fredericton and Halifax, and the Canada Council for the Arts. Thanks as well to our members, including our boards of directors, for their commitment to the Beaverbrook and the AGNS and the mission that this publication represents.

Finally, a heartfelt thank you to Colleen Wolstenholme, whose decades-long commitment to her practice has resulted in this remarkable exhibition and the publication that documents it. Without artists of such dedication and skill the world would be a poorer place.

BERNARD J. DOUCET
Executive Director
Beaverbrook Art Gallery

SARAH MOORE FILLMORE
Chief Executive Officer
Art Gallery of Nova Scotia

Valium, 1997

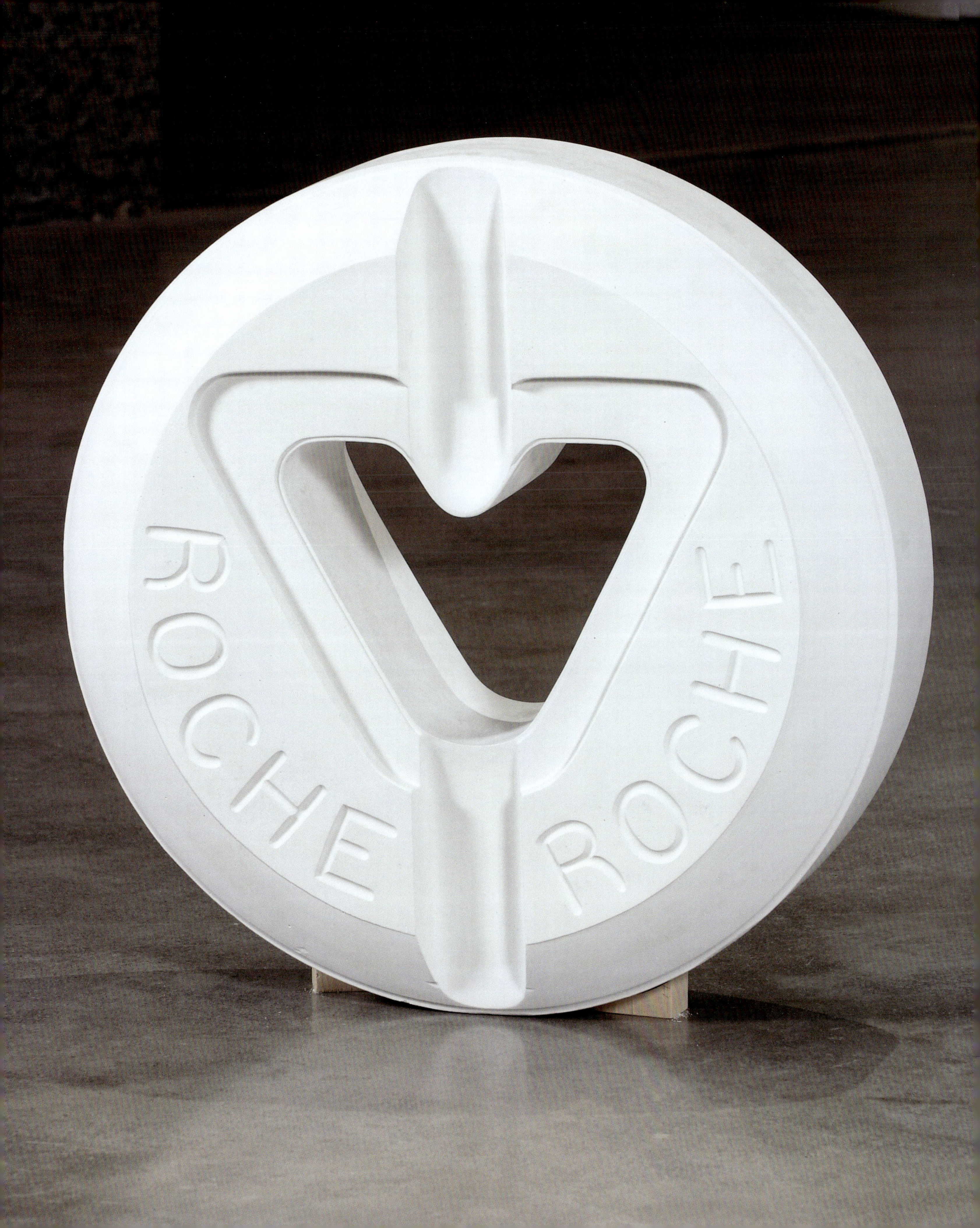
ROCHE
ROCHE

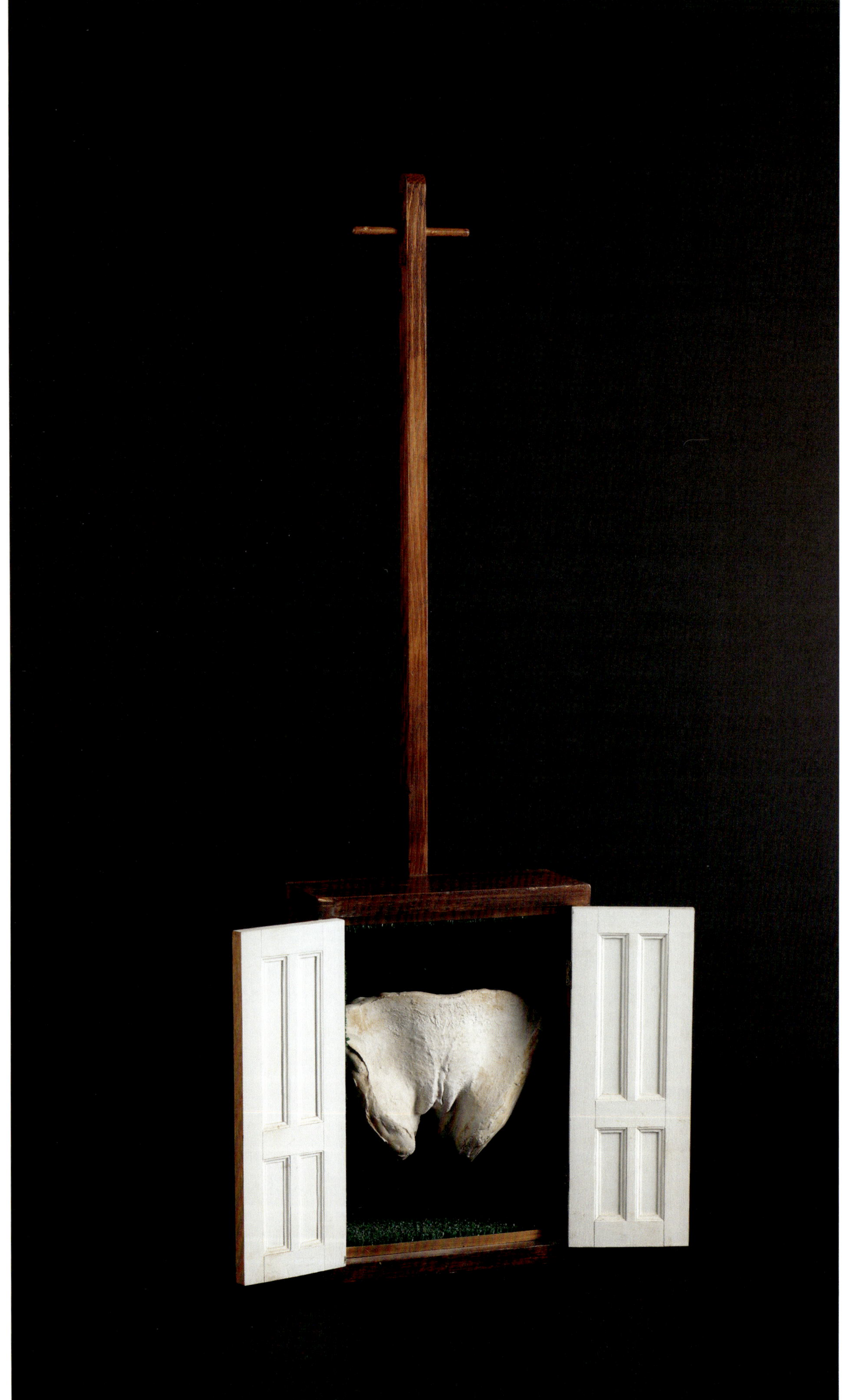

Hyperobjectivity

RAY CRONIN

For many artists, especially those who were trained in the intellectual hothouse of the Nova Scotia College of Art and Design, art is a way of thinking. Whatever expressive or poetic elements may survive in the artist's work, it is thought that is paramount. It comes as no surprise, then, that Colleen Wolstenholme makes thoughtful, powerful, subversive, and ultimately hopeful work. She makes us see more than we ever bargained for, and in so doing can inspire new and more active ways of looking – and thinking. Her work is cerebral and direct, esoteric and popular, easy to look at and hard to forget. As an artist who came into her own in the late 1980s and early 1990s, she is steeped in the postmodernism that marked this period in the art world, sharing a generation's distrust of systems, hierarchies, styles, genres, markets, and other illusions of control.

Being seen, heard, and understood amidst the biases and conventions of history are key goals of any feminist project, and feminists rightly insist on them. That insistence, in the arts as much as any other field, can be dismissed as strident, misread as special pleading, and actively fought and suppressed. Nonetheless, if history has taught us anything, it is that unless feminists insist, men do not listen (if they do even then). Firmness is as necessary as their feminism. Colleen Wolstenholme, like so many of her generation, reluctantly calls herself a feminist, but she knows that history depends on the tellers and that tales can be weapons.

Pud', 1992

In Linda Nochlin's essay *Why Have There Been No Great Women Artists?*, the art historian explores the tale that for most of Western visual art history, women were not allowed to work from the nude model, tracing the institutional roots of how women have been excluded from the possibility of achieving "greatness." Nochlin further acknowledges how that very notion is gendered. She neither sells acquiescence nor provides excuses. "What is important," she writes, "is that women face up to the reality of their history." The goal has to be to change the institutions of control: "[U]sing as a vantage point their situation as underdogs in the realm of grandeur, and outsiders in that of ideology, women can reveal institutional and intellectual weaknesses in general, and, at the same time that they destroy false consciousness, take part in the creation of institutions in which clear thought — and true greatness — are challenges open to anyone, man or woman, courageous enough to take the necessary risk, the leap into the unknown."[1]

•••

A great artist must be both destroyer and creator, as Nochlin recognizes. And destroying false consciousness, disrupting habit, upsetting convention, and discomfiting the comfortable are things postmodern artists do all the time. As feminists, as ethnic and cultural minorities, as non-binary individuals, as revolutionaries and from so many other positions of rebellion or subversion, generations of artists have taken up a version of Nochlin's challenge, have chosen to speak their truths to power and make their own leaps into the unknown.

Colleen Wolstenholme has been doing just that over a career that spans more than thirty years. Whether in her native Nova Scotia, New York, Vancouver, Montréal, Toronto, or now Fredericton, she has been a working artist her entire adult life. She is usually referred to, and refers to herself, as a sculptor. But she works across many genres. *Colleen Wolstenholme: Hyperobjectivity* includes sculpture, textiles, paintings, drawings, video, paper constructions, jewellery, and installation. Her work can be representational, figurative, or abstract, and her imagery (when present) can be created, adapted, or appropriated. From her first solo exhibition in 1996, her work has defied expectations and resisted easy categorization. "Conceptual" is just about the only descriptor that is consistently accurate when discussing her practice.

This thoughtful artist is interested in the philosophical concept of hyperobjects, a term coined by environmental philosopher Timothy Morton. According to Morton's thinking, hyperobjects are identified as things so vast that we can neither physically see them nor cognitively comprehend them in their entirety. In other words, we cannot perceive a hyperobject, only its effects. Indeed, we can barely conceive of a hyperobject as a thing at all. For Morton, an ecosystem is a hyperobject. So, too, is a storm system and perhaps harder to grasp, global warming or the COVID-19 pandemic.

Thinking of systems as objects — or perhaps more accurately, expressing systems' effects through objects — has been Wolstenholme's artistic strategy throughout her career. Her work has always been predicated on the fact that objects can mean more than they appear to, and while function informs meaning, it doesn't limit it. Objects contain and transmit cultural information: they are never neutral. This is true for humans as much as it is for our artifacts. Surely for the worse, women's bodies, whether clad or nude, are rarely just their own bodies, being held up to stultifying cultural standards, onerous expectations, and sexualized codes that society uses to transform those bodies into objects that can be possessed. However categorized, and whatever the medium Wolstenholme chooses to use at any particular time, her work is always concerned with subverting control, exposing the systems that exercise that control, and putting the lie to the cultural contexts that justify it.

Subversive and rebellious, her work refuses to accept the status quo, whatever that may be in any given moment. It is activist, uncompromising, and often perceived as difficult because it rejects any convenient collaboration with power. Wolstenholme sees a problem and shines a light on it, revealing the powers that hide behind the curtain. Through her work we see the world as she sees it. In the process, we are empowered, and we, too, are exposed.

•••

Colleen Dawn Wolstenholme was born in Antigonish, Nova Scotia, on March 15, 1963. Her parents, John (Jack) Daniel Wolstenholme and Alberta (Sue) Mary Carter, were living in Antigonish while Jack finished his degree at St. Francis Xavier University. They later lived in Moncton, Toronto, and then Dartmouth before settling in Halifax, where Wolstenholme spent her youth. She was six when her parents separated, and they divorced in 1973. She was raised by her mother and was very close with her paternal grandparents.

From the age of fourteen Wolstenholme rebelled against authority, particularly at school. She described her mid-teen years, from fourteen to seventeen, as "rocky."

In grade 9 she mostly stopped attending school. "It was the '70s – it would have been '77 – and there was a lot to distract young people at that time from school," she recalled. "I stopped going to school and started experimenting with drinking, smoking, and various other things."[2] Her mother never gave up on her recalcitrant daughter. "Mom, to her credit, went and found a school psychologist and got everything worked out so that I could actually graduate from junior high by doing the exams at the end of the year." Wolstenholme's school principal, the noted Halifax historian Dr. Lou Collins, worked with Sue Wolstenholme to ensure that Colleen would be able to stay in school. "It was my mother and him that kept me from dropping out of school in grade 9 like a lot of my friends had done," she remembered. After attending summer school, she was able to start high school in the fall of 1978.

It was in high school that she had her first formal exposure to art instruction: "I had Fred Sayeau as my art teacher. I crawled through high school, but I had Fred and history. I liked history... It kept me coming back." In high school Wolstenholme decided that she wanted to study art, applying for entry into the Nova Scotia College of Art and Design (NSCAD), as it was called then, while she was still in grade 11. That attempt was unsuccessful, and she reapplied after graduating. "I don't think I was a strong candidate really," she recalled, "so they let me in, in January, and I started in January of 1982."

After her foundation semester, she first tried painting but soon gravitated to sculpture. "I was really attracted to sculpture," she said. "Still now, if you look at the philosophy I'm interested in right now, it's all about objects. All to do with considering objects in the same type of vein as we consider our own ego. I think I had fallen in love with objects at a very young age." She came under the influence of Robin Peck, a charismatic artist and writer who had a large following among the sculpture students at NSCAD. "I had interactions with Robin," she said, "and that was huge – it gave me a huge sense of acceptance in a way, like, 'Oh I can get away with this, being this, this is OK, maybe I'm meant to be this.'" Her relationship with Peck spanned decades, and he remains one of the more influential figures in her development, as mentor, supporter, and sometimes foil.

Another key influence was David Askevold, who returned to teaching at NSCAD in 1984 after a stint in Minneapolis. "David came, and that was a whole different influence. That was video, including an introduction to Michael Snow's work, which had a big impact on me," she remembered. "There was this idea of the physicality of media," which she gleaned from Snow and from Askevold.

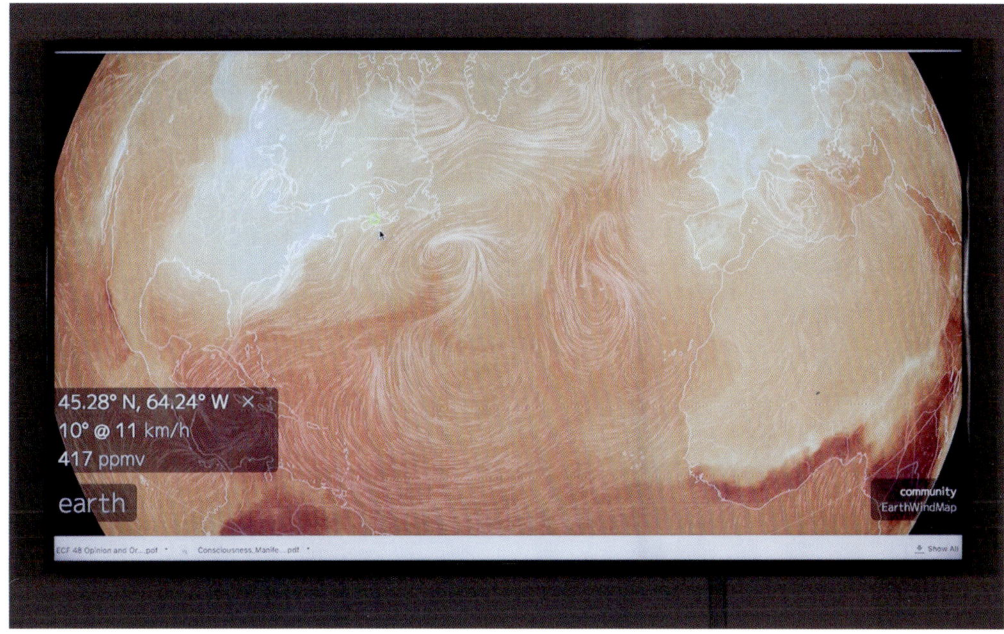

A Year of the Air I Breathe, 2018
(video still)

Her interest in video has lasted, and she has gathered footage since that first introduction. Despite her ongoing interest, it wasn't until 2018 that she actually showed a complete video (*A Year of the Air I Breathe*). John Greer, Gerald Ferguson, Garry Neill Kennedy, and Eric Cameron were other teachers who made an impact on her development. She sees elements of their influence to this day: "I thought John was very interesting, and if you look at my art you can see his influence in it – and also because of the humour. And Robin's too, and Garry's, and Jerry's. And Eric, he was a huge influence on me."

•••

As an undergraduate Wolstenholme's influential teachers were male artists. The reality was that there simply were very few women teaching at NSCAD at that point. "There were definitely women artists that I was influenced by, it's just that they didn't happen to be teaching in sculpture." Her work at this time was influenced by minimalist sculpture. "I made sculptures like Rachel Whiteread, only not as good," Wolstenholme said. "Basically, the negative casting thing is what I did as my sort of minimalist thing when I was studying under Robin and John." Casting blocks with negative spaces in them was, for Wolstenholme, a response to the minimalist "boy's club" at NSCAD. "Part of the reason I was doing this negative casting thing was a

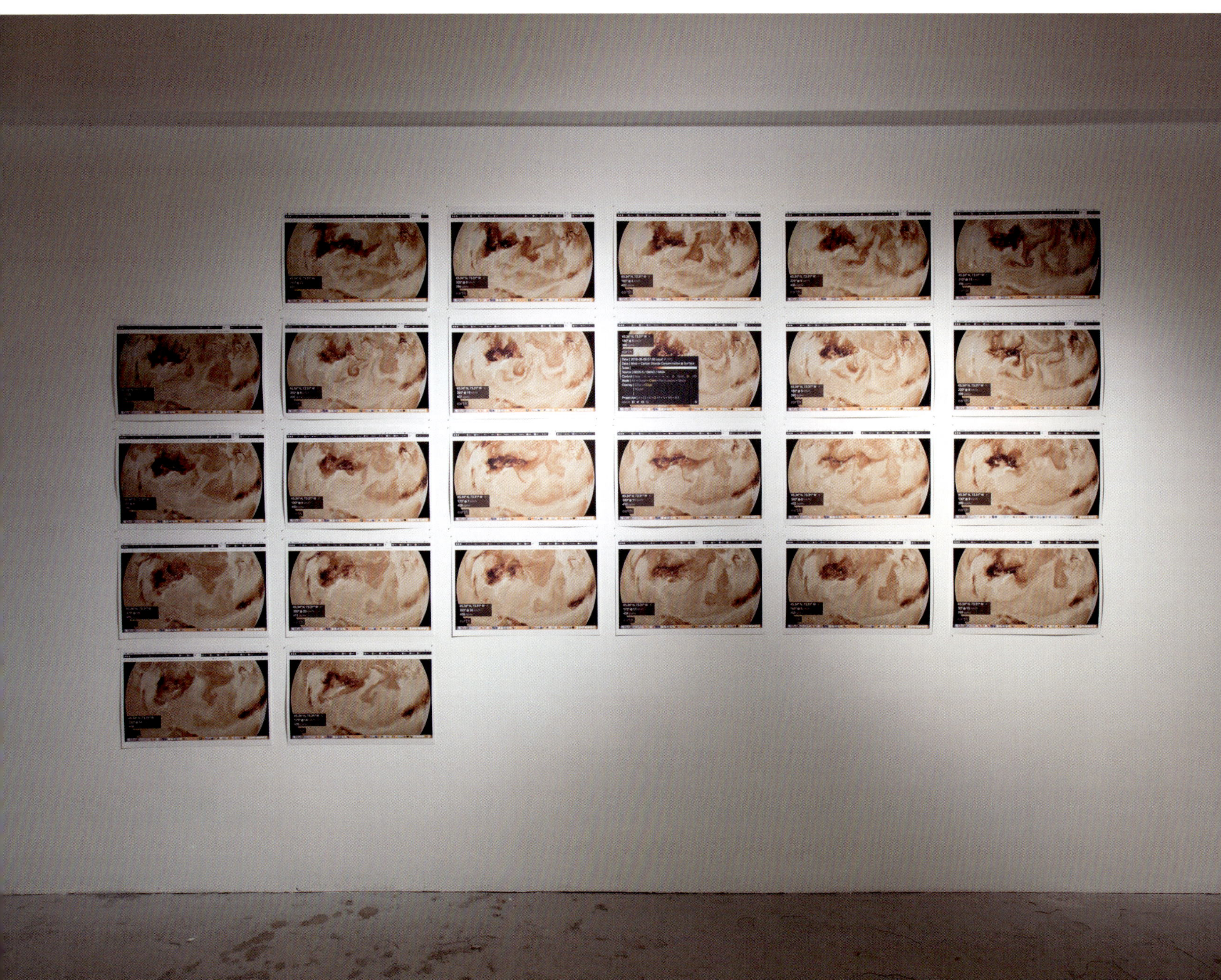

A Month of the Air I Breathe, 2018 (installation)

reaction to sculpture being a sort of monolithic erection. I wanted to do some sort of female ideal, and the negative casting was the answer to me."

She graduated as a fine arts major (concentrating on sculpture) in 1986, and in 1987 she participated in NSCAD's New York Studio program, staying in New York until 1989. In the summer of 1987 she worked for Andy Warhol's printer, Seymour Berlin, at Record Offset. She was exposed to a much wider range of contemporary art in New York than she had seen in Halifax. "I'd been into minimalism," she recalled. "I recognized that that was not really where the art world was at all." At that time the art world was in the midst of a deliberate postmodern critique of culture that conflated high art and consumerism, what critic Hal Foster has dubbed "commodity sculpture." Sculptors such as Robert Gober, Jeff Koons, Ashley Bickerton, and Haim Steinbach were showing objects that combined the ready-made of Marcel Duchamp with conceptual art's idea-based aesthetic. Some of these sculptors, Gober and Bickerton in particular, used high-end fabrication to make objects, a return to a certain ideal of craft that had been all but abandoned since the advent of minimalism in the early 1960s. "I started to be influenced by that heavily, and also because I saw the relationship between that and craft," Wolstenholme remembered. "A lot of it was super high-crafted stuff, especially Ashley Bickerton's stuff. It might look quasi-carpentry oriented but it's pretty skilled fabrication."

She worked at various jobs in New York and spent a lot of time going to galleries, but found it left her with little time to make her own work. "I was floundering as an artist," she recalled. While at NSCAD, she had taken a few jewellery courses, and she had brought a torch and other tools with her to New York. Lacking proper studio space, she found herself making objects at home.

A break-up, her realization that her partying was getting out of hand, and frustration with her lack of progress as an artist all combined to prompt her decision to return to Nova Scotia: "I wanted to be an artist, I knew that, so... I knew that I wasn't equipped yet to do it. I'd seen enough in New York to make it clear to me that I didn't have a clue what I was doing."

She returned to Halifax in 1989 and re-enrolled at NSCAD, completing a major in jewellery in two semesters: "That was when I really learned how to make stuff. That was really important because, not being a rich person, I couldn't afford to hire people to do it for me. I figured that I was going to have to do everything from scratch, just like the poor sort of street urchin that I was, really. And that gave me a lot of power, learning how to control fire and metal and make shit, and it still does. It's amazing."

•••

In 1990 Wolstenholme started graduate studies in jewellery at the State University of New York (SUNY) at New Paltz, about an hour and a half north of New York City. While there she worked primarily with the well-known jeweller Fred Wohl: "Fred was a great jeweller who made brooches and different things using the parts from say a car model, but he would do something to it, make it look like it had been in an accident.... He would take these little parts, but he would put two of them together, affect them somehow."

Wohl's approach would influence Wolstenholme profoundly, but initially she focused on making hybrid objects that expressed a feminist approach to artmaking. Two artists whose work she admired were Rebecca Horn and Roni Horn. These artists defied traditional genres in their work and exemplified women who achieved success while making critical, activist work. Wolstenholme's work in graduate school combined jewellery techniques such as holloware construction in copper with cast plaster and cabinetmaking. One work, for instance, was a wooden cabinet that contained a plaster cast of the artist's torso, with a zoetrope at eye level. When one looked into the eye slot, the zoetrope flashed an image of Manet's *Olympia*, a close-up of the model's eye, so that it appeared the sculpture was winking. Wolstenholme positioned a mirror where the torso's vagina would have been, so that it is the viewer's genitals that appear in the piece as they step up to look at the zoetrope. The work is called *The Bride Stripped Bare by Herself, Even* (p. 19), in homage to the French artist Marcel Duchamp's *The Bride Stripped Bare by Her Bachelors, Even* (1915–23). This piece was included in Wolstenholme's graduating exhibition in 1992. She remembered the work in that exhibition as "pretty good... I mean I thought it was competitive, somewhat competitive." Competitive, that is, with what she was seeing in New York.

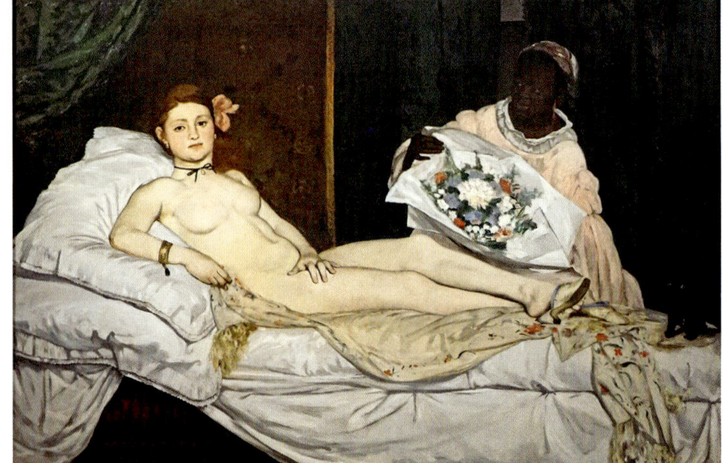

Édouard Manet, *Olympia*, 1863 (Musée d'Orsay, Paris)

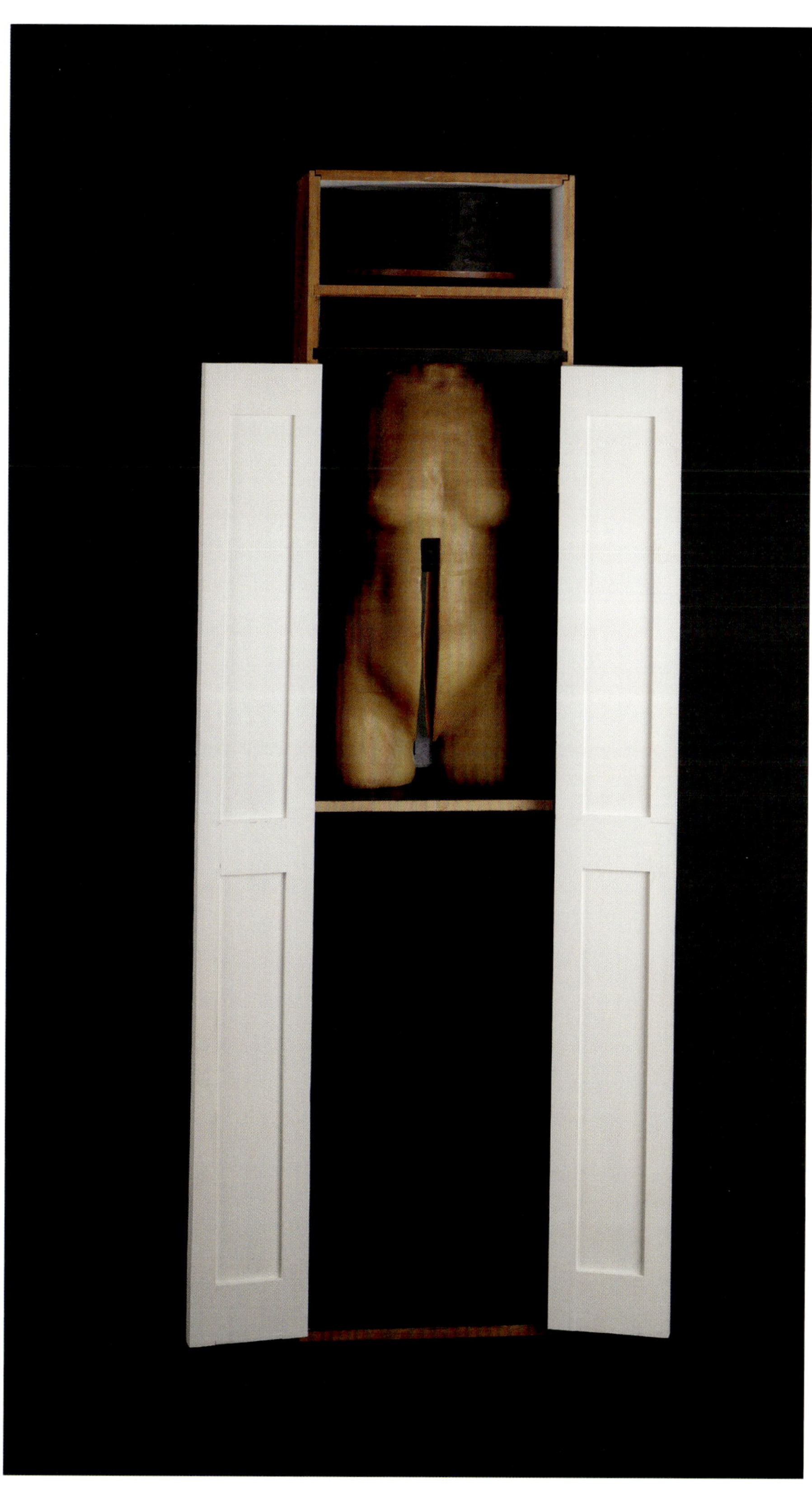

The Bride Stripped Bare by Herself, Even, 1992

In February 1993 she moved back to New York. "I remember it was a bad snowstorm. We had to carry my crap up five flights of stairs. But that was nothing compared to what we had to do to the apartment to fix it up. It was a dive. I actually cried when I saw it."[3] One of the things hauled up those stairs was a large sculpture she had begun just after finishing graduate school. She worked on it during the two years she lived in New York, eventually bringing it back to Nova Scotia with her in 1995. For those two years she was part of the installation crew at the Dia Center for the Arts, working on exhibits of internationally renowned artists such as Ann Hamilton, Dan Graham, On Kawara, Robert Gober, and Katharina Fritsch, among others. For an ambitious emerging artist, close access to internationally acclaimed artists and their work was a significant opportunity. NSCAD welcomed many well-known artists as visitors, but a lecture or even a studio visit could not compare to spending a period of weeks installing large and complex sculptures. "That was an incredibly important period," Wolstenholme said.[4]

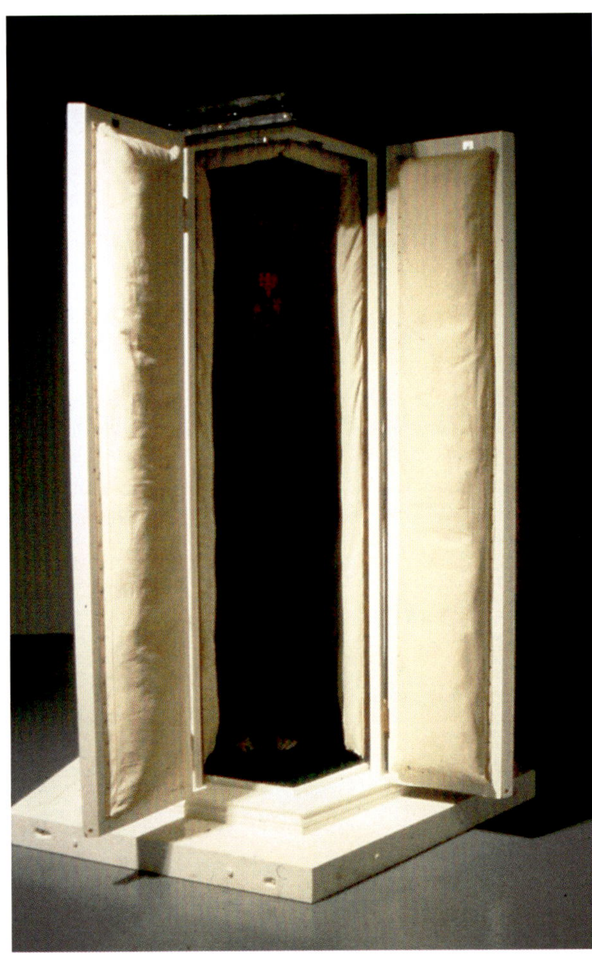

Patience, 1992–1995

Health issues prompted her return to Nova Scotia, where she struggled to overcome an environmental illness that took a year of recovery. In the summer of 1996, she was hired at NSCAD to teach in its jewellery department. At that time, guest faculty were offered an exhibition at the school's Anna Leonowens Gallery. The show included Wolstenholme's first pill sculptures and the copper pillows with embroideries, as well as *Patience* (1992–1995, right), the completed large sculpture she had brought with her from New York.

Patience is a wooden construction with a shingled roof and twin doors that is exactly large enough to hold one person. Its interior is thickly padded with canvas cushioning. The only light that enters when the doors are closed is through a small window in the apex of the roof, and through other small windows on the sides set at the height of the screen in a confessional. The work functions much like a pedestal in traditional statuary, except that rather than being elevated by a plinth the figure is contained by it. Both architecture and sculpture, *Patience* evokes not only the systems of control exercised on persons with mental illness – a personalized treatment or holding centre – but also the intense loneliness and anxiety of those suffering. This cell is at once restrictive and protective, an allegory for depression itself.

The three copper "pillows" combine traditional jewellery techniques with needlepoint embroidery. Feminist artists have been using the so-called domestic crafts in fine art since the 1960s, playing on the complicated history of "women's work" in Western art. From Penelope unravelling the burial shroud she is weaving to postpone selecting a new husband in *The Odyssey*, to the ever-present baskets of needlework in the hands of the Victorian fiction heroines, handwork has for millennia served as a defining feature of femininity, part of the construct of a "feminine ideal." Art historian Rozsika Parker notes: "There is a significant difference between acknowledging the construction of femininity in the family and its maintenance in social institutions, and accepting the cultural representation of women imposed on us."[5] The difference between weaving cloth from which to make the family clothes and making a decorative sampler to frame and hang on the wall is, of course, profound. Handwork, as it came to be understood, could only flourish when women had leisure time; as such, it was a form of work for women to do when they weren't doing other work — when they weren't being useful.

"I had been doing the needlepoint while I was sick," Wolstenholme said. "I hadn't known when I started the needlepoints what I was going to do with them. I just started the needlepoints because I couldn't do anything else." *Phenobarbital Pillow* (1996, p. 23) is the size of a small decorative throw pillow, with copper tassels at each corner and an embroidered design taken from the descriptions of drugs from a medical textbook. Wolstenholme's allusions are to decorative handwork — needlepoint cushions or chair backs, for instance. Through the late 1990s and early 2000s, Wolstenholme made a series of needlepoint panels depicting drug company logos, as well as images drawn from other corporate sources. The transformation of corporate symbols into forms that our culture has conditioned us to regard as benign and comforting carries a powerful punch.

Wolstenholme's use of needlepoint as a subversion of socially acceptable women's work reflects a prevalent trend in feminist artmaking from the 1970s on, a strategy found in work by artists as diverse as Judy Chicago, Mary Kelly, Irene Whittome, Nancy Edell, and Mary Scott. Many of Wolstenholme's artist contemporaries also use such strategies, for instance, Pandora Vaughan, Sarah Maloney, Janice Wright Cheney, and Anna Torma. In fact, after a struggle, domestic needlework (including embroidery, needlepoint, rug-hooking, knitting, felting, and weaving, among other techniques) has gradually gained acceptance as a fine art practice, although it is all too often relegated to a lesser status than, say, painting. It's often considered a "craft"

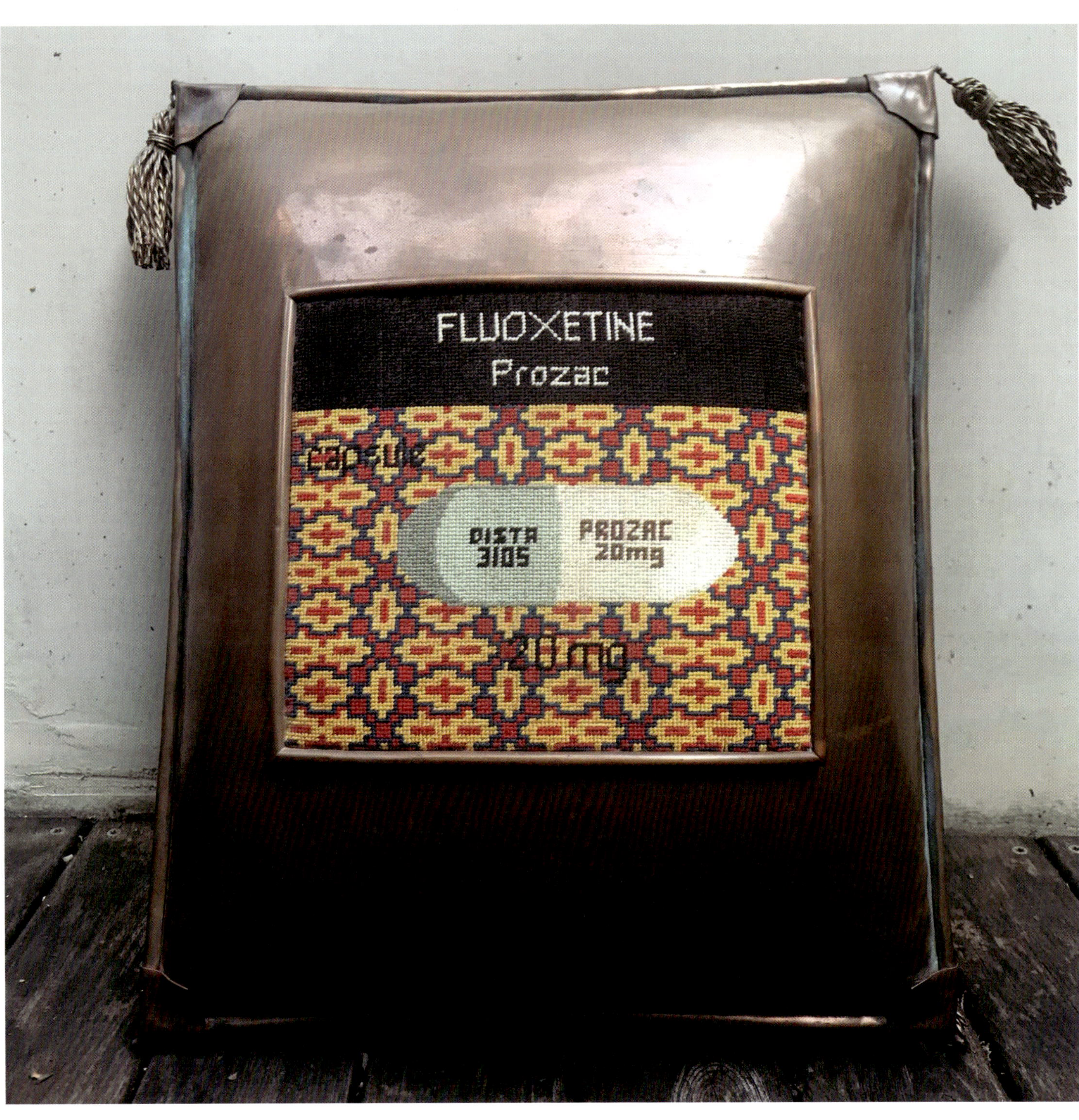

Prozac Pillow, 1995

(opposite)
Phenobarbital Pillow, 1995

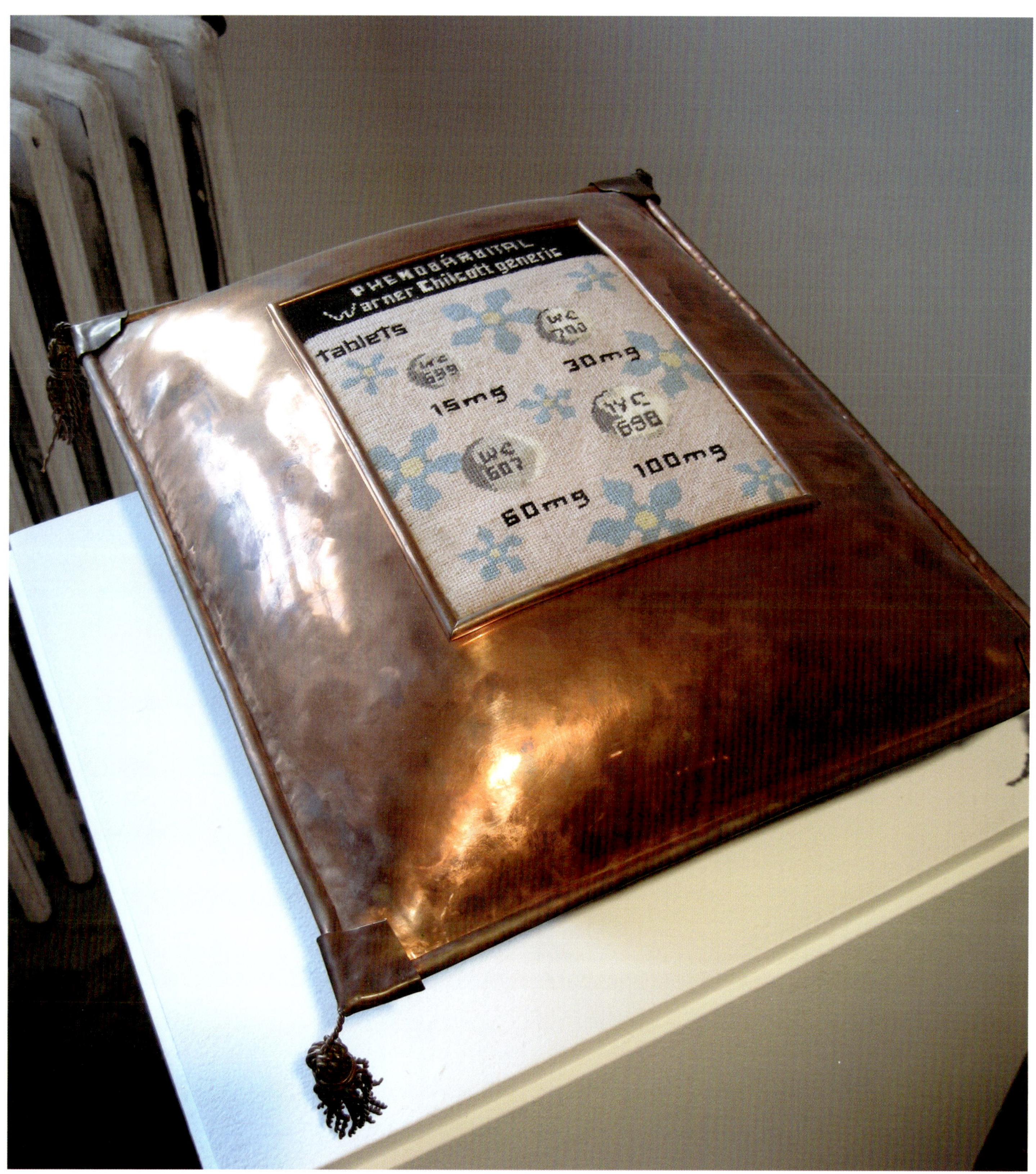
PHENOBARBITAL
Warner Chilcott generic
tablets
15mg
30mg
60mg
100mg

(as is jewellery). As Rozsika Parker points out, "Limited to practising art with needle and thread, women have nevertheless sewn a subversive stitch – managed to make meaning of their own in the very medium intended to inculcate self-effacement."[6]

Partly as a demonstration for a class Wolstenholme was teaching at NSCAD, she began making casts in sterling silver of individual antidepressants and anti-anxiety medications such as Zoloft, Paxil, Valium, and Dexedrine. These she made into pendants, necklaces, and bracelets, assembling the disparate forms into geometric patterns. The ubiquity of legal drug use among young women first became apparent to Wolstenholme in the mid-1990s, when she realized that most of the women she knew, herself included, were medicated. Her response was to start making casts of these pills in silver and gold, "charms" to be worn publicly, bringing into the open what had been hidden. As much small sculptures as pieces of jewellery, these works mimicked familiar forms such as charm bracelets and rosaries:

> The jewellery, that was a real feminist thing. Jewellery was invented for women, basically, to show that they were the property of a man in some way or other. I had been watching television, and this De Beers diamond ad came on for a diamond solitaire necklace, and I remember it because they flashed "Take her breath away" and then the word "Forever" flashes on the screen. And that just triggered me, "Are they really playing with death here, is that what it is? It's either love or death?"

To make moulds of the individual pills, she used techniques she had learned from her teacher Fred Wohl at SUNY New Paltz: "If it hadn't been for taking courses with him it never would have occurred to me that I could take the pills and make jewellery out of them, by casting the way I did it, which is how a jeweller would do it."

Later in 1996, Wolstenholme took a studio on the Halifax waterfront in Pier 21, a decommissioned immigration centre that was a popular space for artist studios throughout the 1990s. There, she made a series of works that would eventually bring her international attention. The new work utilized the traditional sculptural techniques of casting and carving. The sculptures were vastly scaled-up versions of the pill forms she had been using in her jewellery and small sculptures for the past year. What began as dinner-plate-sized versions of Valium tablets were scaled up even more, and she expanded the range of pills she was using as subjects. The final versions were roughly the size of human torsos. Her carved pills – pristine, clean, beautiful — were also carefully calculated affronts to certain ideas about sculpture, to the minimalist-conceptual school of NSCAD sculpture in particular. Carving plaster was almost deliberately obtuse, using what was traditionally an intermediary material between clay or wax and bronze as the end material: "I was interested in the pills because pills seemed to be becoming a big thing at the time. It was the early '90s and everybody was going on antidepressants, correlating that with what was going on in the world, different generational cohorts, and the problems that they might be up against. So, I was interested in how the pills reflected that, without saying anything, just the pill itself. And it brought that into focus."

•••

Wolstenholme uses plaster, bronze, and cement to create her monumentally scaled pills. The modernist designs of their shapes, the clean lines and slick typography, hark back to the design precepts of the Bauhaus. Yet, her use of these forms owes as much to Duchamp's ready-mades as it does to late modernist sculpture. These are essentially "found" objects, for all the painstaking craft that goes into making them.

However, pills as subjects were never the sole aim of these works. As with General Idea's pill works from the early 1990s (such as *Placebo* and *Pharmacopeia*), Wolstenholme's use of pills was politically motivated. These charged objects were chosen for representation because of their power to provoke. And while the specific political point was different for these artists, the familiar forms of medication served them all.

In early 1997 Wolstenholme's friend Sarah McLachlan, who was having a successful career as a singer-songwriter, was visiting her parents in Halifax. She saw Wolstenholme's jewellery and convinced her to come and sell it on the Lilith Fair tour. McLachlan, internationally renowned by that time, was organizing a music tour featuring only women artists. Wolstenholme moved to Vancouver and joined McLachlan's entourage for the three summers that the festival travelled around North America (1997–99). Initially reluctant, Wolstenholme eventually decided that she could approach selling at the fair as a kind of performance piece: "I thought, I'll just make a whole bunch of different antidepressants and have a little booth. I had this big red cross. Some people actually thought it was for real, that they could get Band-Aids there. It was called 'Damage Control.'"

Wolstenholme sold her jewellery from this booth at each venue. The response from people who visited was immediate: "It was a liberational thing for some people who were on medications, to see this. And they sent me letters. I've got letters from people saying how it just changed their life. Just because it became acceptable."

Her exposure at Lilith Fair led to a spate of positive attention from the mainstream media, as well as a series of letters from law firms ordering her to cease and desist in her use of trademarked imagery. Wolstenholme's art was featured in *Psychology Today* and in the pages of *The Guardian* and the *Los Angeles Times*, as well as in more traditional art venues, such as *C Magazine* and *Border Crossings*. Newspapers and magazines began to feature articles about prescription drug dependency, how women were more likely to become dependent, alongside visual art and pop culture responses, particularly Wolstenholme's aggressive, highly critical work.

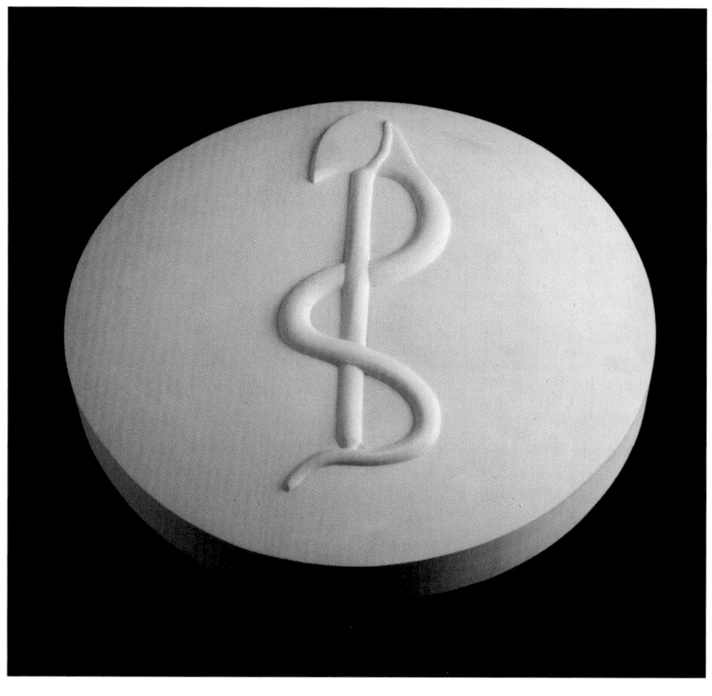

Leritine, 1997

The pill sculptures had tapped into the zeitgeist, achieving a kind of popular success she had never known before or since: "When that happens to somebody in the beginning of their career it's really hard, because you keep looking for that same kind of trigger, and there aren't many of those." The threat of legal actions from large multinational companies gave her work a certain outlaw credibility – though it made for a stressful time for Wolstenholme. None of the threats ever resulted in court action; the use of trademarked images by artists was a bit of a grey area in both Canadian and American law. The letters eventually stopped, and they never had the desired effect of regulating her behaviour.

While living in Vancouver, Wolstenholme exhibited a series of her carved plaster pills at one of that city's artist-run centres, grunt gallery. Her exhibition *Pills* (1998) featured sculptures of such drugs as Valium, Xanax, Dexedrine, Paxil, and Leritine. It was curated by Robin Peck, who had also written "Scattered Across the Floor," an article on Wolstenholme's work for *C Magazine*, the cover of which featured the artist's work. Wolstenholme's polemical intent was clear: "This sculpture is a powerfully reasoned indictment of the collaboration between corporate pharmaceutical firms and contemporary psychiatry," Peck observes.[7]

Peck was also alert to the feminist implications of all Wolstenholme's work, and her revisiting of sculpture's history, particularly early modernist sculpture, with the fresh eyes of the formerly excluded: "This sculpture is made by repetitive hand labour, gendered within the discourse of traditionally female pre-capitalist domestic crafts."[8] Women played little role in the heroic early story of modernist sculpture, usually confined to the role of muse, mistress, or patron. Wolstenholme was having none of it: "I mean to notice the gendered history of labour,"[9] she stated. The exhibition, retitled *Pharmacopoeia*, was remounted in Hamilton in 1999.

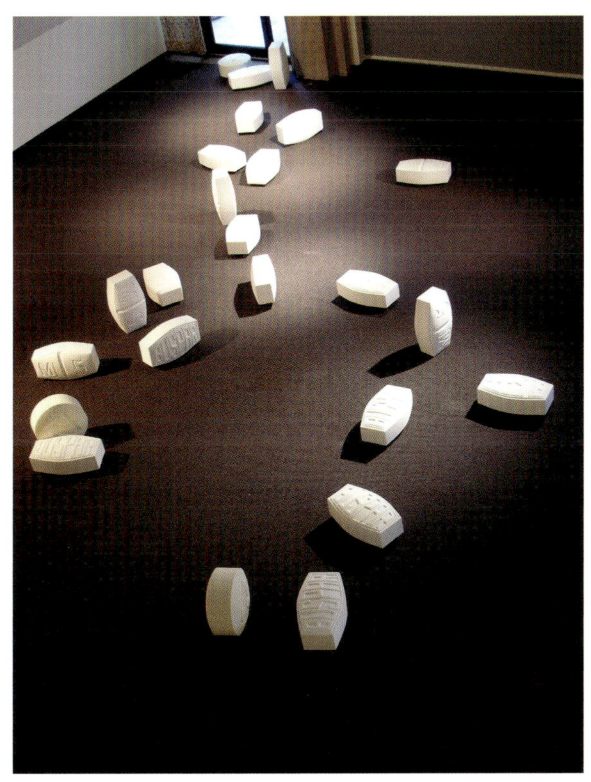

Spill, 2001

In 2001 Wolstenholme started to make large constructions from the pill forms. *BuSpar Column* (2001, p. 29) is a 2.5-metre-high bronze sculpture depicting BuSpar tablets stacked end to end, its stacking of rhomboid shapes referencing Constantin Brancusi's *Endless Column* (1937), his war memorial assemblage at Târgu Jiu, Romania, while wryly commenting on the addictive nature of the subject matter. It is in the collection of the Montreal Museum of Fine Arts and is permanently installed outside along with works by Antony Gormley, David Altmejd, and Auguste Rodin, among others. *Daisy* (2002) is a cement sculpture made up of seven petals (again modelled after BuSpar tablets) and one central, yellow circle (the antidepressant amitriptyline hydrochloride), suggesting the happy promises arising from much of the drug advertising. The authority of the medical community — doctors, pharmacists, and the pharmaceutical industry — is based in part on a sense of trust. That trust can easily be abused, as the present opioid crisis makes all too clear.

There is irony in presenting a string of antidepressants as a monument, more a warning than a celebration. As Virginia Eichhorn points out, "Wolstenholme reminds us to challenge these authorities and to, above all, question how something is presented."[10] *Daisy*'s irony is won only at the cost of hard labour, and is so unflinching that the work avoids being merely cynical, instead making a genuine cultural criticism that resonates on several levels. This work, and the works that precede it, are, as Peck has described, "sculpture as an alternative healing process."[11] The labour of making these objects is key, both to the artist's reasons for making them and to our eventual reception of the sculptures. This is the way things are, Wolstenholme observes, all the while suggesting that they could be better.

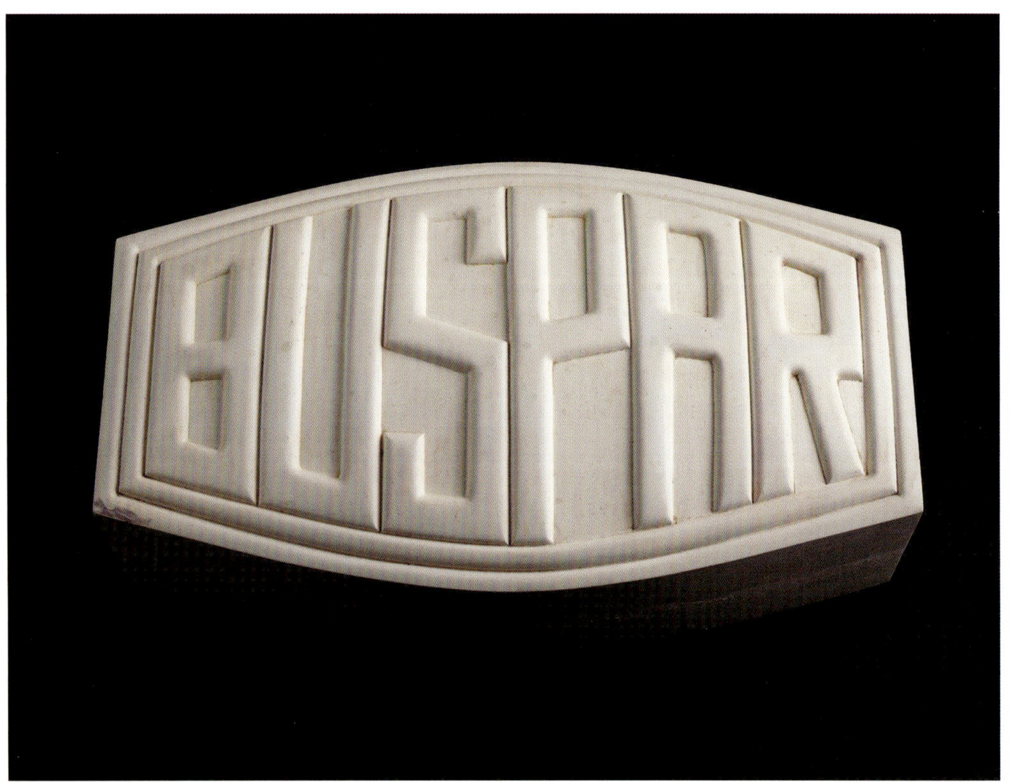

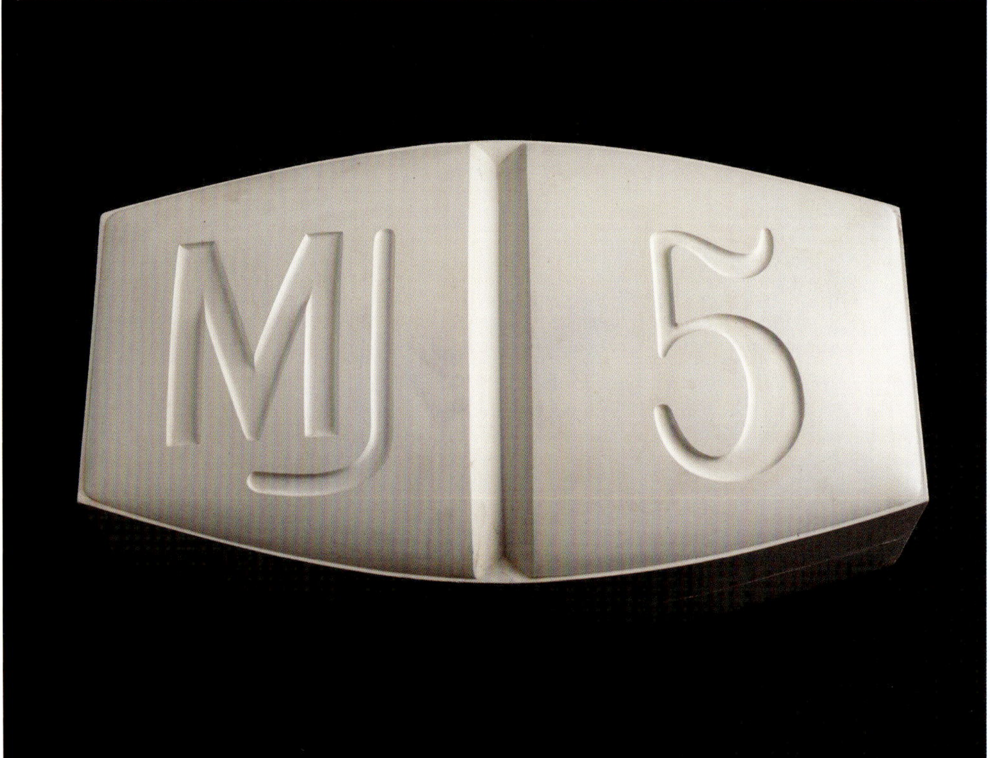

Recto and verso of *BuSpar*, 2001

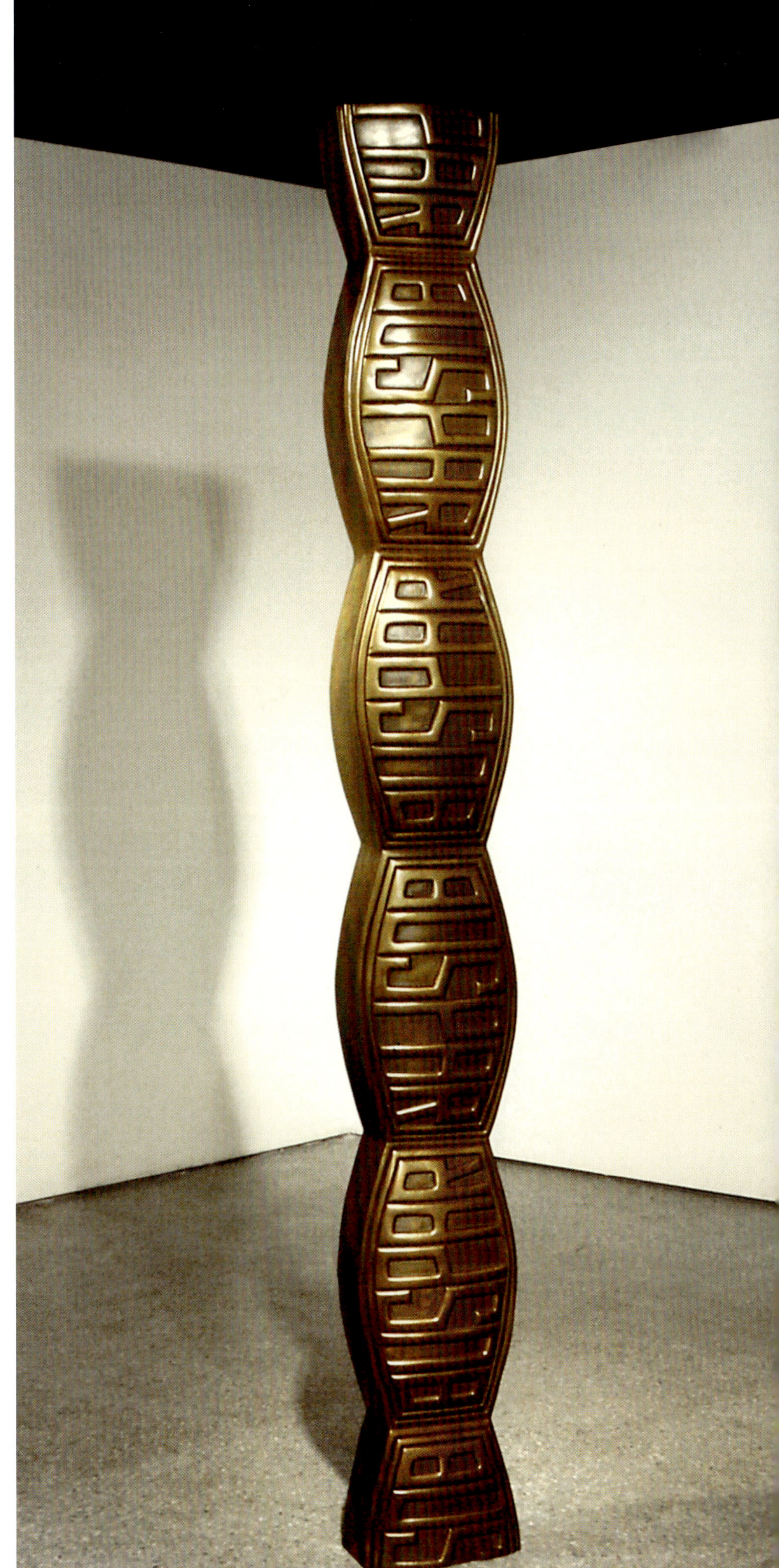

BuSpar Column, 2001

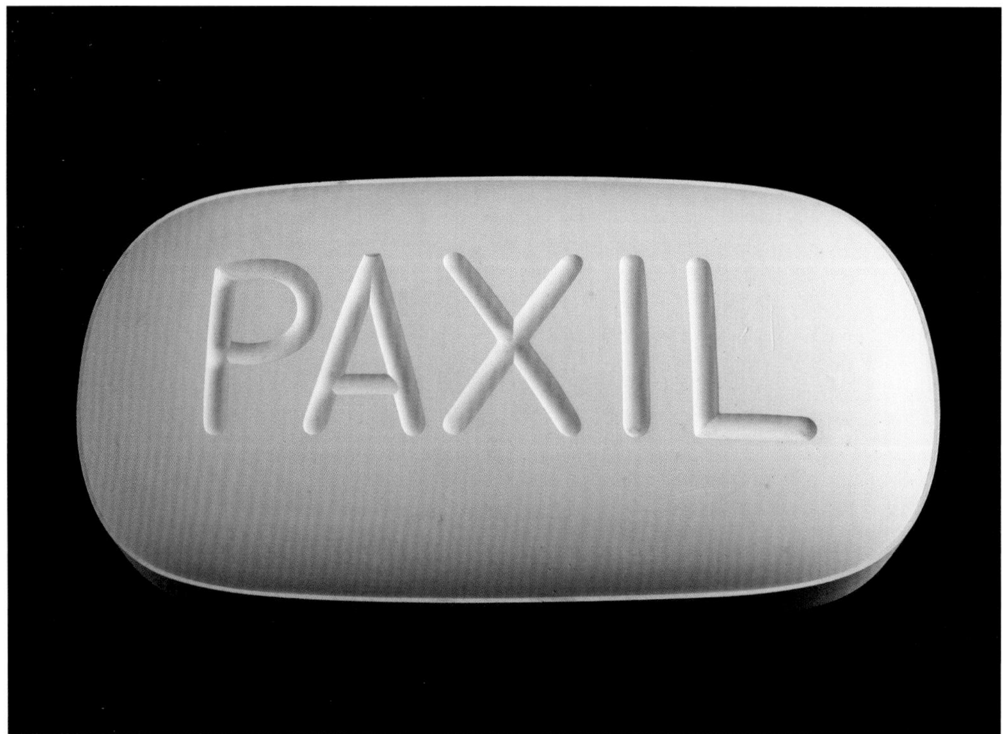

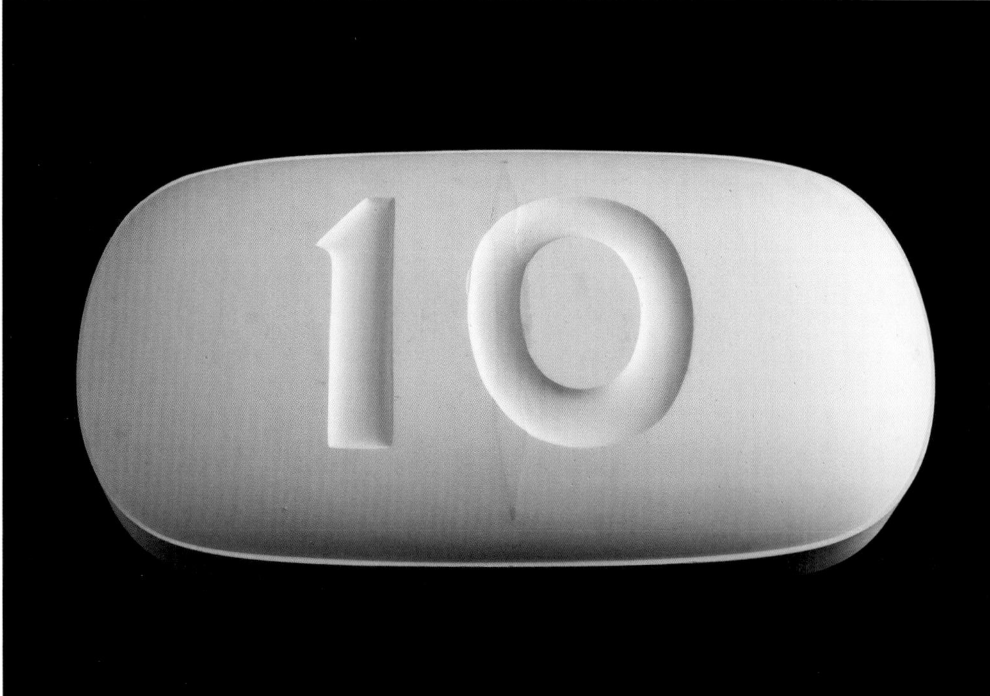

Recto and verso of *Paxil II*, 1997

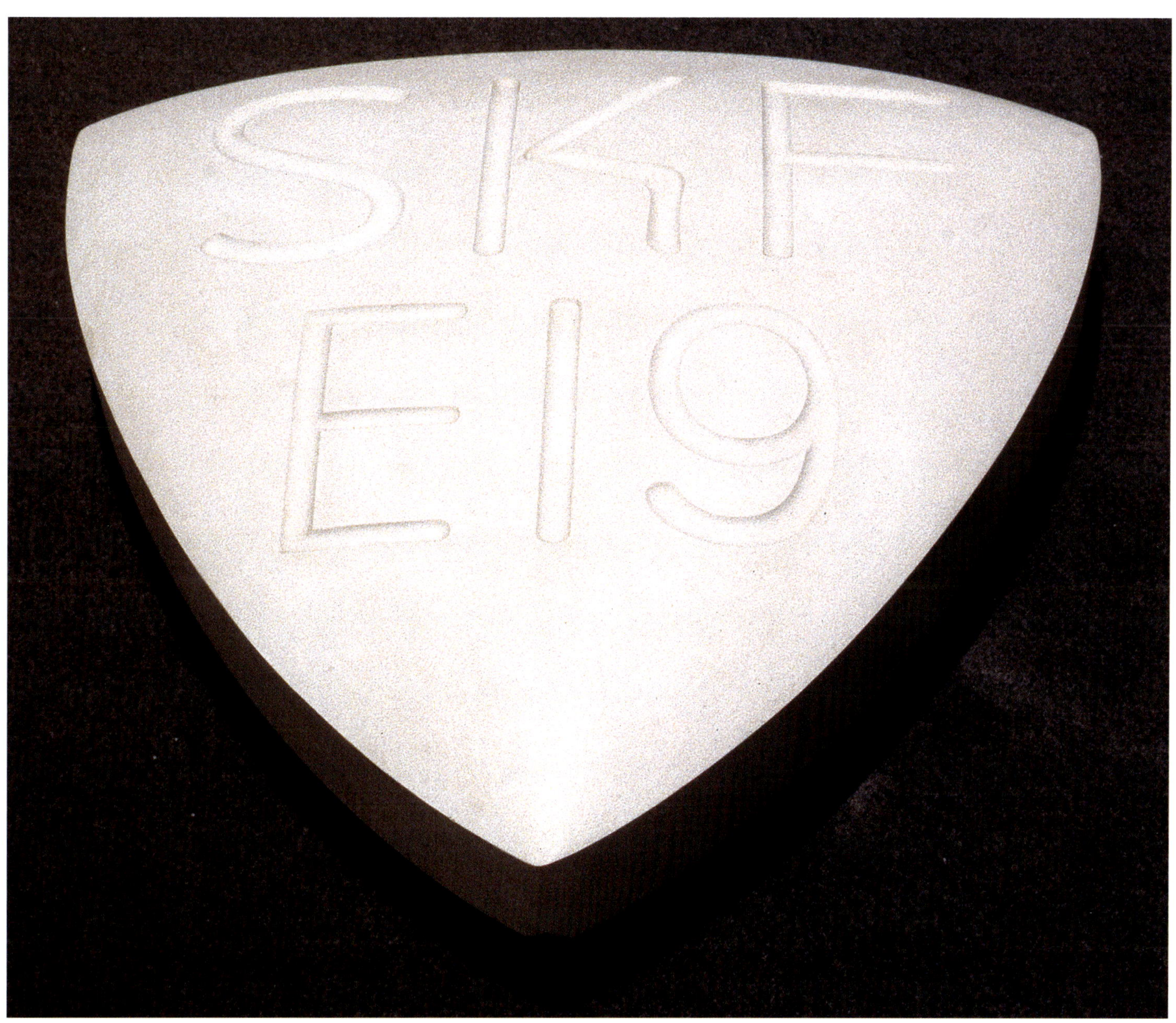

Dexedrine, 1997

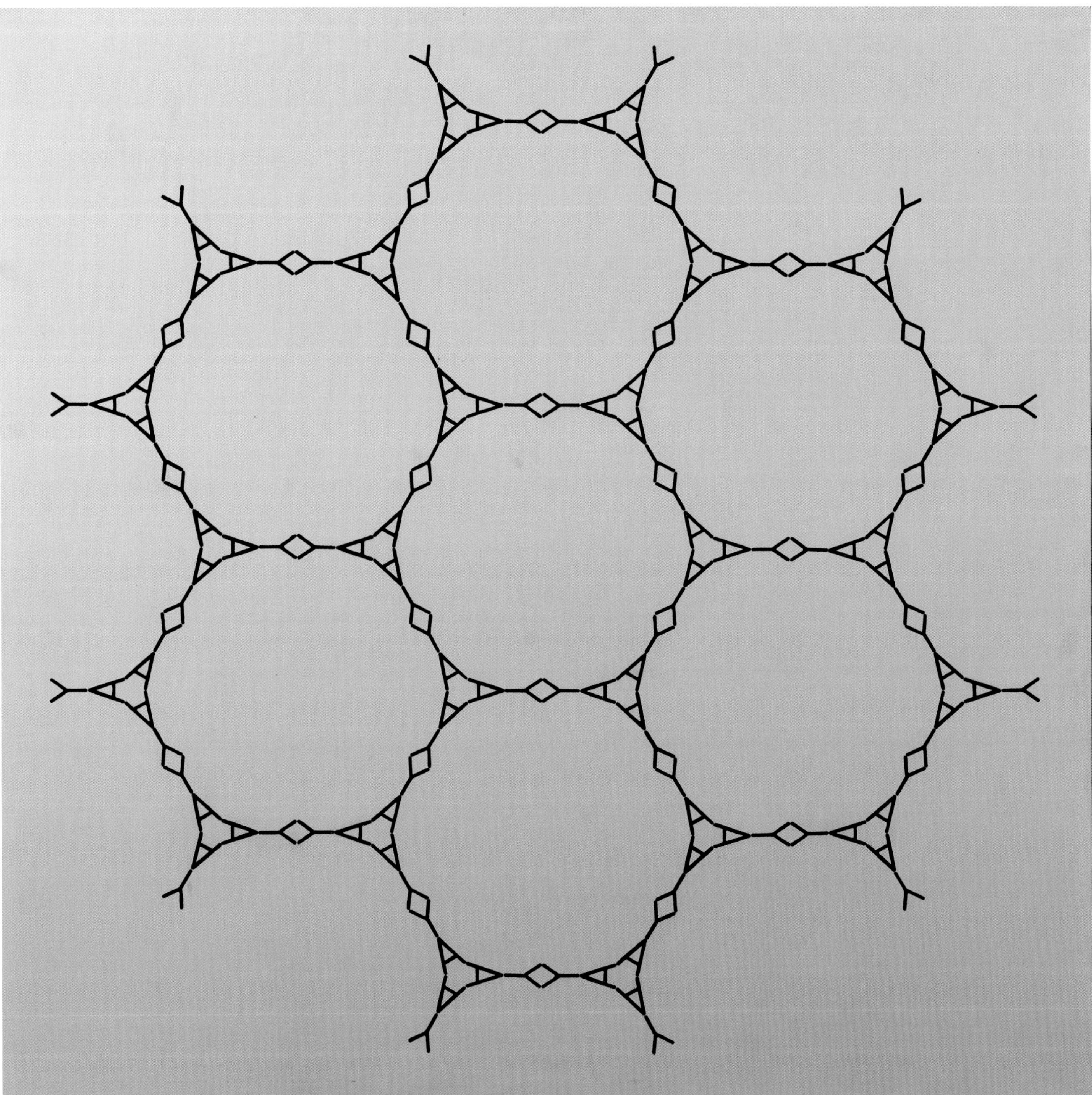

Ya, 2001

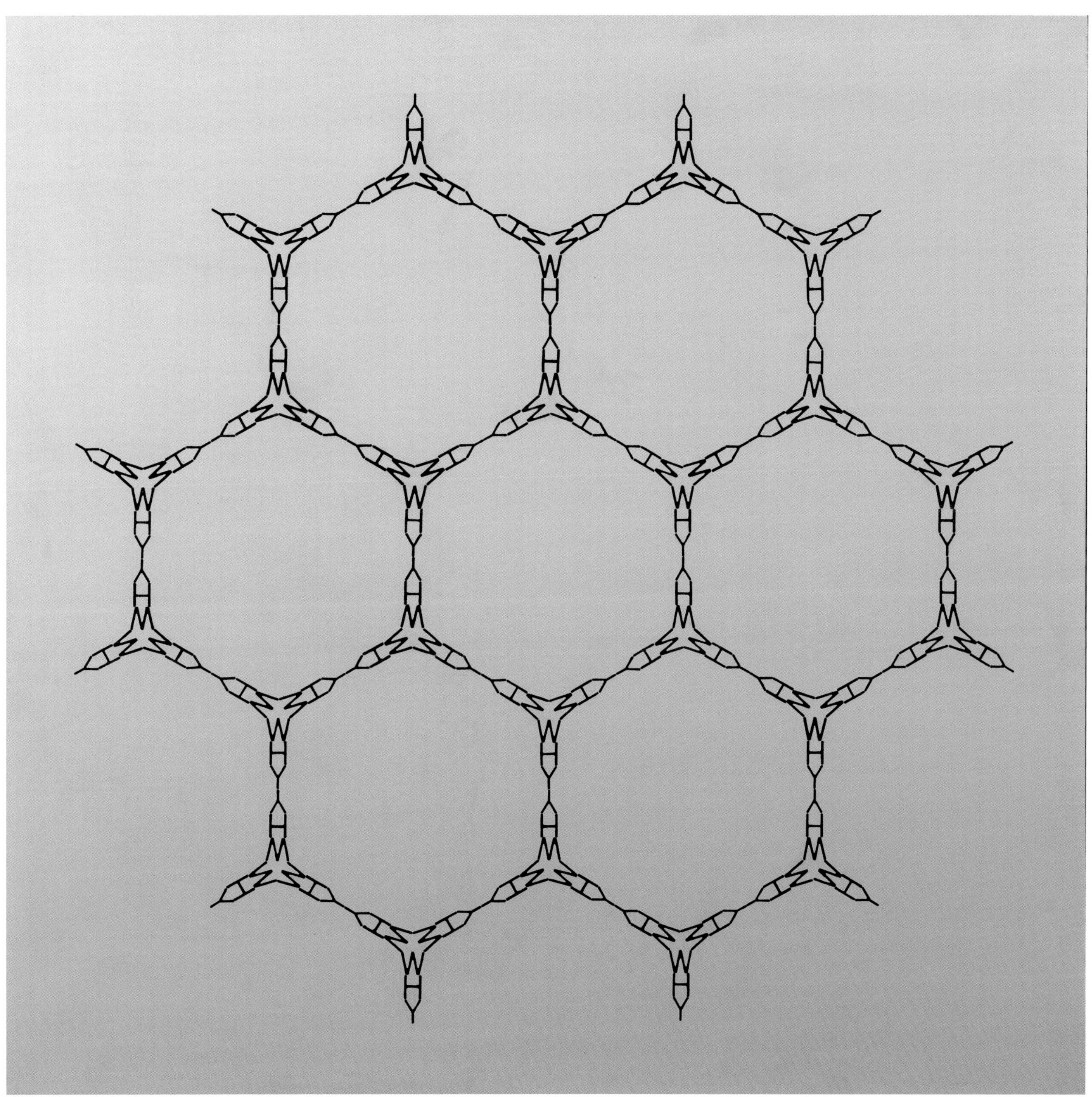

Why, 2001

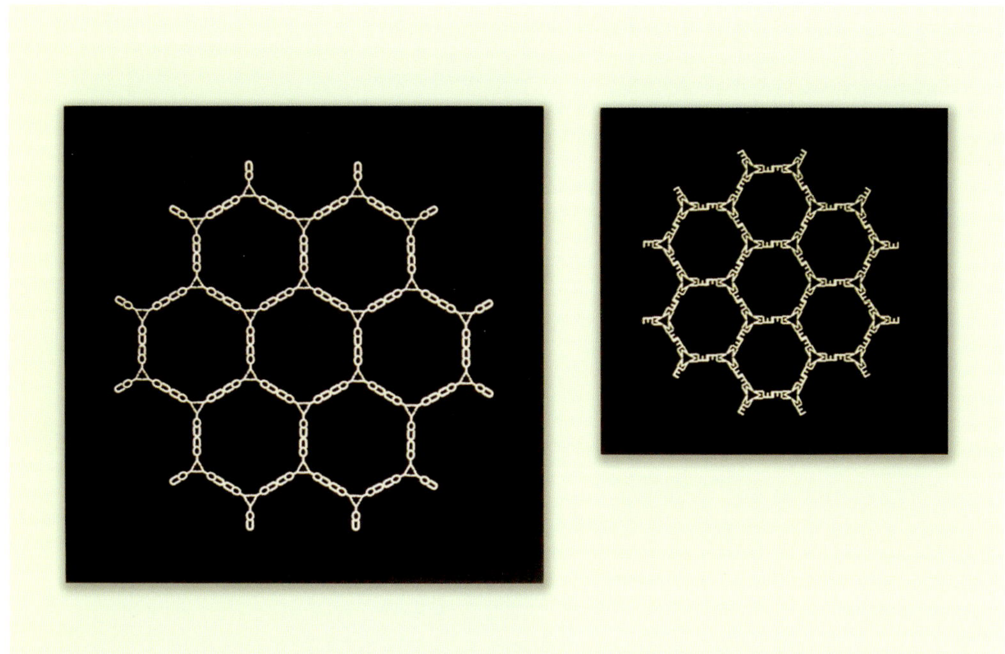

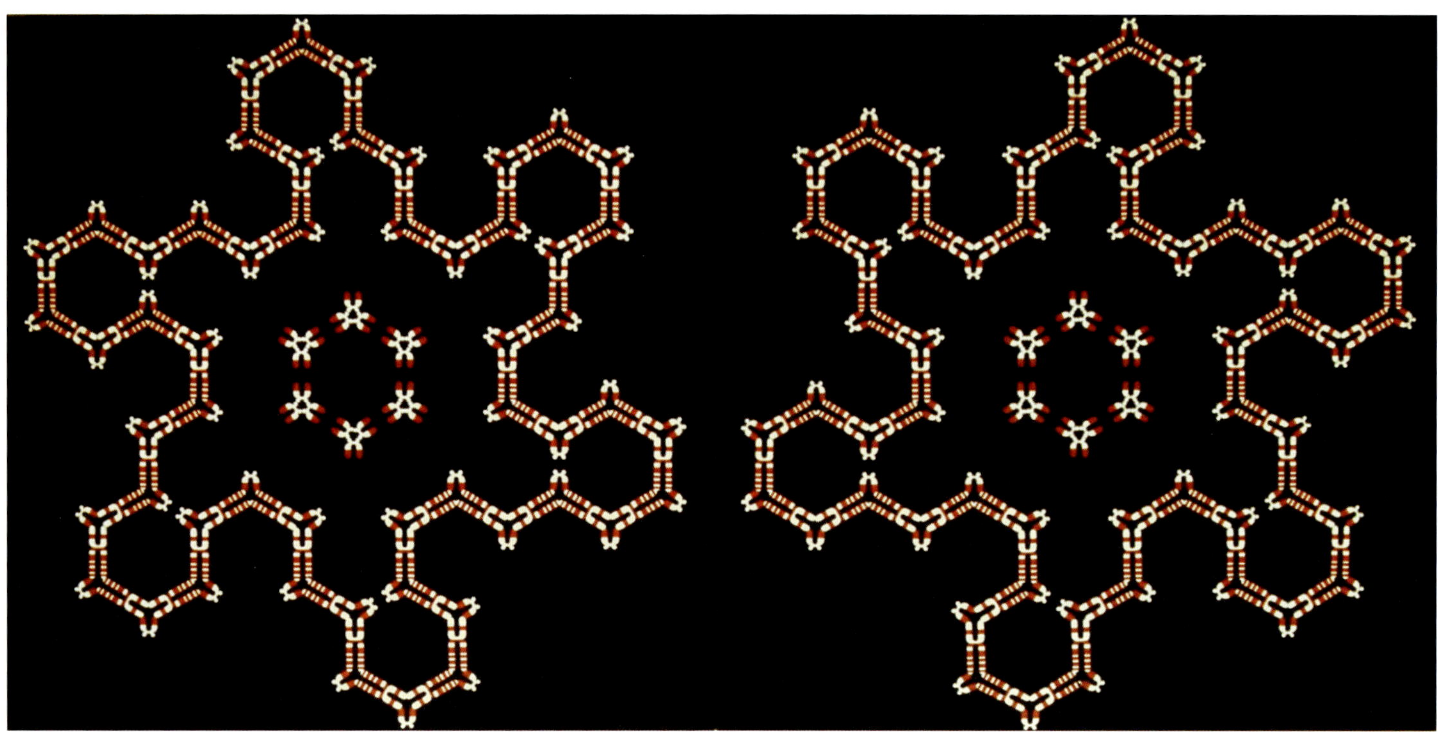

(left)
You and Me, 2002

(below)
SeXY , 2002

Wolstenholme returned to Nova Scotia in 1999 after three years in Vancouver and the last iteration of Lilith Fair. "It rained in Vancouver every day in 1999, and it was very expensive to live there. I was not happy and kept finding crazy roommates. I went to visit Mom after she'd moved to Hantsport and resolved to move back there too."[12] Hantsport, a small town on Nova Scotia's Fundy shore, would be Wolstenholme's home for the next twenty years.

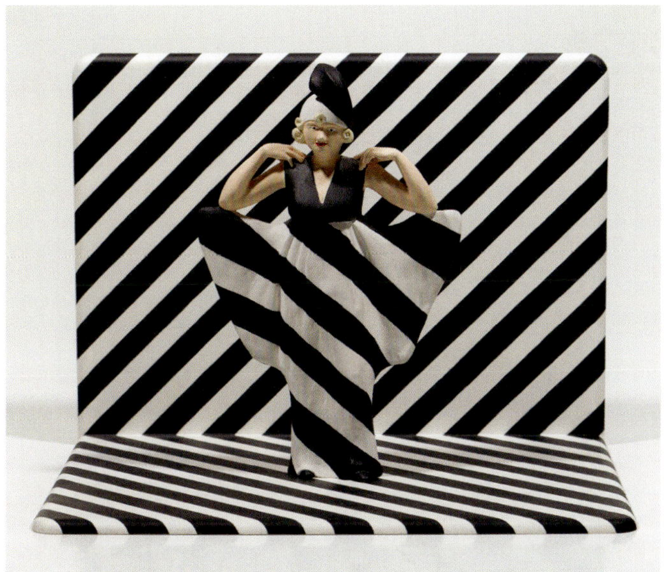

Dazzzled, 2003

In 2000 Wolstenholme was one of three artists in the exhibition *Desire*, which I curated for Charlottetown's Confederation Centre Art Gallery. She displayed six of her plaster pills and six needlepoints of drug company logos. The show later toured to Halifax's Saint Mary's University Art Gallery. In 2002 Wolstenholme was the Atlantic nominee for the inaugural Sobey Art Award (which was won that year by Vancouver-based artist Brian Jungen). Although the pills continued to receive the most attention, Wolstenholme worked in many other modes throughout the 2000s. Painting became more prominent in her studio, as evidenced by her 2002 exhibition *"AH"* in Ottawa. *You and Me* (p. 34), *SeXY* (p. 34), and *Om Am Hum* used painted letters to reference the genetic code, while in painted sculptures such as *Fast Lane* and *Dazzled* (above) she painted camouflage patterns on figurines and their bases. Camouflage was also the starting point for her *Camouflesh* series (2005, pp. 37–39, 96) and for a series of paintings based on sports logos and currency that she created in the mid-2000s.

Also in the early 2000s Wolstenholme began to make figurative sculptures, modelled in clay and then cast in plaster and ceramic. These small figures, all women, were approximately the size of the Royal Doulton figurines popular in many Canadian homes. Rather than Regency belles in flowing gowns, though, Wolstenholme chose more controversial subject matter: figures wearing burkas, the full-body covering mandated by many fundamentalist Islamic sects, that were accurately researched to reflect several styles from across the Islamic world. And rather than just focusing on one instance of culturally mandated clothing for women, Wolstenholme also made nuns wearing habits particular to specific religious orders, as well as stereotypical figures such as a flapper and a Victorian matron. She eventually made larger, burka-clad figures, such as *Triad* (2005, p. 70) and *Shrouded Figure* (2005), now in the collections of the National Gallery of Canada and the AGNS respectively.

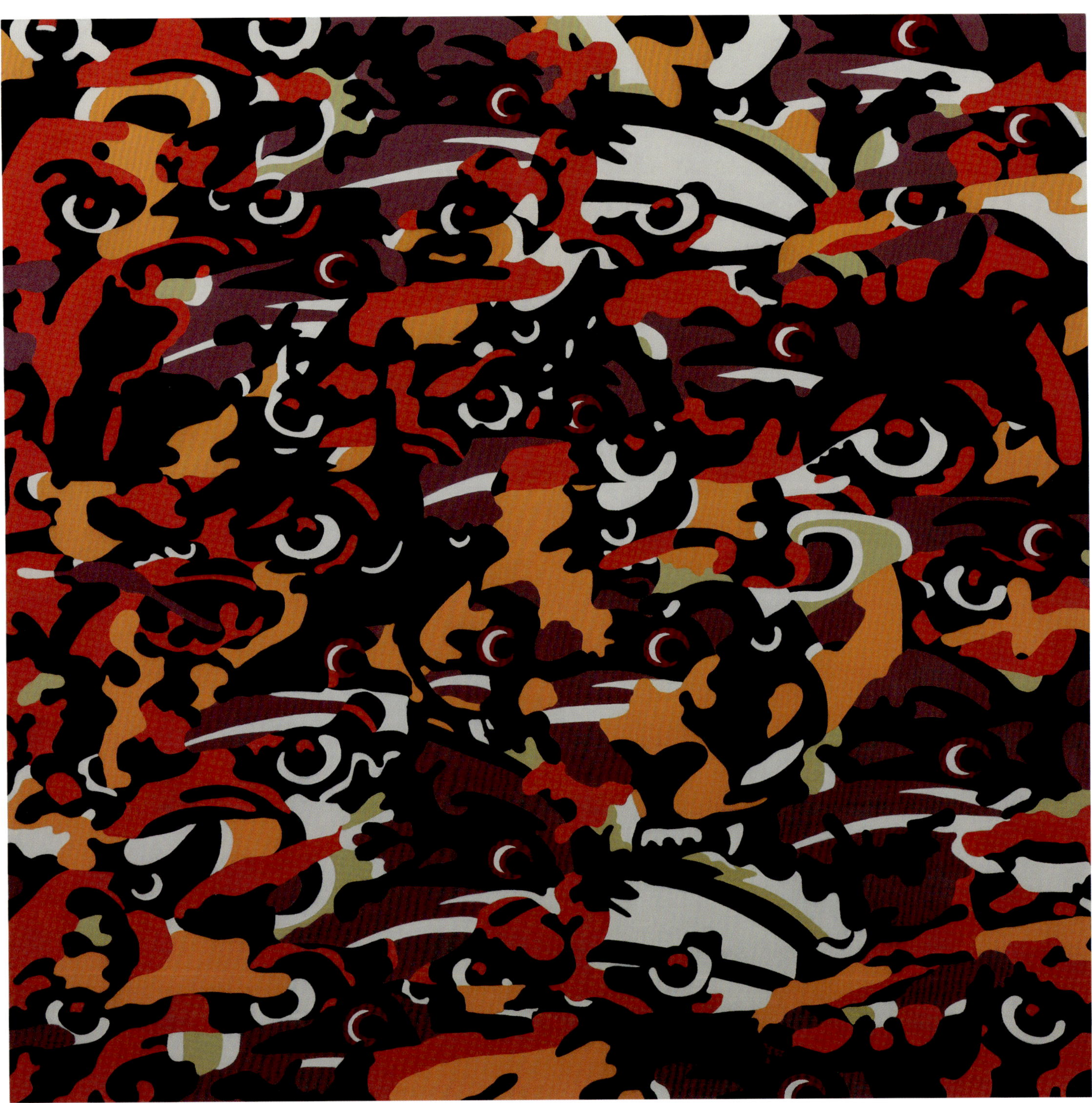

Line of Scrimmage, 2004

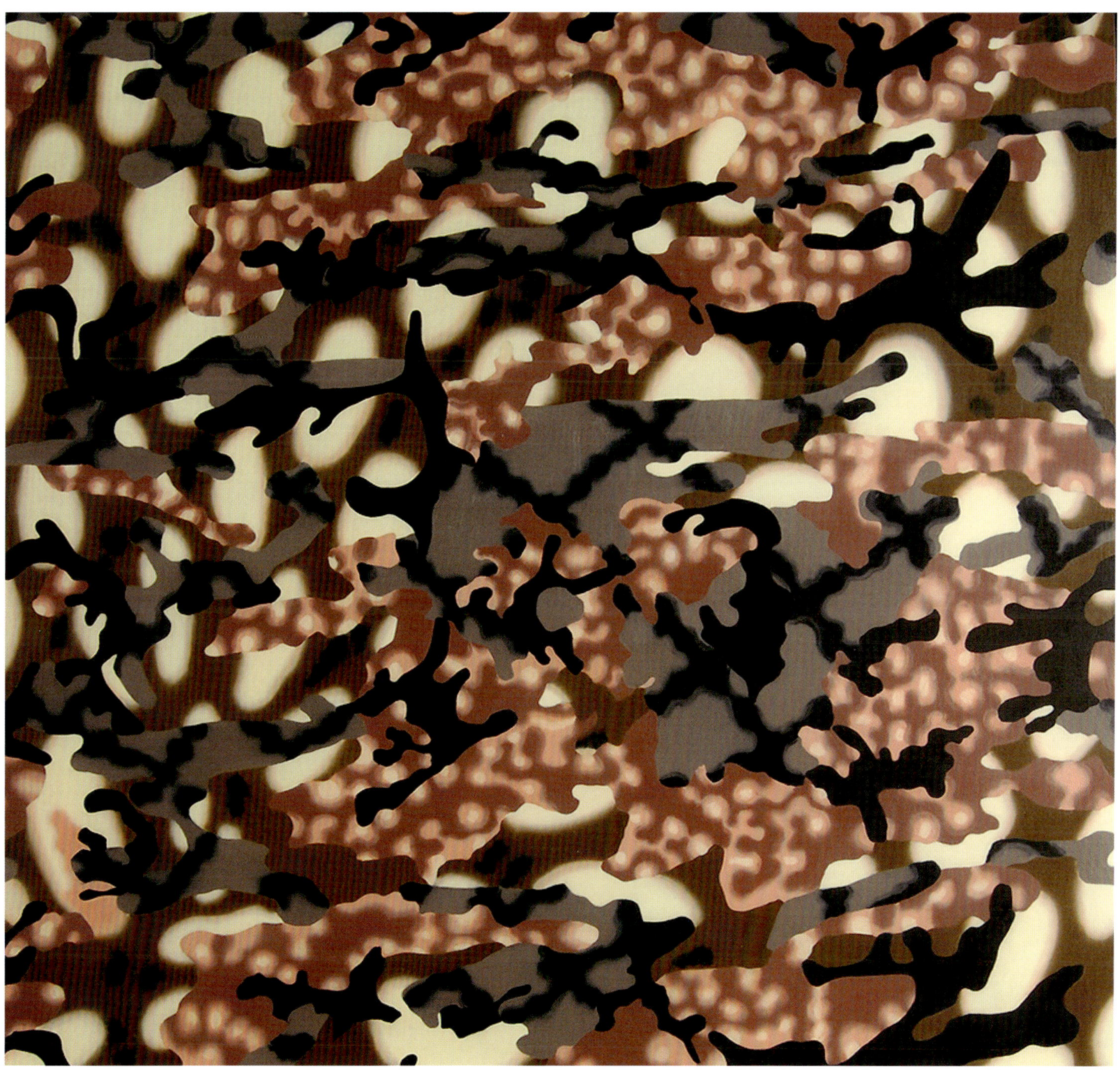

Camouflesh USA, 2005

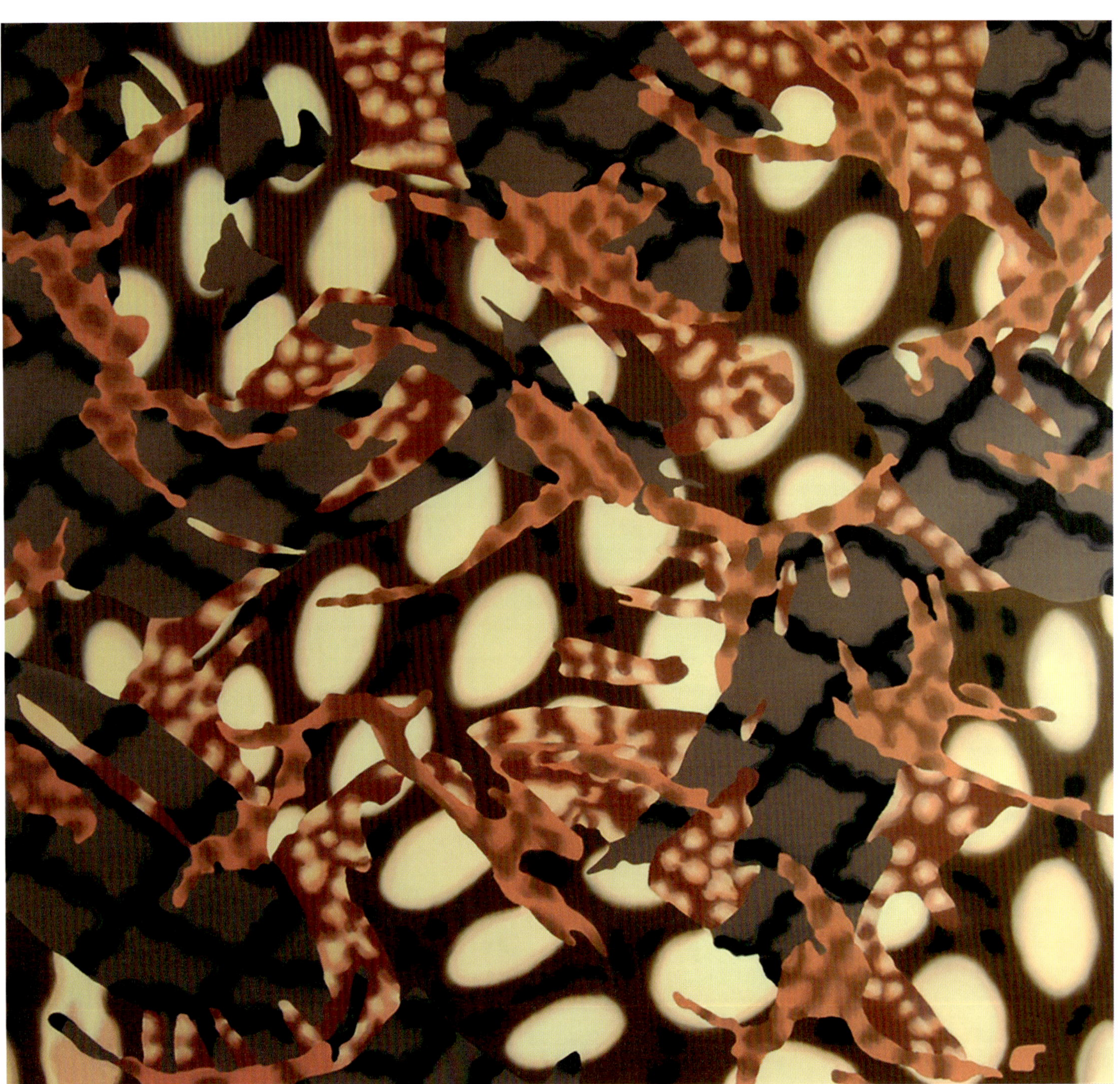

Camouflesh Great Britain I, 2005

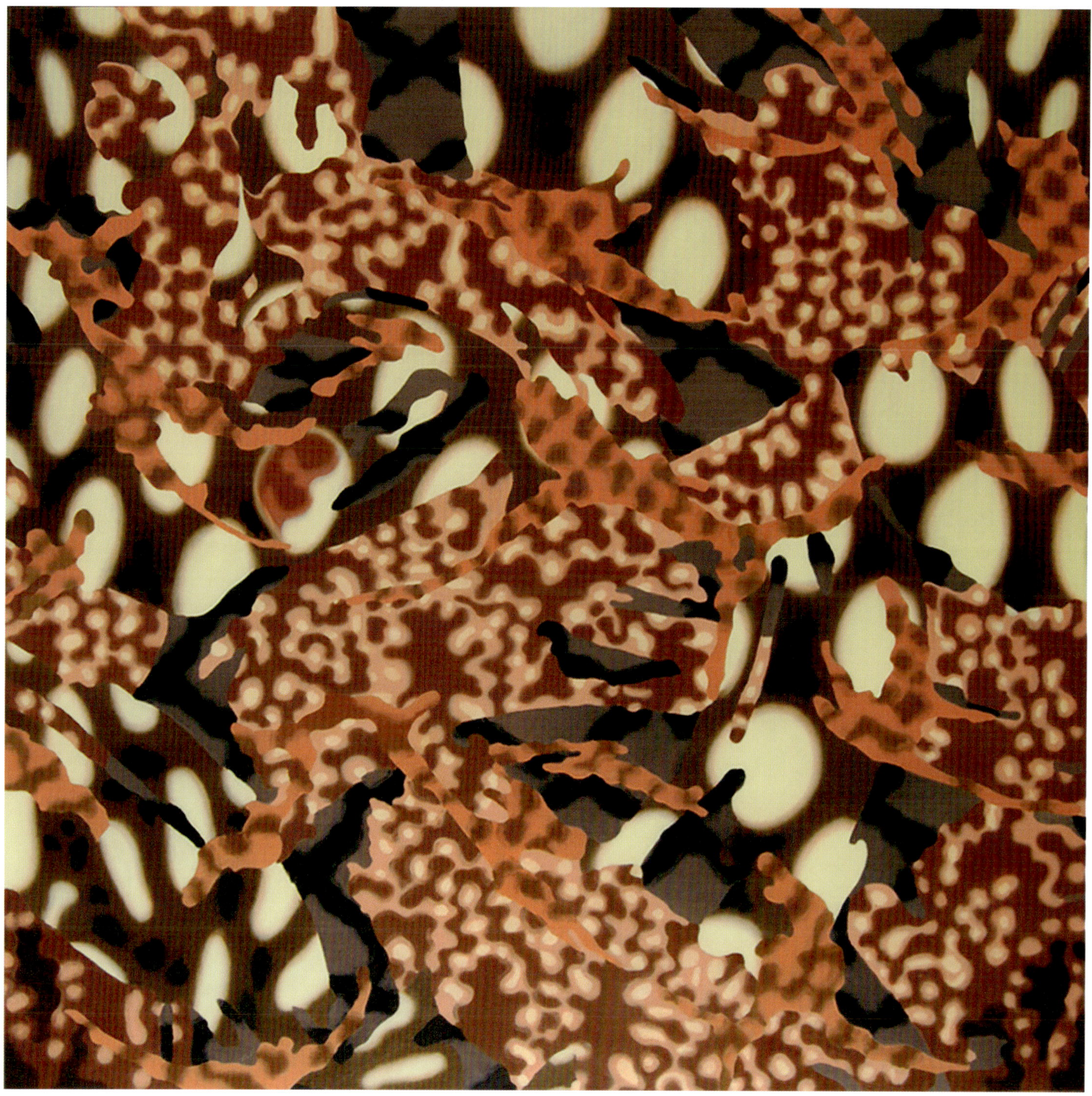

Camouflesh Great Britain II, 2005

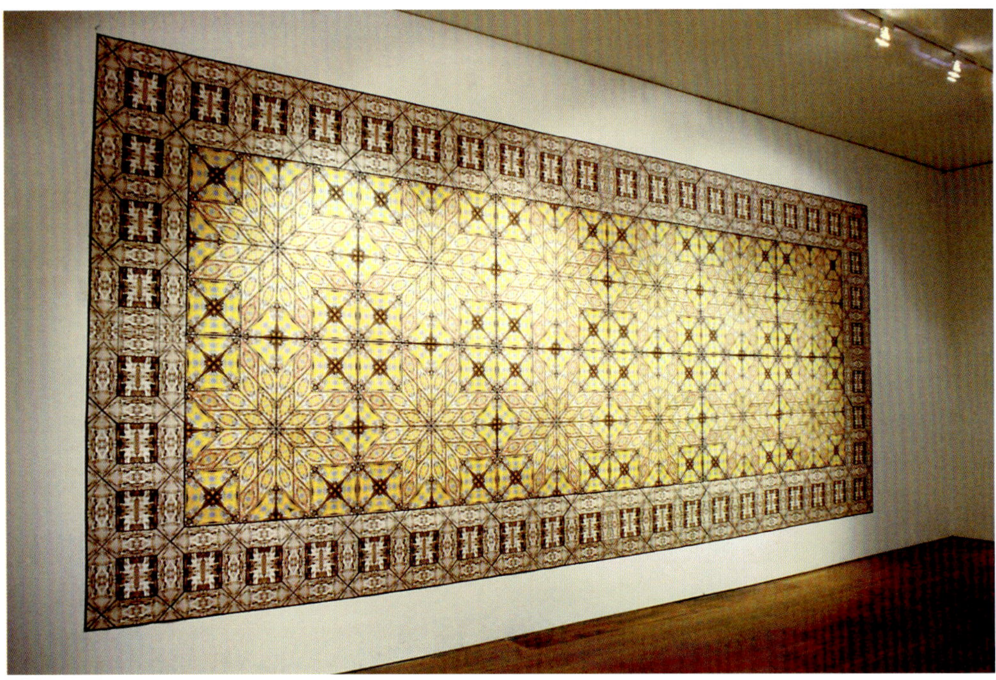

...they often tend to resemble plants, 2004

Wolstenholme was also making paintings at the same time, many based on camouflage patterns that she created from various sources (for instance, logos of sports teams as in *Line of Scrimmage* [2004, p. 36], or from different currencies). In a 2004 show in Fredericton she exhibited five works in which the figures were painted in various camouflage patterns, as were the shelves on which they were displayed. The clothing, meant to obscure the female figure, disappeared into the repetitive patterns of the camouflage. In these works, camouflage is not designed to hide things in the landscape. Instead, the artist is interested in the concealment practised in the social sphere. These works maintain that fashion, uniforms, and gendered roles and positions are all cut from the same cloth. Such conventions subsume the individual underneath a collective identity. These varied costumes are worn by women and dictated by men – or at least by the conventions of male-centred societies. Designed to either mask the body or present it in a stereotypical, sexualized manner (another form of masking, Wolstenholme would say), these are costumes eroticized by men.

Paintings made during that period, such as the *Camouflesh* series (2005, pp. 37–39, 96), also use the camouflage motif, combining pornographic images pulled from the internet with corporate logos and imagery derived from banknotes, fashion, and advertising. The surfaces of these paintings, which at first glance seem merely

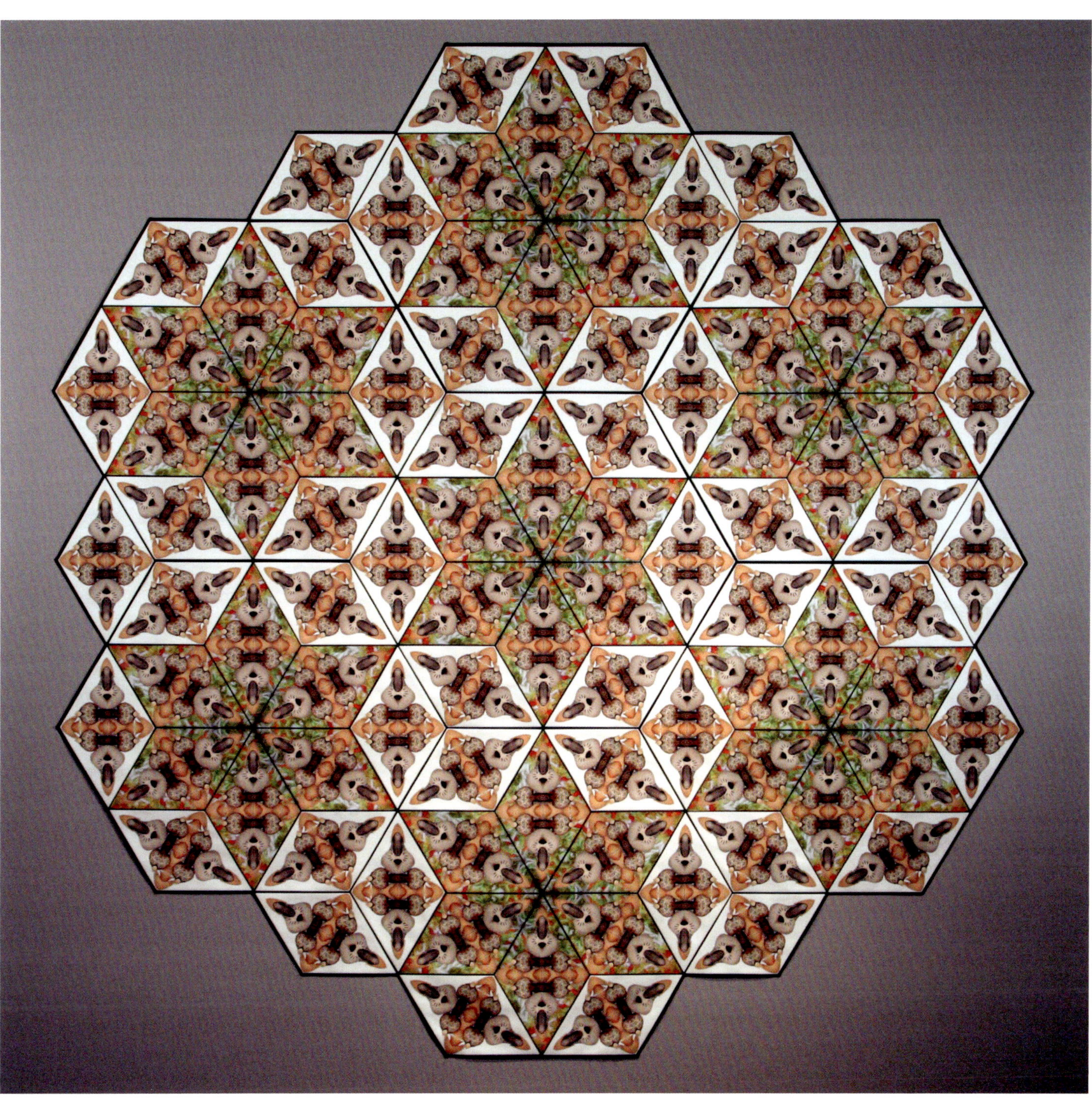

Homesse, 2005

decorative patterns, break up into their constituent parts upon closer inspection, disrupting any attempt by the viewer to have a "proper" response.

The paintings led to large paper collages, made from numerous cut-out image fragments and basted together the way one would a patterned quilt. In works such as *they often tend to resemble plants* (2004, p. 40) and *Homesse* (2005, p. 41), Wolstenholme employs images from a diverse range of sources (art history, advertising, and pornography) to create dense geometric patterns. As with her paintings, the compositions are intricate, decorative, and at first glance abstract. It is only on closer inspection that the imagery from which they are made becomes apparent. As Pan Wendt describes them, "The wall pictures present the generation of pattern and form, as well as the process of seeing, as interwoven with the need to contend with the generative power and allure of the female body."[13] Reminiscent of classical Islamic art, from which the human figure is banned, it is nonetheless the figures of women that provide the foundation for the patterns in these works, a critical stance based in Wolstenholme's feminism. As critic Alex Keim writes, "In an increasingly volatile world where women's voices are often stifled or marginalized through abstract and mostly masculine-dominated systems, Wolstenholme, through her art, speaks loud and clear."[14]

Sugar and Spice (2007, p. 43) in the National Gallery of Canada collection is a large bronze screen, made up of sixteen repeated forms, themselves comprised of casts of bones, nail polish bottles, a powder compact, and small figures of the singer Posh Spice from the Spice Girls. Harking back to the "quilted" paper works such as *Homesse*, *Sugar and Spice* bridges the gap between the two strains of Wolstenholme's work, the abstract and the figurative. It was inspired in part by her ongoing jewellery practice. As in the large paper constructions, in this sculpture Wolstenholme is veering away from the minimalist look of her pill work to something more ornamental. Suspended from the ceiling when shown, the sculpture is both screen and barrier, open to the eye but physically obstructive. Also like the paper constructions, this sculpture references quilting – another nod by the artist to the history of women's domestic crafts. She told the National Gallery, "I infuse these technologies into my work because they are appropriate to my practice, a component of which seeks to notice the fact that they have generally been undervalued and seen as less significant art historically, partially due to their association with the feminine."[15] The work, reflecting what curator Josée Drouin-Brisebois calls a

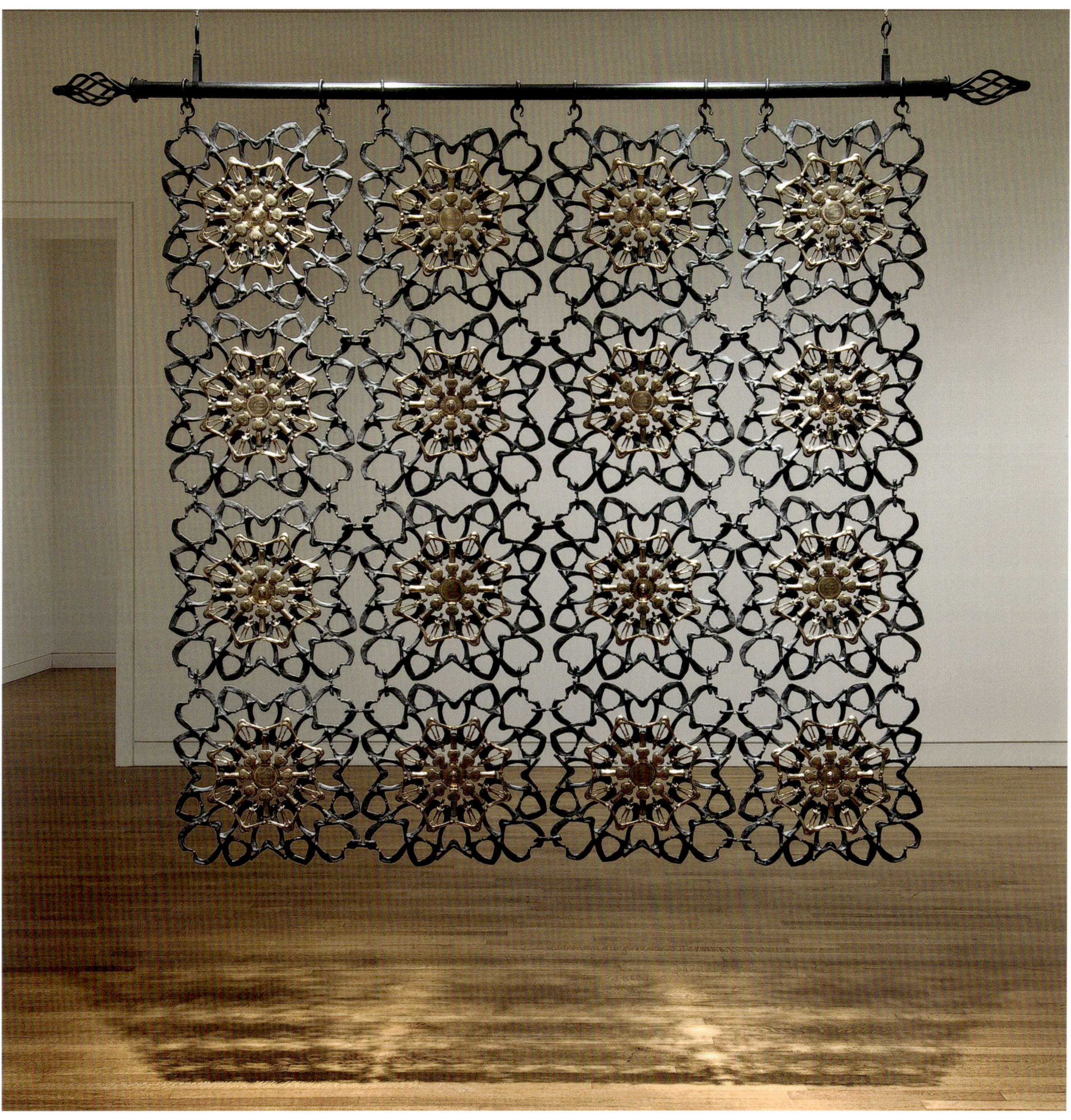

Sugar and Spice, 2007

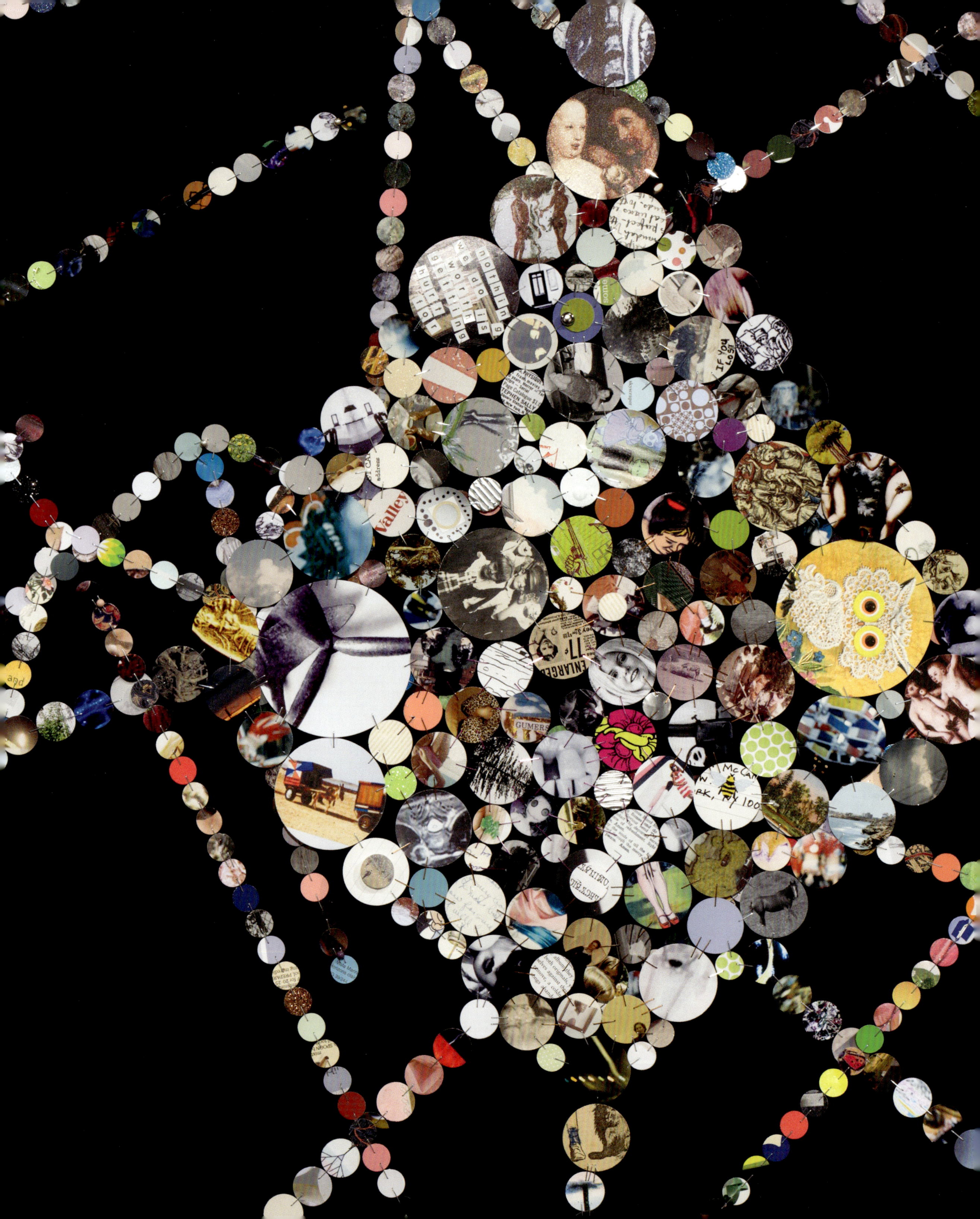
Valley
some
and

(opposite, right, and overleaf)
Neuraesthezia, 2011

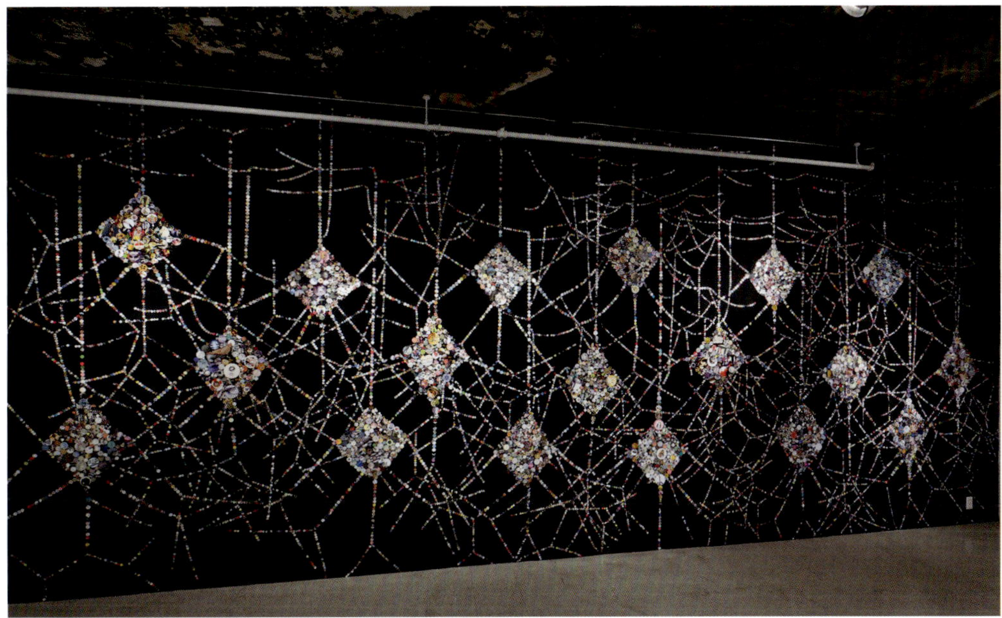

"baroque sensibility,"[16] also points forward to later work, a series anchored by the large sculpture *Hexagraphy* (2018, pp. 53, 54–55).

From 2000 through 2020, Wolstenholme had numerous solo exhibitions across Canada. In addition, she was included in several large group exhibitions, one of which, *Arena: The Art of Hockey*, toured the country. Her work of this period was primarily figurative, or at least representational, including the continued use of pill imagery. She made a series of porcelain, burka-clad figurines glazed in bright colours that sat on a long shelf mounted on the wall. Loosely based on images she had seen of women lining up to vote in Islamic countries, the pieces were titled *Suffrage* (2005) and *Undercover* (2011, pp. 74–75). *Exposé* (2011, p. 73) is a life-sized nude figure with a cow's head, modelled in plaster, reclining on a chaise lounge. *Exposé* references the Egyptian fertility goddess Hathor. Wolstenholme has deliberately disguised the gender of the work; it easily reads as either male or female.

Exposé was first exhibited in Montréal in 2011, with a large paper construction. *Neuraesthezia* (2011, pp. 44, 45, 46–47) was made from punching images out of magazines and stapling them into disks of varying sizes. It was a process developed collaboratively with Wolstenholme's friend Gillian McCain. Based on a visual representation of a neural net, the form reflects the physical neurons, while the imagery reads as content — the random thoughts, memories, and impressions that fire through our brains at all times. As another construction loosely based on a grid,

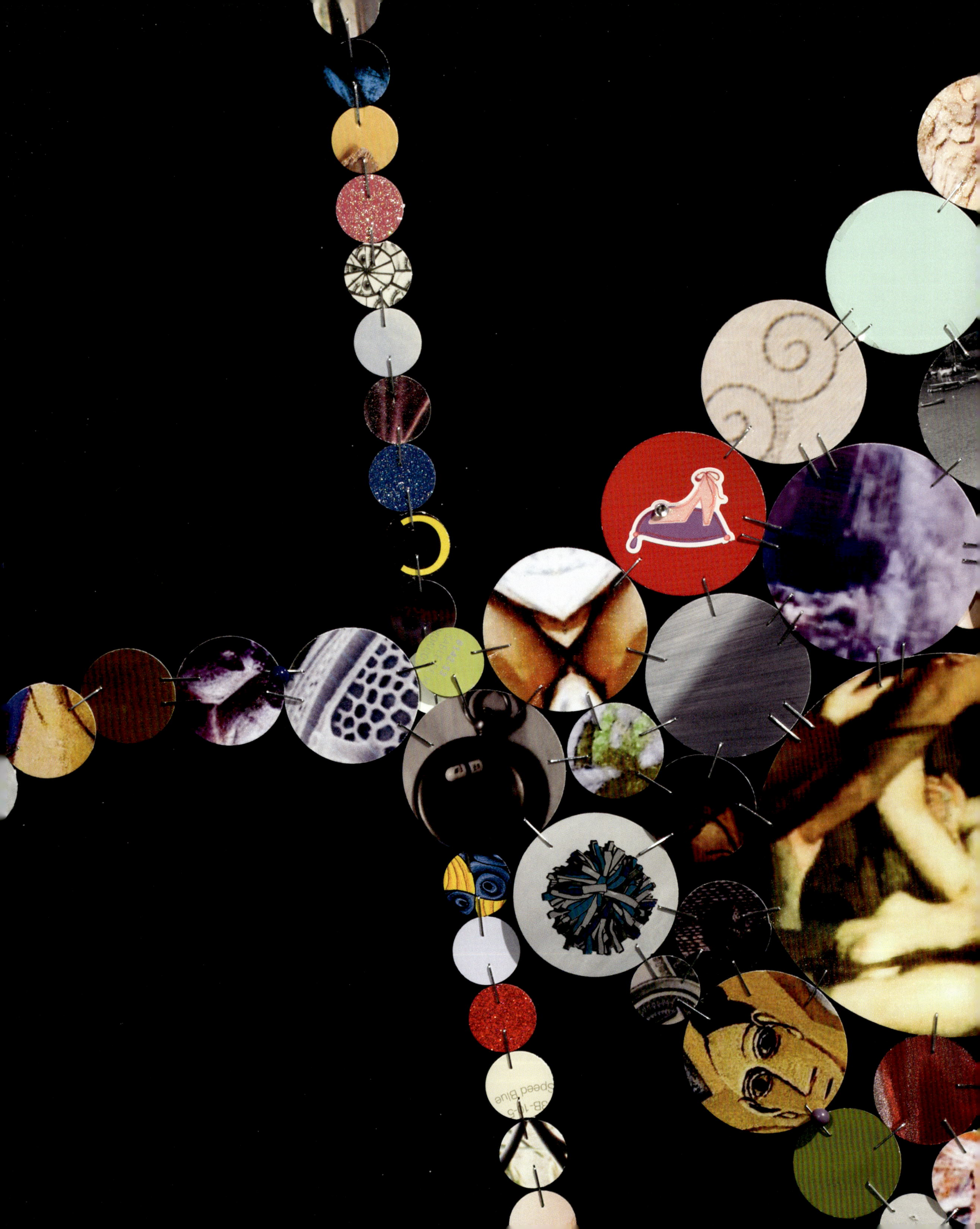

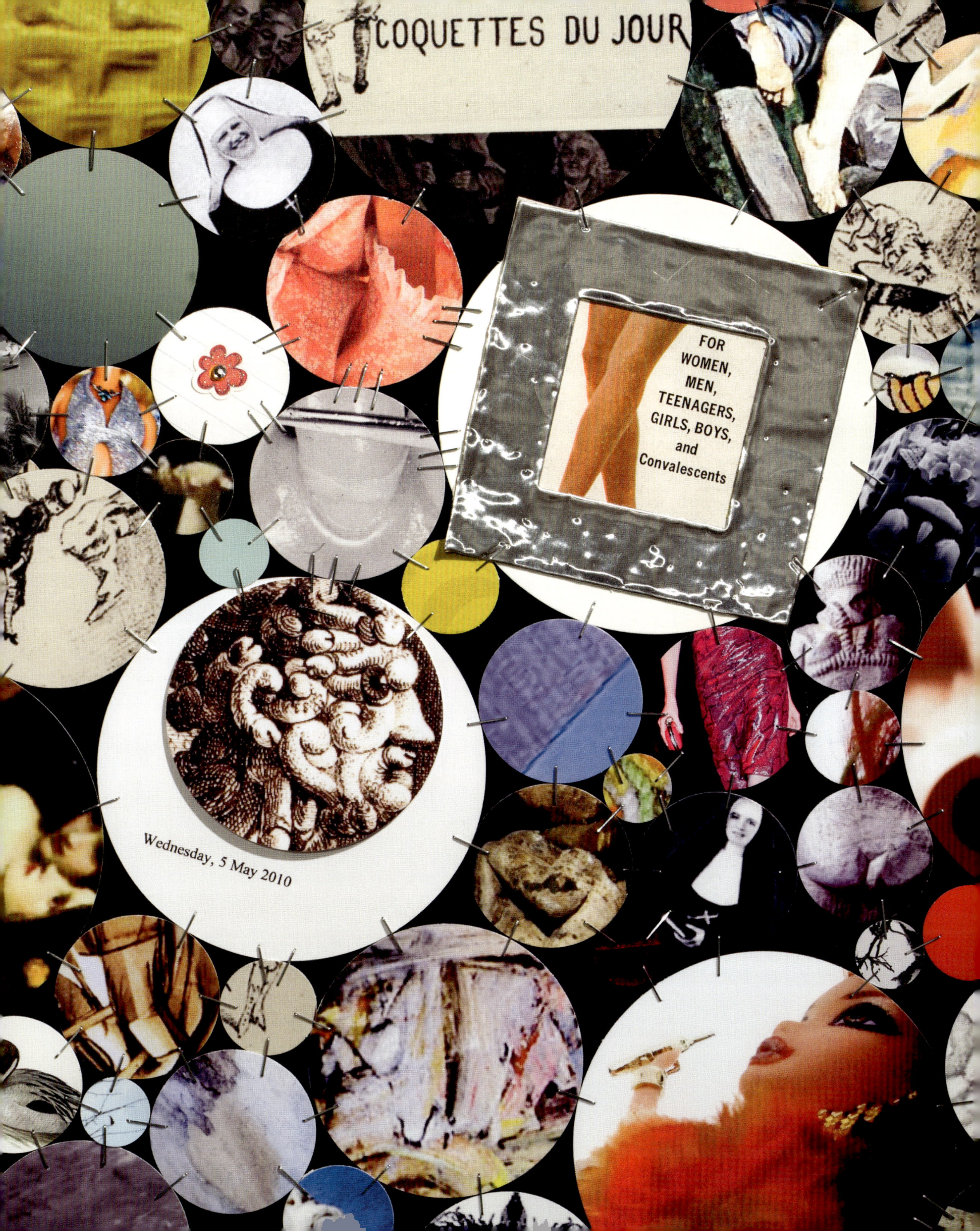
COQUETTES DU JOUR
FOR WOMEN, MEN, TEENAGERS, GIRLS, BOYS, and Convalescents
Wednesday, 5 May 2010

the work refers back to the "quilt" pieces of the mid- 2000s, and looks forward to the steel and plastic grids of the later 2010s. *Hexagraphy*, in particular, is indebted to this work, as it starts from a similar point: the neural activity of the human brain. However, where *Neuraesthezia* takes the content of that activity as its subject matter, presenting a kind of map of the thinking process, *Hexagraphy* looks at the neurological activity itself, the electrical impulses by which content is created, conveyed, and stored.

•••

Hexagraphy has turned out not to be the outlier it may have appeared to be back in 2018. Wolstenholme, of course, never thought of it in that way. In fact, she sees its roots stretching back to her student days at NSCAD in the 1980s, and to Michael Snow's film *Wavelength*, which David Askevold introduced her to. Shot in one long take, Snow's iconic film takes the length of the movie to zoom in on a postcard of the ocean on the opposite side of a large loft from the camera's position. "My piece for my PhD is a reference to his film, of the picture of the ocean on the wall across the room. And, you know, it's not a huge leap," Wolstenholme observed.[17] The sculpture, with its undulating form and sequential waves of lights, physically references an ocean swell, a section of wave, and a small piece of a massively large phenomenon.

Where *Hexagraphy* can be read as a representation of one part of the ocean environment, the surface that we can see, Wolstenholme's newest works constitute more of a deep dive into marine ecosystems. From the early 2020s, painting was a major focus, spurred in part by the COVID-19 shutdowns and by space limitations in her Fredericton house. She also was spending a lot of time with her mother in hospital then, and she could do small paintings while they watched television together. One of the things they watched was footage of deep-sea exploration. The watercolours she created while watching the documentary were later worked up into her large series of paintings *Into the Deep Blue Sea* (2023, pp. 49–50, 84–86). Without the large studio she had enjoyed in Hantsport, painting was a strategy to continue making work.

In 2025 she built a new studio in her Fredericton home and began making plans to return to welding and other ways of making sculpture. She is working on an immersive video for her retrospective exhibition, a hexagonal "tent" that will feature "sea snow," the constantly sinking organic matter that is the base of the food chain

Into the Deep Blue Sea: Triptych 1
(Piglet Squid, Ctenophore, Jelly), 2023

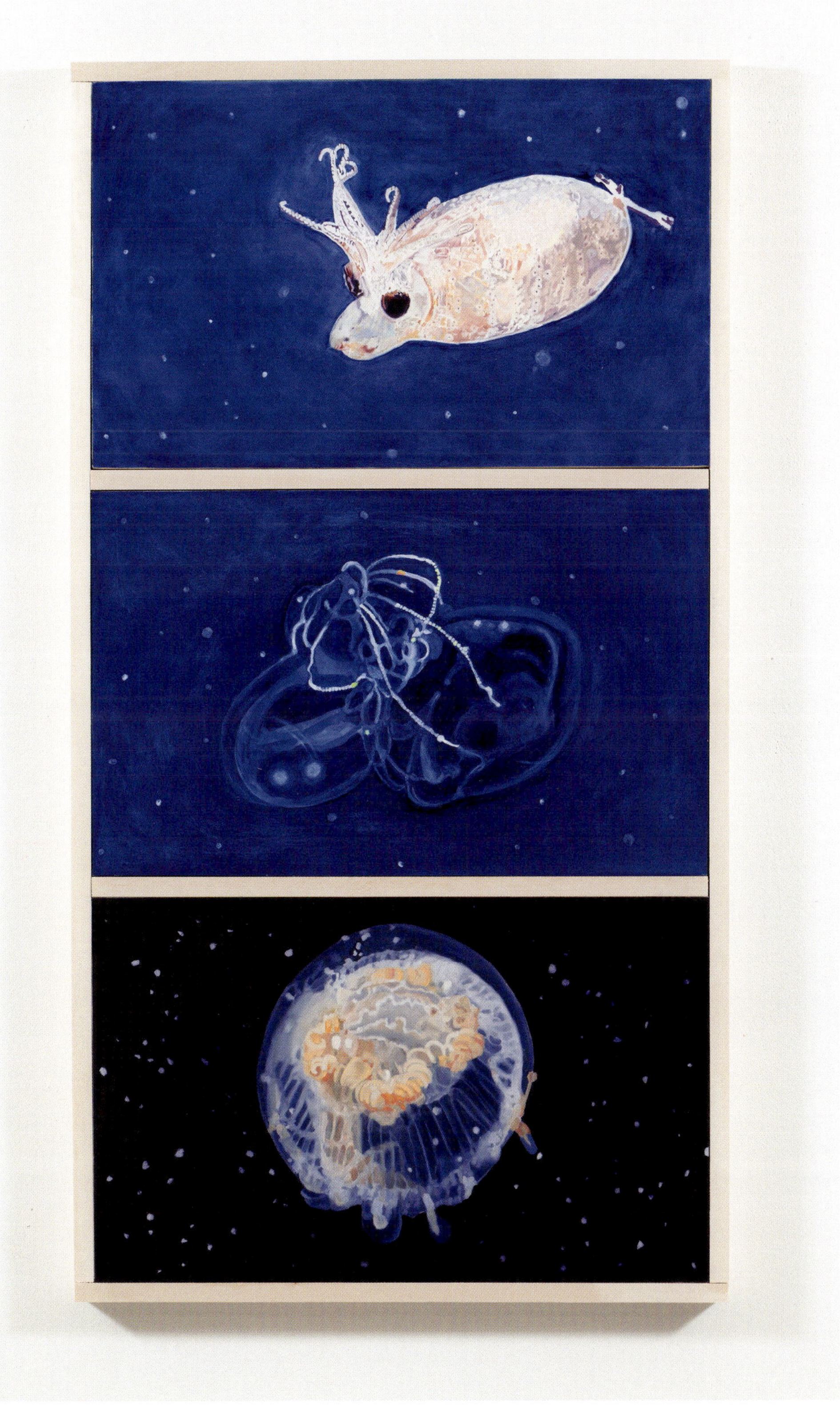

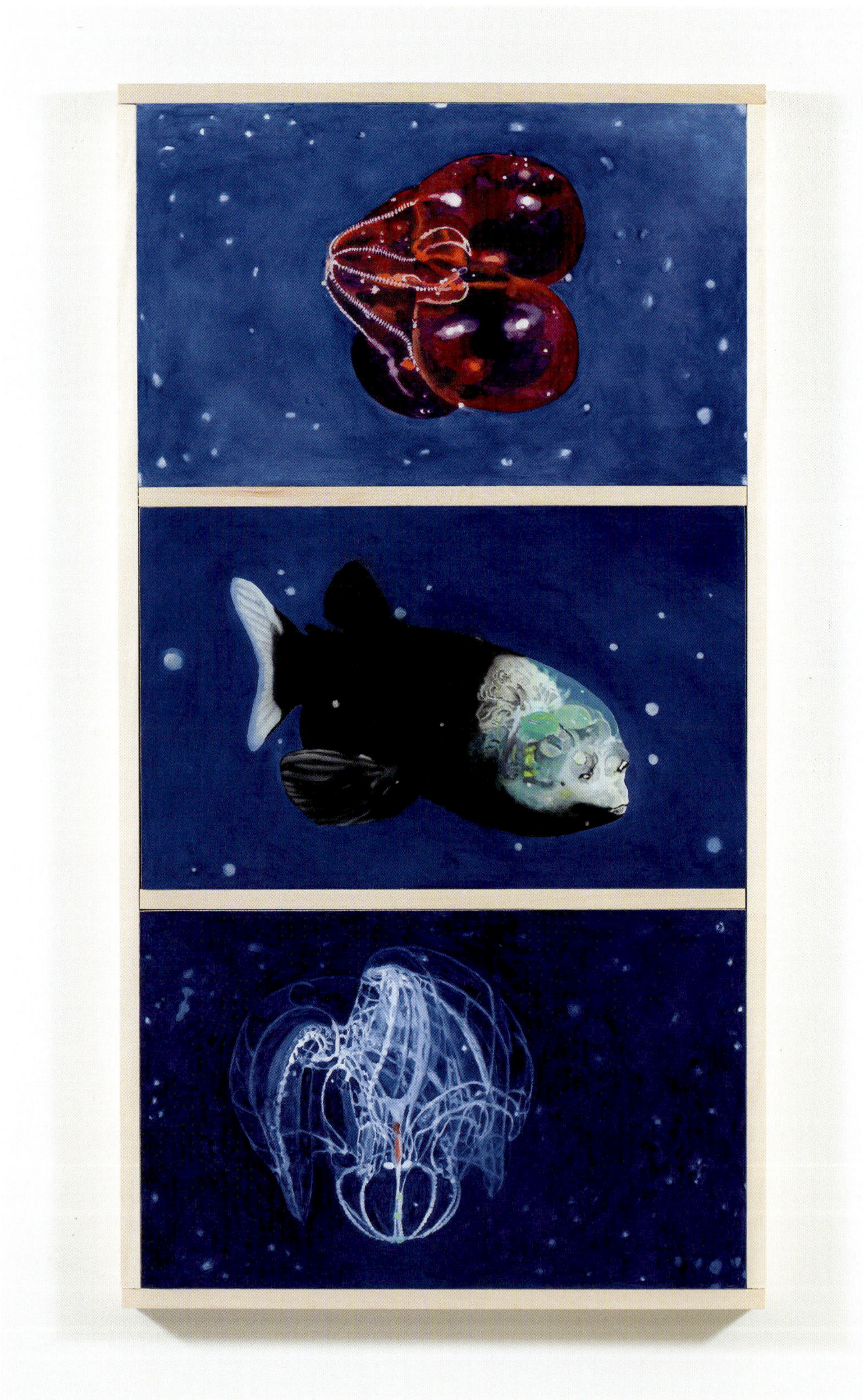

Into the Deep Blue Sea: Triptych 2 (Bloody-Belly Jelly, Barreleye Fish, Lobate Ctenophore), 2023

in the deep ocean. An enclosing space that harks back to *Patience* (p. 20), the video also points forward, though she does not know where to. Yet.

"Whatever opportunities are offered to me, I take them up, wholeheartedly," Wolstenholme says. "I don't tend to go looking for opportunity, because there's so much rejection there, like you just get reject, reject, reject, and you start to feel like you're just a nobody, and that you have no place."[18] But the fact is that Wolstenholme has been carving out her place for decades.

Subverting the levers of control is never easy. Nevertheless, some artists continue to try, making that leap of faith into what they hope will be a better world. Colleen Wolstenholme is such an artist. She has steeped herself in the history of European art – whether modernist, classical, or ancient – in order to deflect the patriarchal views that have dominated art across centuries. So much of her work exposes the forms of coercion that limit women's possibilities and circumscribe their potential for action. In Wolstenholme's hands, sculpture, the art of the object, becomes a powerful means of countering the objectification of women, thereby opening new paths and new insights into how thought can provoke action, and, ultimately, inspire change.

NOTES

1 Linda Nochlin, ***Women, Art, and Power and Other Essays*** (Harper & Row, 1988), 176.

2 Colleen Wolstenholme, interview with the author, May 10, 2021. All other quoted excerpts from Wolstenholme are taken from this same interview, unless otherwise indicated.

3 Colleen Wolstenholme, email to the author, April 5, 2021.

4 Colleen Wolstenholme, email to the author, May 28, 2021.

5 Rozsika Parker, ***The Subversive Stitch*** (Routledge, 1984), 4.

6 Parker, ***Subversive Stitch***, 215.

7 Robin Peck, "Scattered Across the Floor," ***C International Contemporary Art***, no. 61 (1999): 8.

8 Peck, "Scattered Across the Floor."

9 Colleen Wolstenholme, quoted in Peck, "Scattered Across the Floor," 8.

10 Virginia Eichhorn, "Colleen Wolstenholme, Iconophobia," ***Espace Sculpture***, no. 77 (Fall 2006): 40.

11 Peck, "Scattered Across the Floor," 8.

12 Wolstenholme, email to the author, April 5, 2021.

13 Pan Wendt, "Colleen Wolstenholme: A Divided Room," in Pan Wendt, ***Sugar & Spice*** (Confederation Centre Art Gallery, the Art Gallery of Nova Scotia, the Robert McLaughlin Art Gallery), 18.

14 Alex Keim, quoted in Pan Wendt, ***Re:collection at Confederation Centre Art Gallery*** (Confederation Centre Art Gallery, 2017), 164.

15 Colleen Wolstenholme to Josée Drouin-Brisebois, October 20, 2009.

16 Josée Drouin-Brisebois, "Sugar and Spice / Sucre et épice, 2007," purchase justification, 2012, artist files, National Gallery of Canada, Ottawa.

17 Drouin-Brisebois, "Sugar and Spice," n.p.

18 Drouin-Brisebois, "Sugar and Spice," n.p.

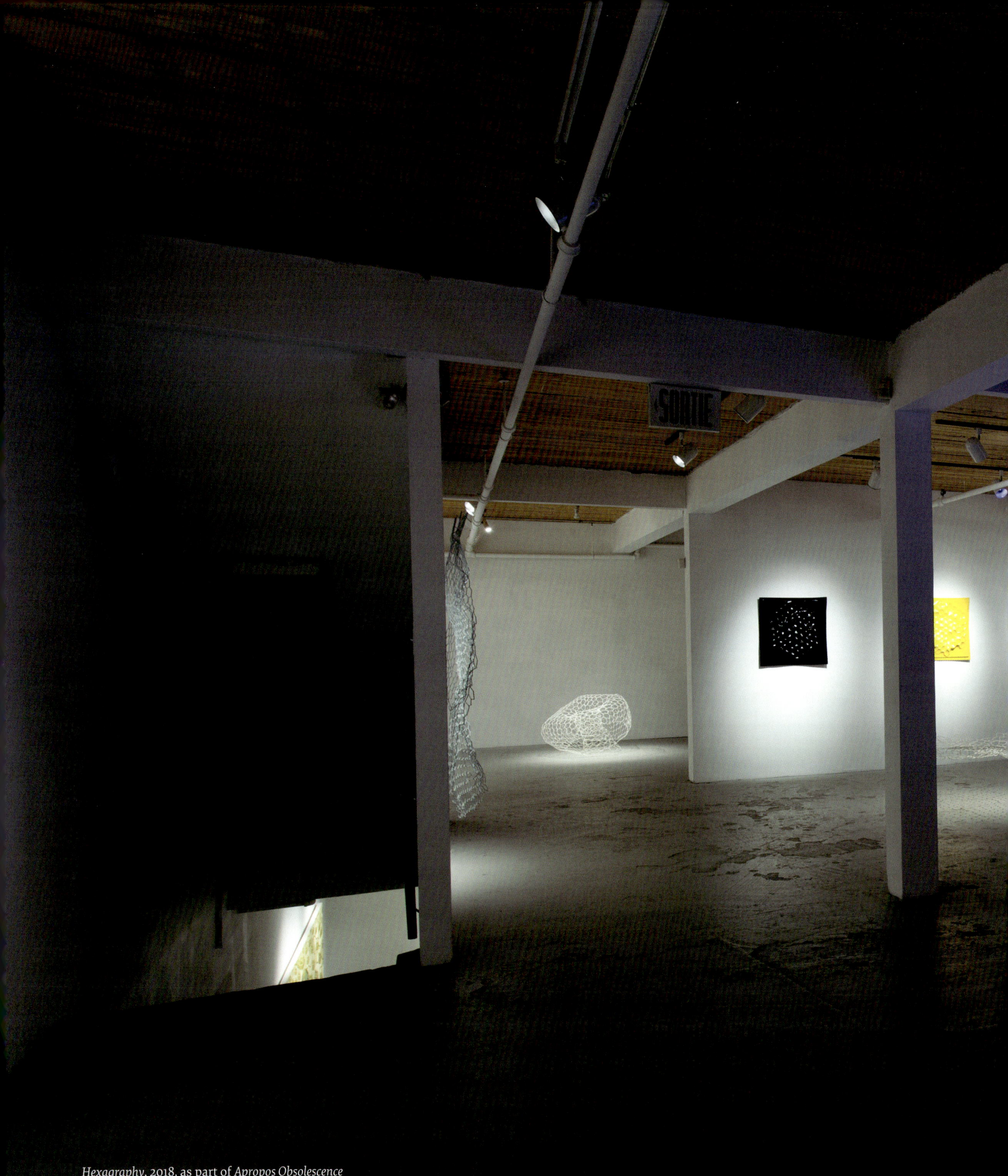

Hexagraphy, 2018, as part of *Apropos Obsolescence*

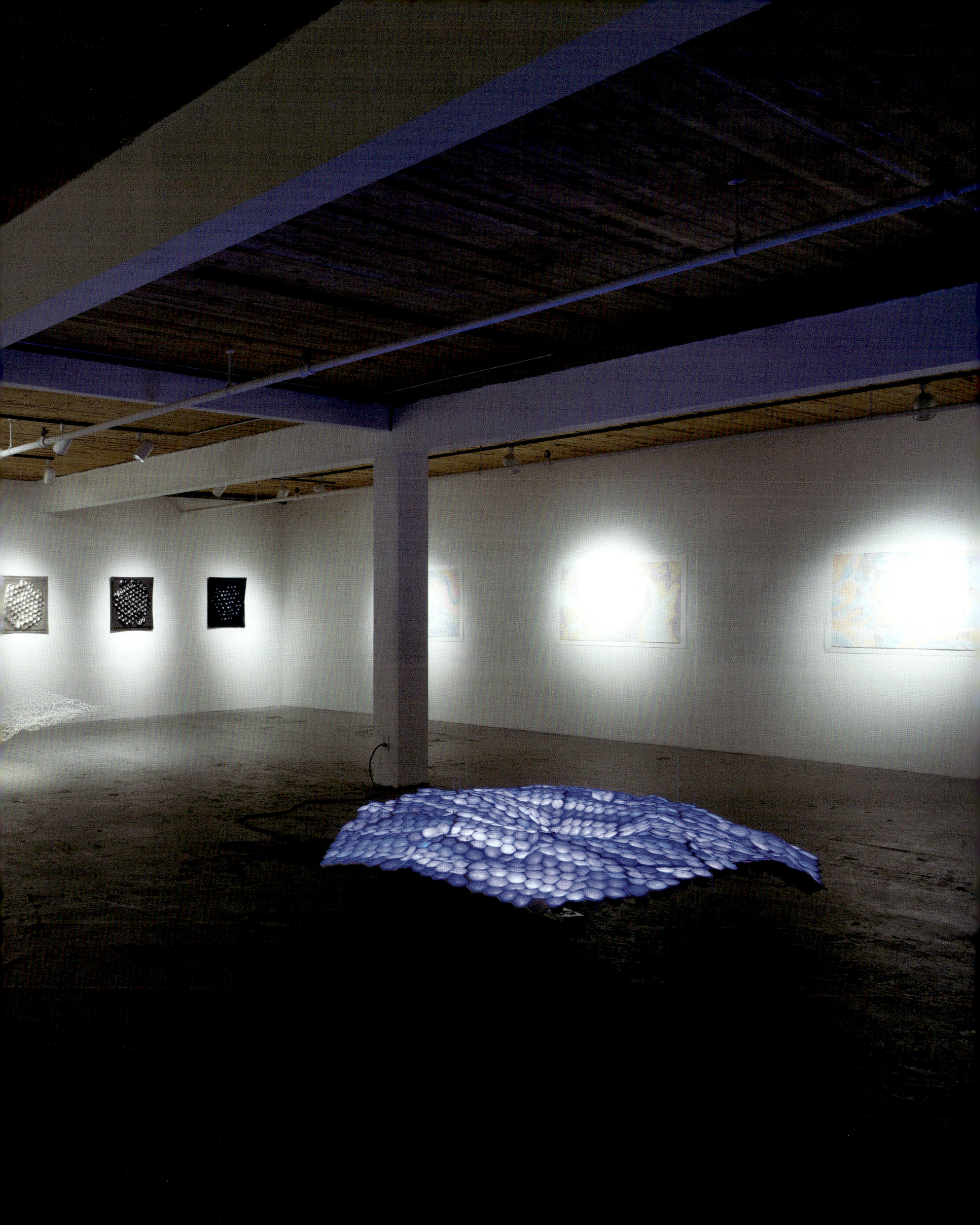

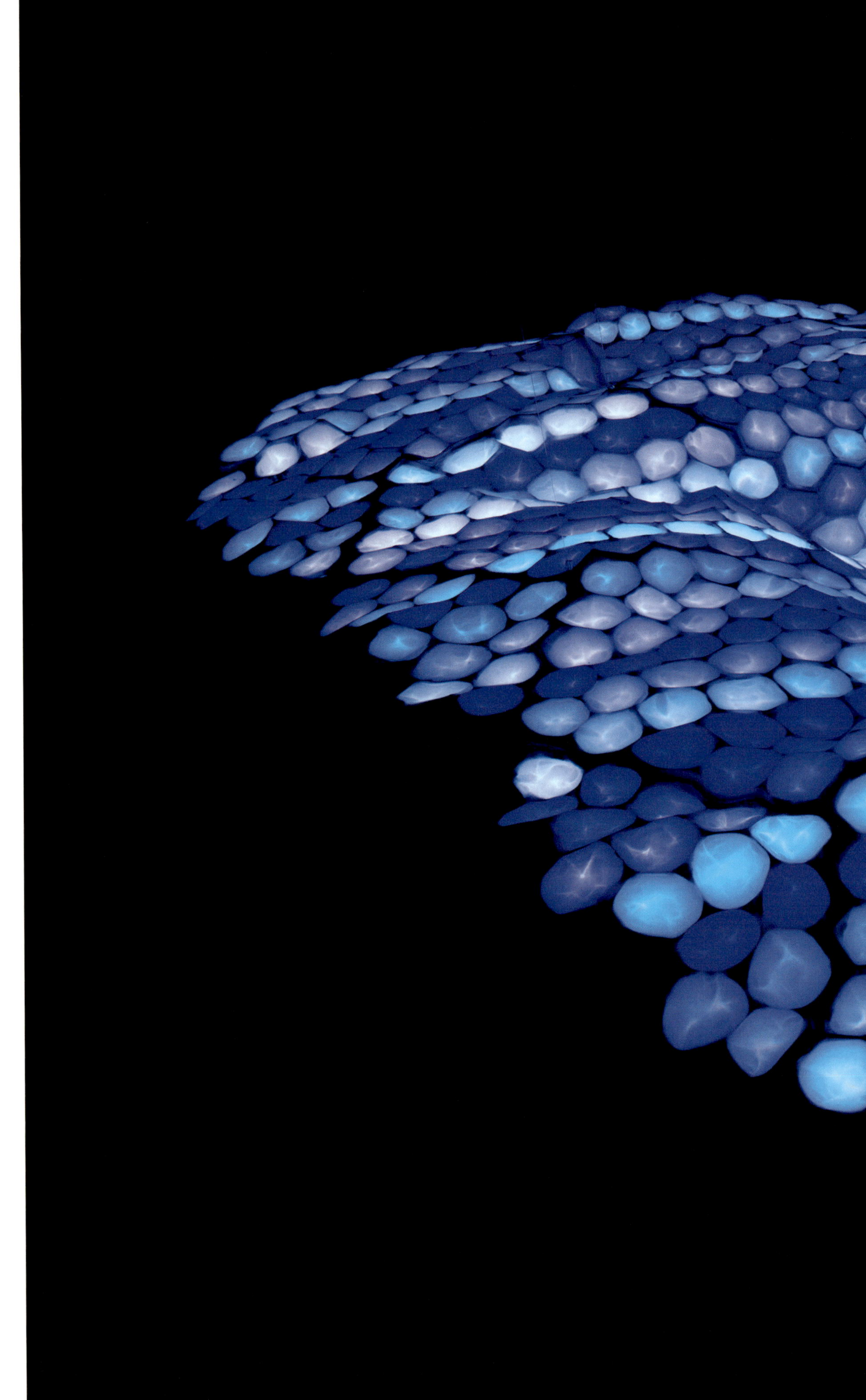

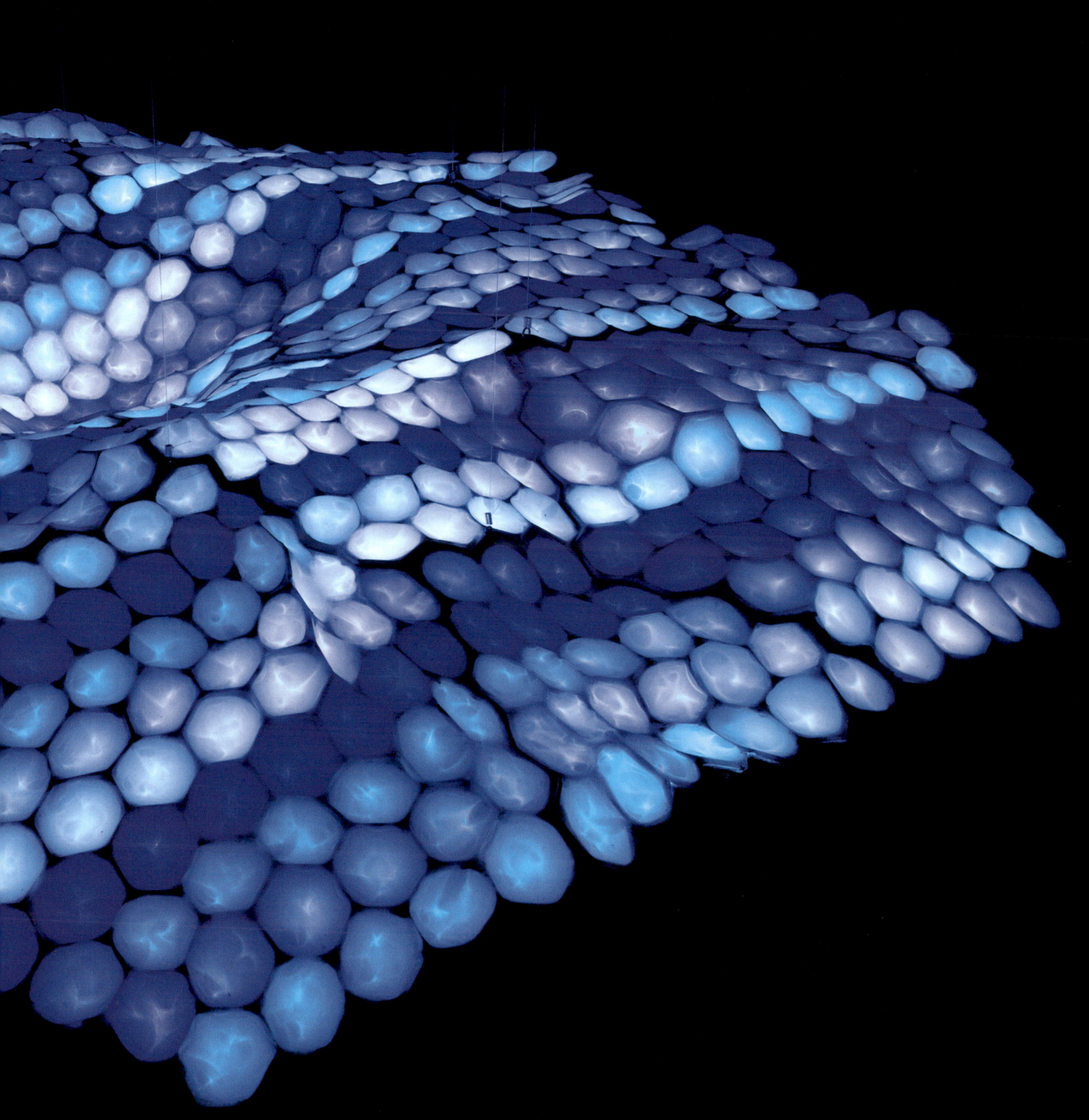

Hexagraphy, 2018

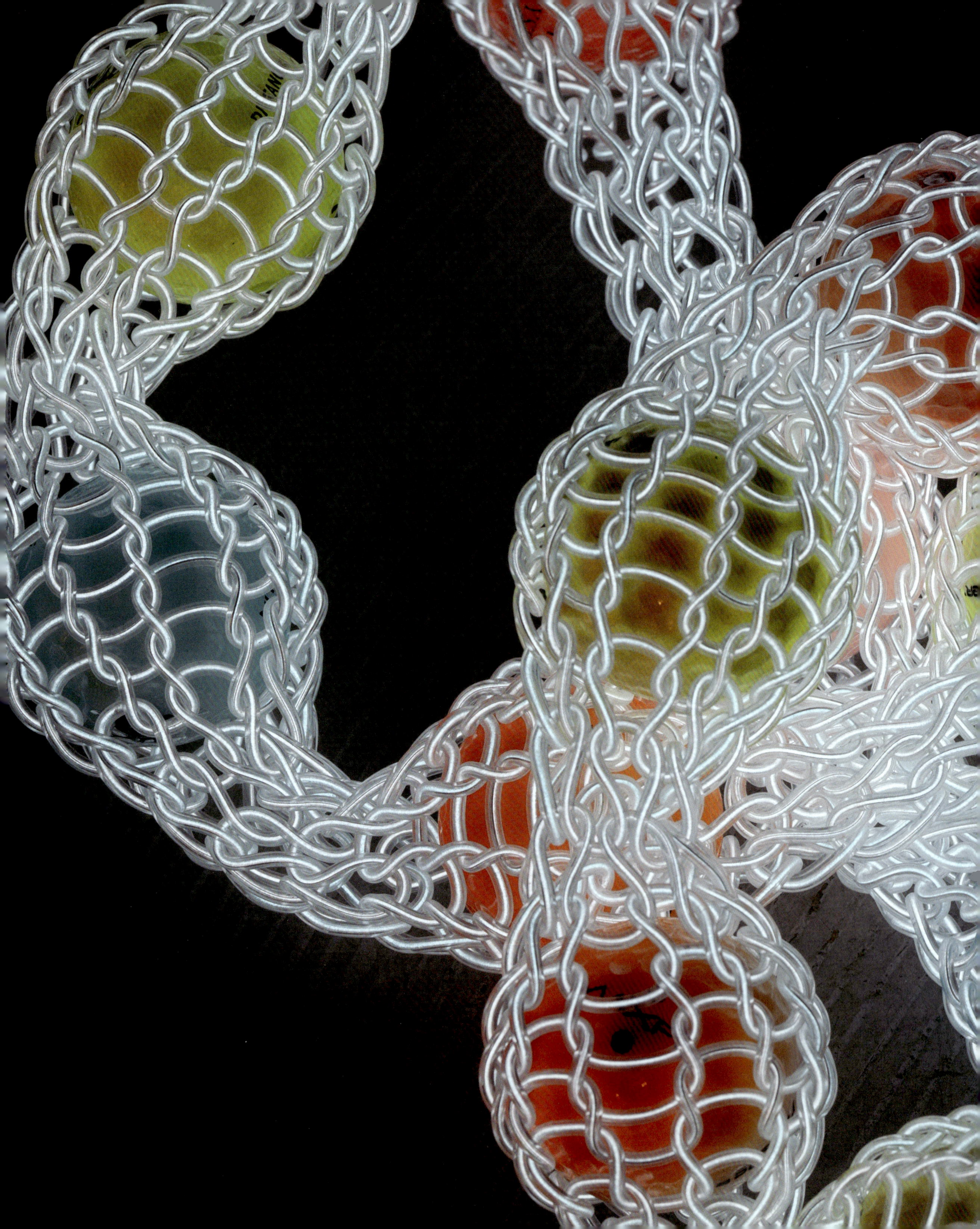

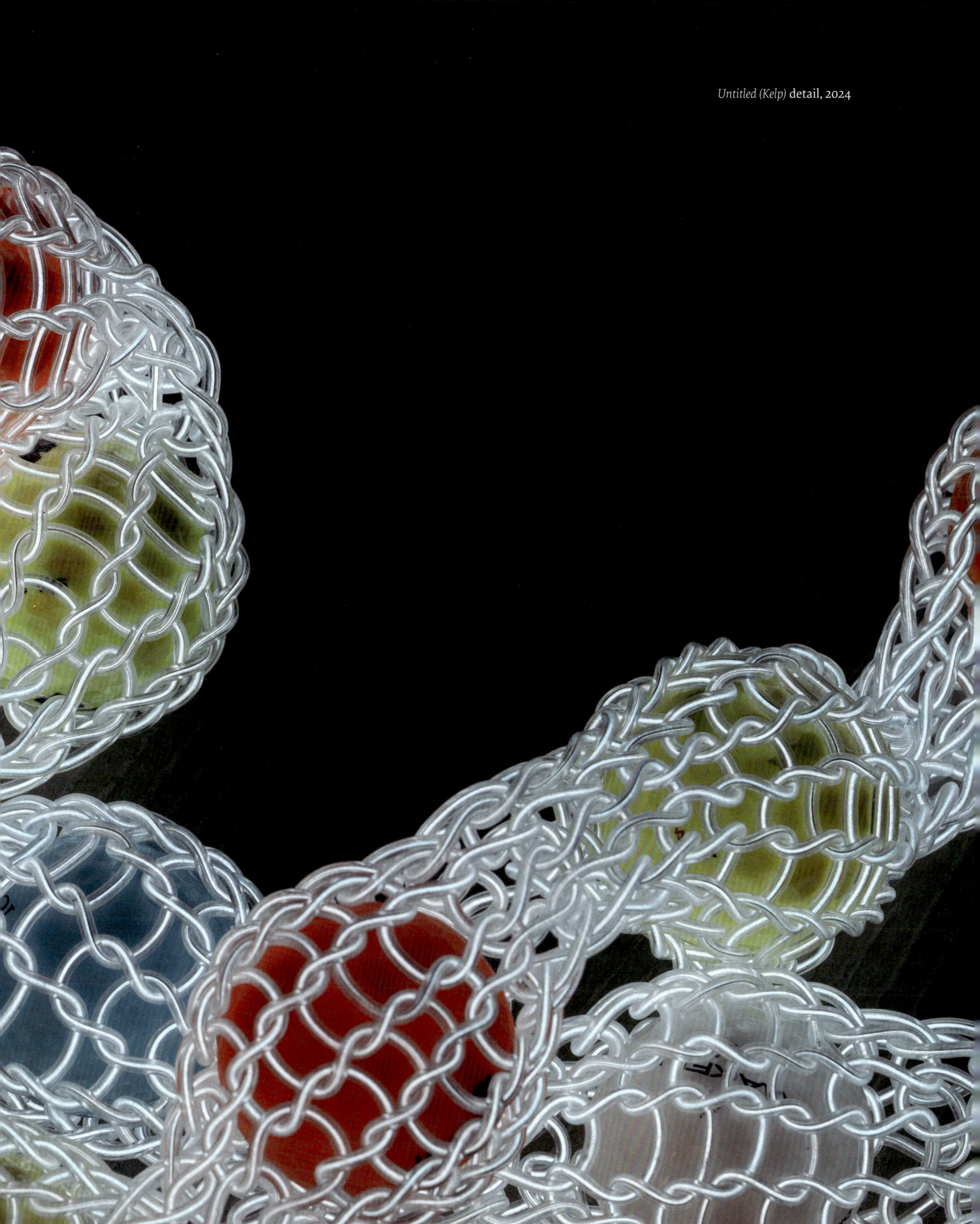

Untitled (Kelp) detail, 2024

Drug Company Logos, 1999
Frosst
Knoll
Roche
SmithKline
Upjohn
Wyeth

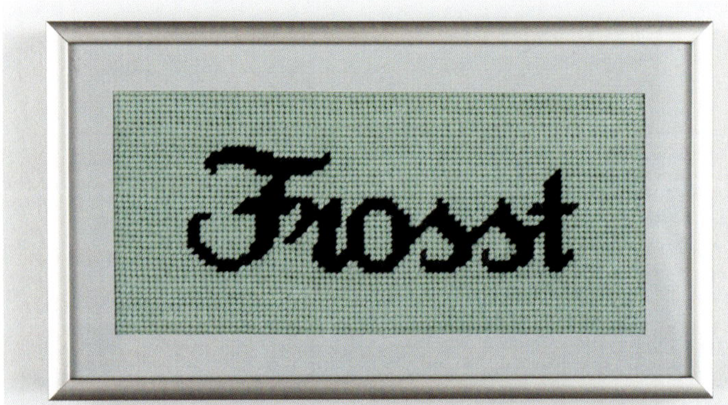

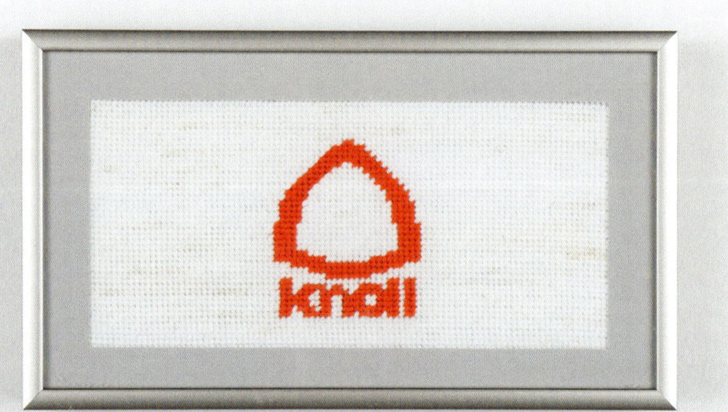

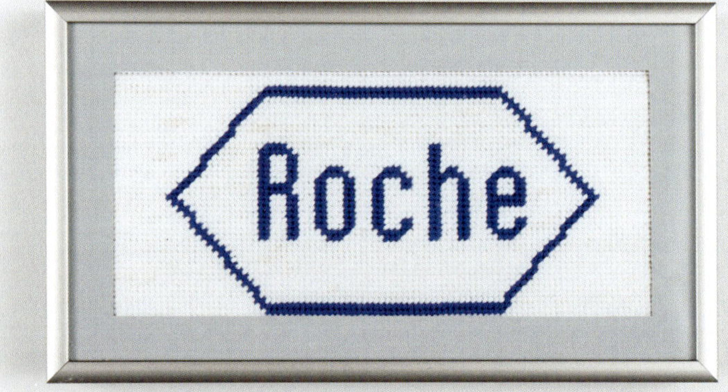

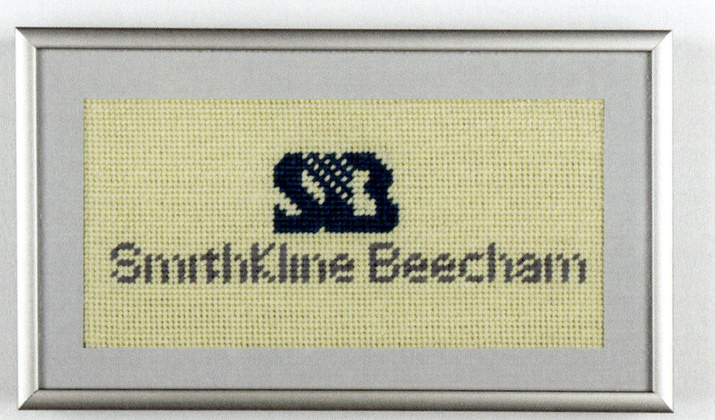

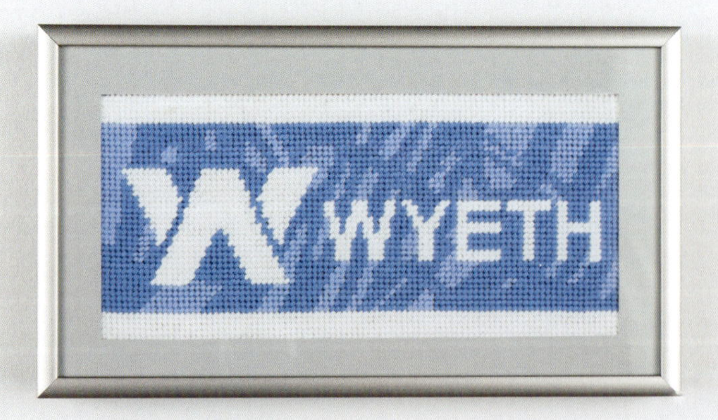

Situating feminism in Colleen Wolstenholme's objects / Situating objects in Colleen Wolstenholme's feminism

LAURA J. RITCHIE

In 1969 American feminist activist Carol Hanisch declared, "The personal is political."[1] A rallying call to collective action for second-wave feminists, the notion contributed to the deneutralization of the subject position in art criticism and artmaking. Where women artists looking to be taken seriously had previously tried to omit the personal from their works, by the 1970s critics such as Lucy Lippard normalized the idea that perspective matters.

Today, in the #MeToo era of the fight against women's oppression — what some call the fourth wave of feminism[2] — the adage still holds: women acknowledge that social and political structures shape individual experiences. Making and reading art are no exception. When asked to write about Canadian sculptor Colleen Wolstenholme's feminism, or about her in the context of feminist art and artists, I confess I struggled with the implications of the structures at play. Assuming her practice to be inherently feminist risks repeating earlier criticism — often by men — that imposed feminism onto her work rather than engaging with it through a feminist lens.

Facing the question of whether an artist's feminism should be addressed at all, I asked first: is feminism relevant in the work itself? Whereas phenomenology would have an artwork's meaning constituted in how it is viewed and perceived — and the subject (viewer) is essential — a feminist phenomenological approach questioning *how* I perceive and interpret the work seemed appropriate. With curatorial interests in art by women and feminist art history in Canada, I could see the utility in tracing the history of women artists[3] and placing Colleen on a timeline.[4] I could imagine

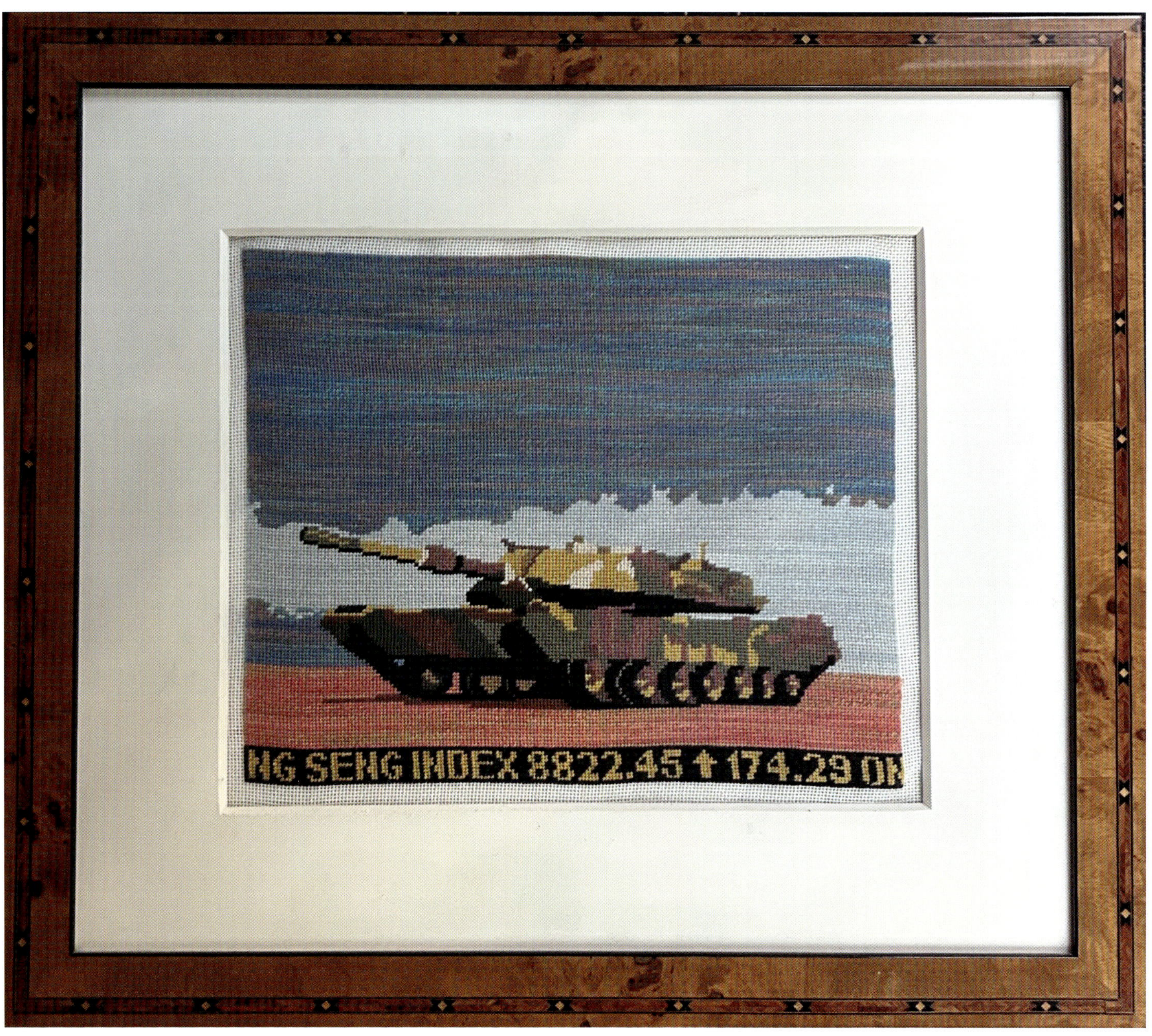

Abrams Tank, 2010

invoking Joyce Wieland and the regularly cited written works of Griselda Pollock and Linda Nochlin. I can, and do, see the value in a biographical approach such as that taken up by Ray Cronin in this publication. But, if I were to defer to facts,[5] if I went to the artist and asked, "Tell me about this work," or delved into a lit review (asking "What has been said about this work?"), I risked reducing the work to biographical artifact or artist's intention, losing some subjectivity, and missing the opportunity to open up a new encounter at the confluence of material, maker, and viewer.[6]

In situating Colleen's feminism, then, I opted to start from a reading of the works as objects — a type of speculative formal analysis given that so many of the now-packed or housed sculptures were inaccessible to me in the round. At first glance, feminist themes in Colleen's objects seem unobtrusive, and the links between her projects over time appear loose. However, the aesthetic of women's labour is present. Often seen in the practices of openly feminist artists, stitching, knitting, or weaving — using traditional craft materials and techniques — become symbols of the domestic sphere and women's confinement to it. This symbolism is evident in the needlepoint-embellished bronze cushions, such as *Prozac Pillow* (1995, p. 22); needlepoint *Drug Company Logos*, (1999, p. 58); the quilting tape assembly of ... *they often resemble plants* (2004, p. 40); and the recent knitted LED rope light surface of *Untitled (Kelp)* (2024, pp. 56–57, 61, 112–114). Repetitive work and process, tropes that reference women's unpaid labour, are evident in the necessary shavings of the oversized plaster pills, such as *Valium* (1997, p. 9) or *Xanax, 2mg* (1998, p. 62–63), or the minute line detail of the *Wind Algorithm* drawings (2018, pp. 66–68). Reading a suggestion of feminist intent in these works is not inappropriate.

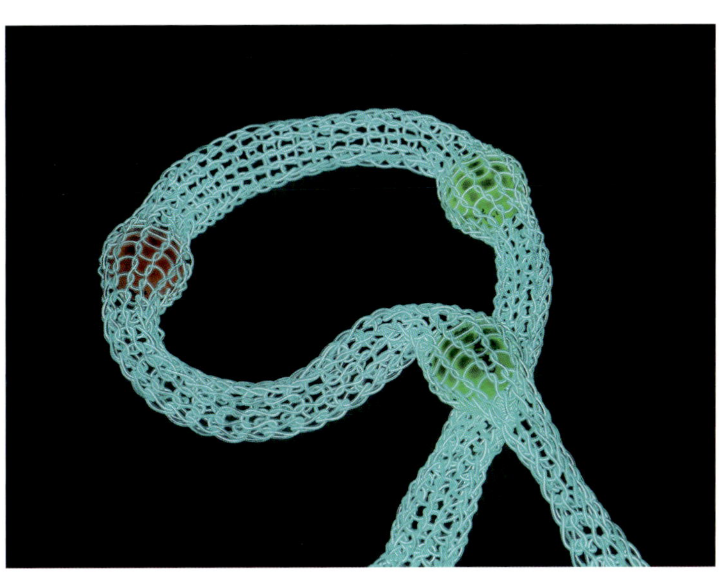

Untitled (Kelp) (detail), 2024

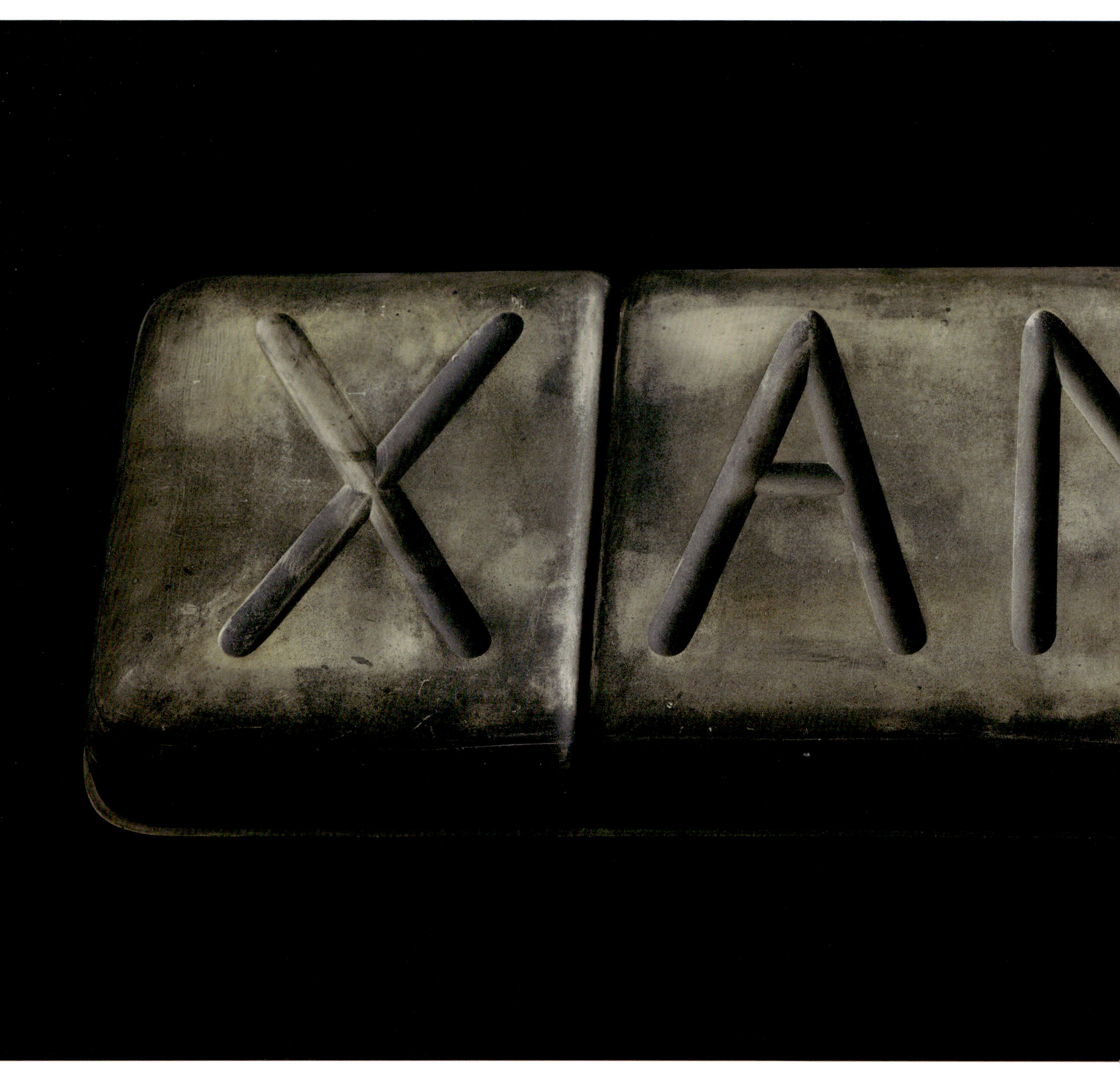
XAN

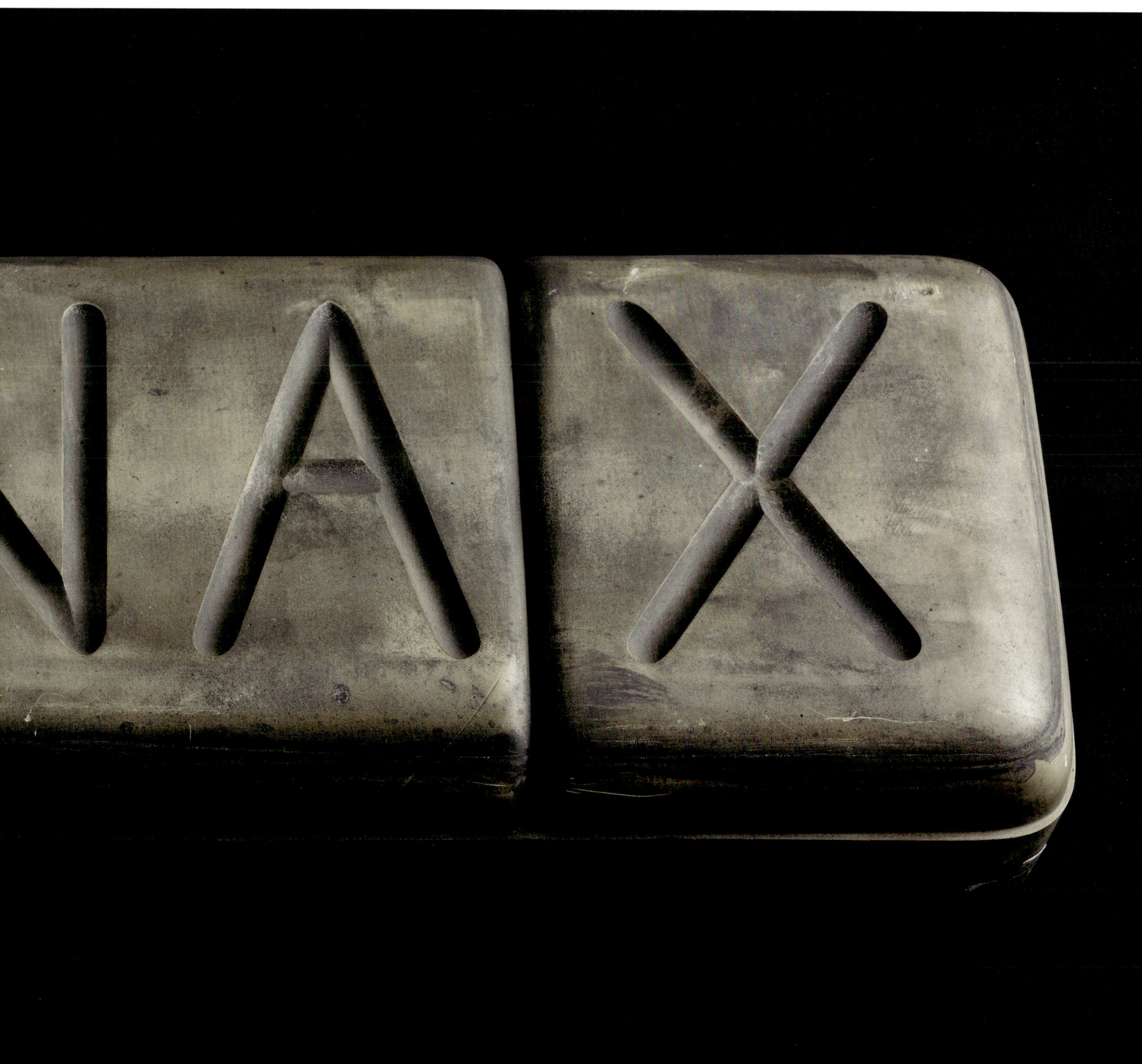

Xanax, 2mg, 1997

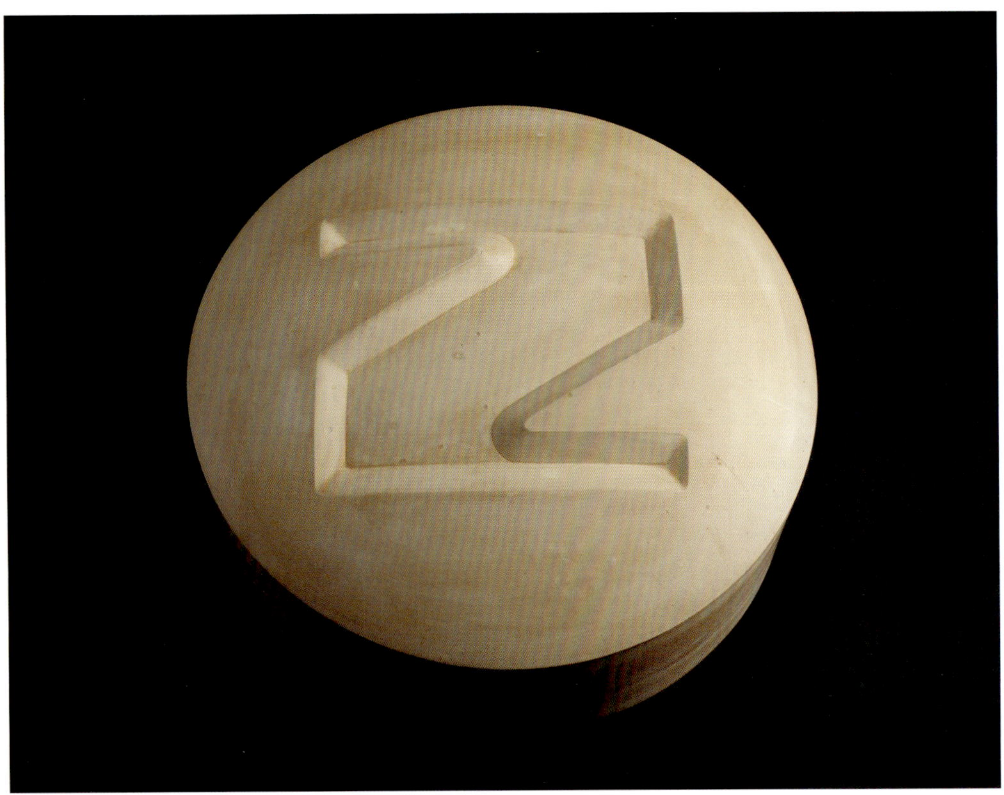

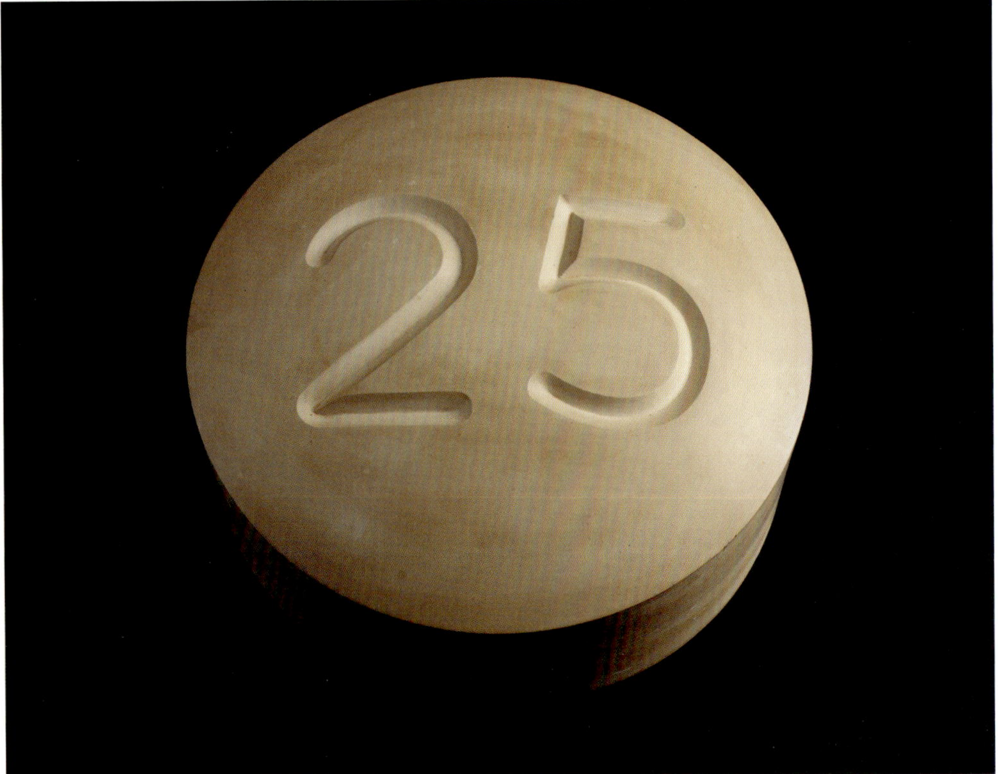

Recto and verso of *Amitriptyline*, 1999

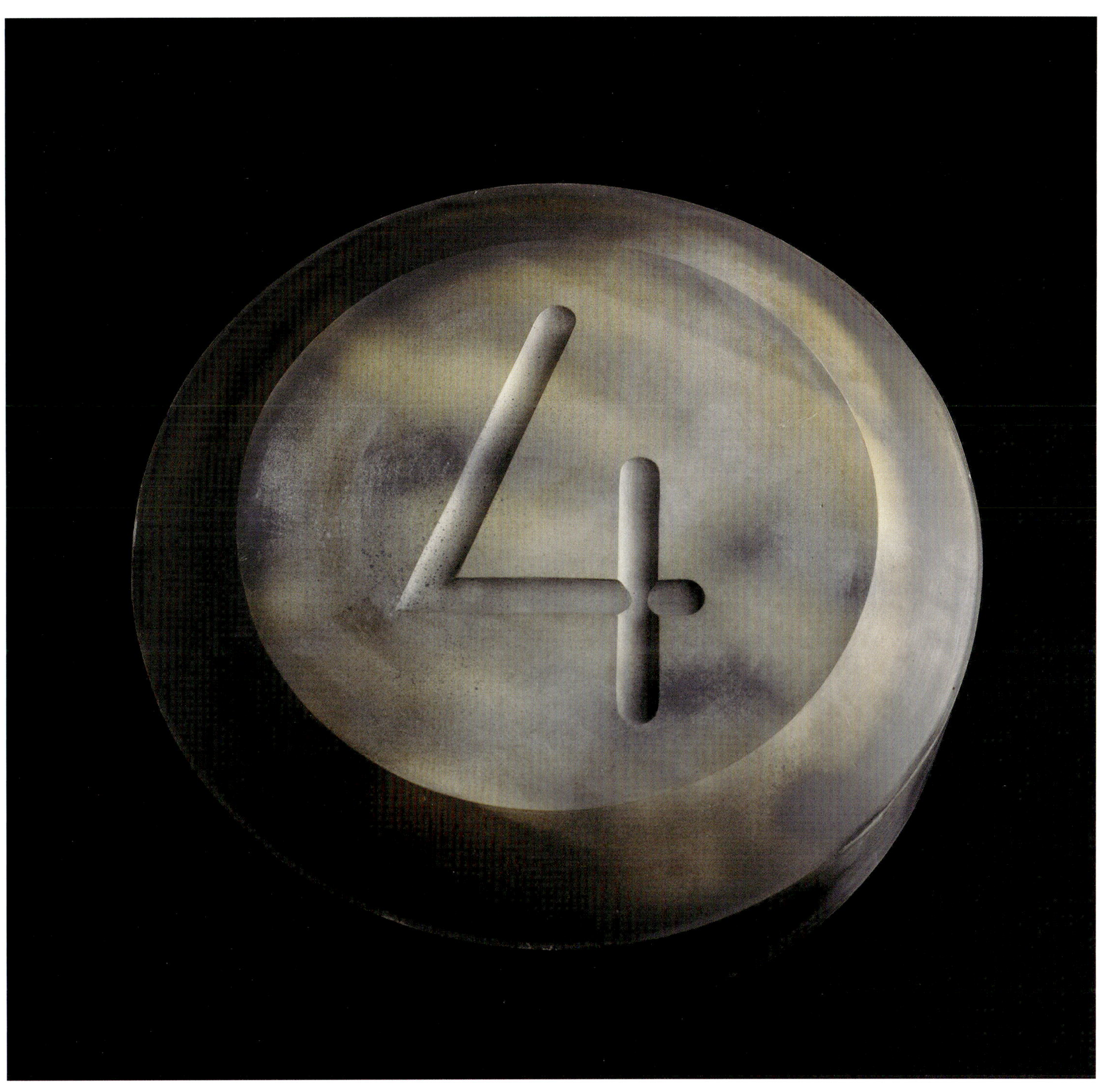

Dilaudid, 1997

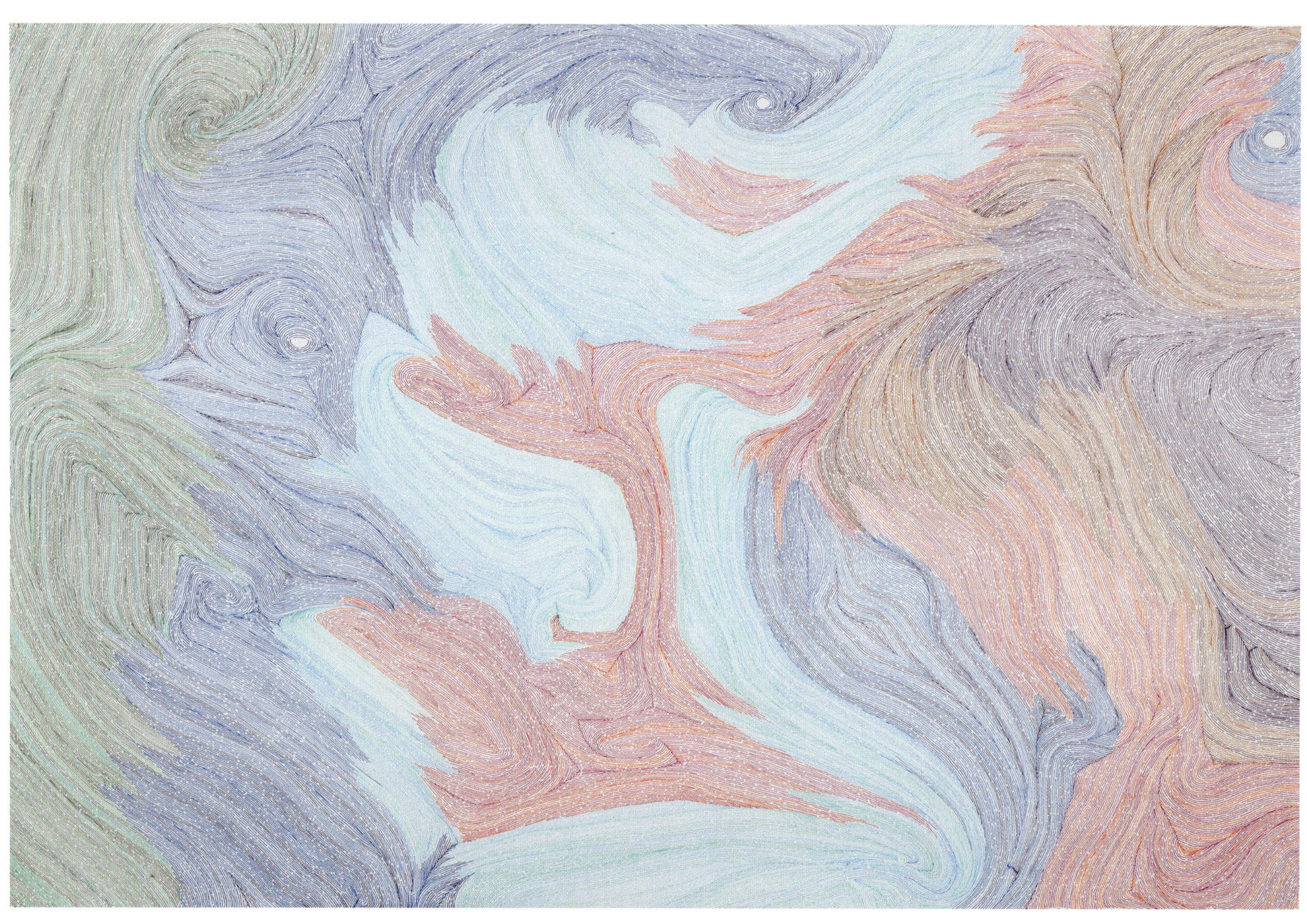

Wind Algorithm 1, 2017

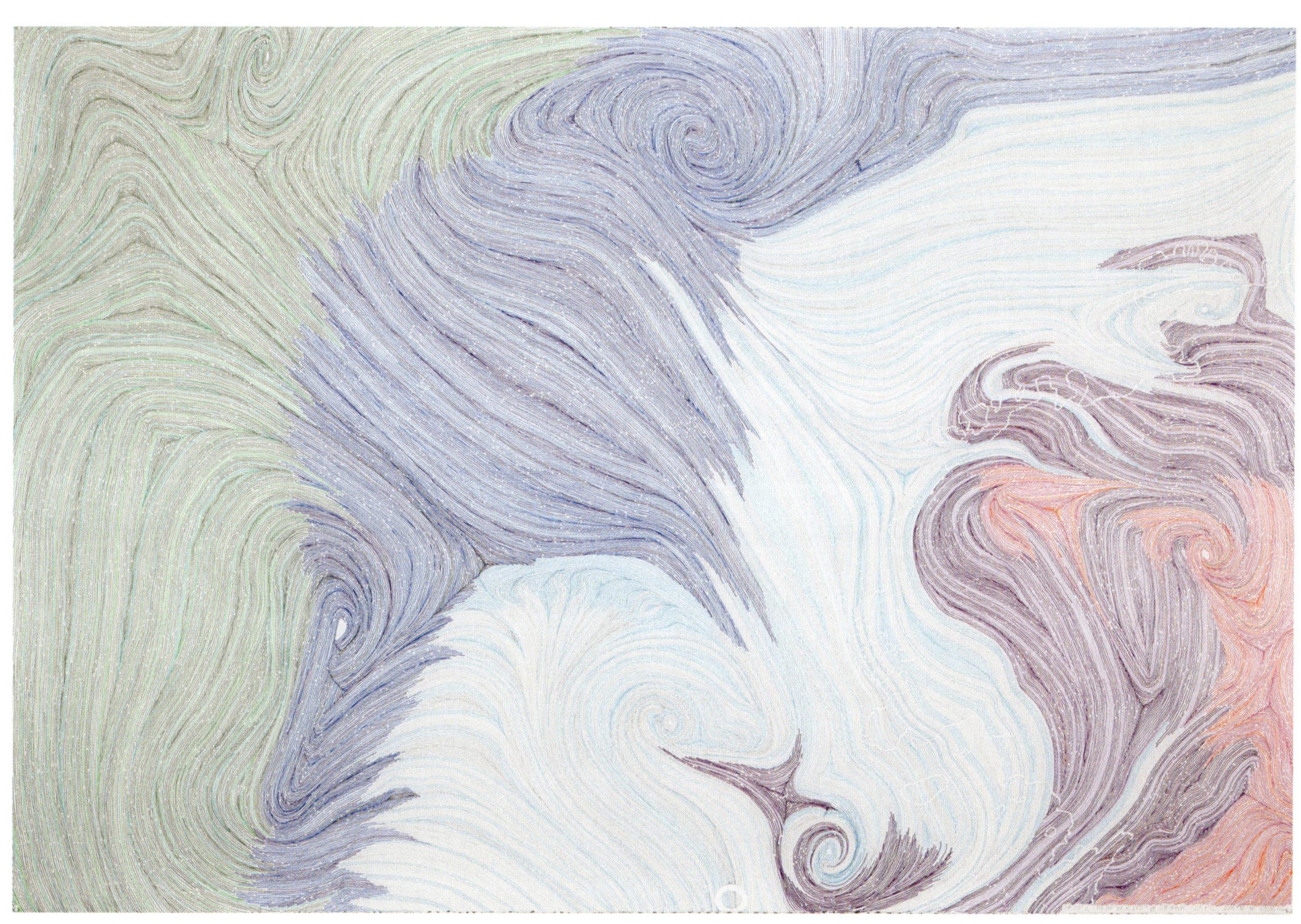

Wind Algorithm 2, 2017

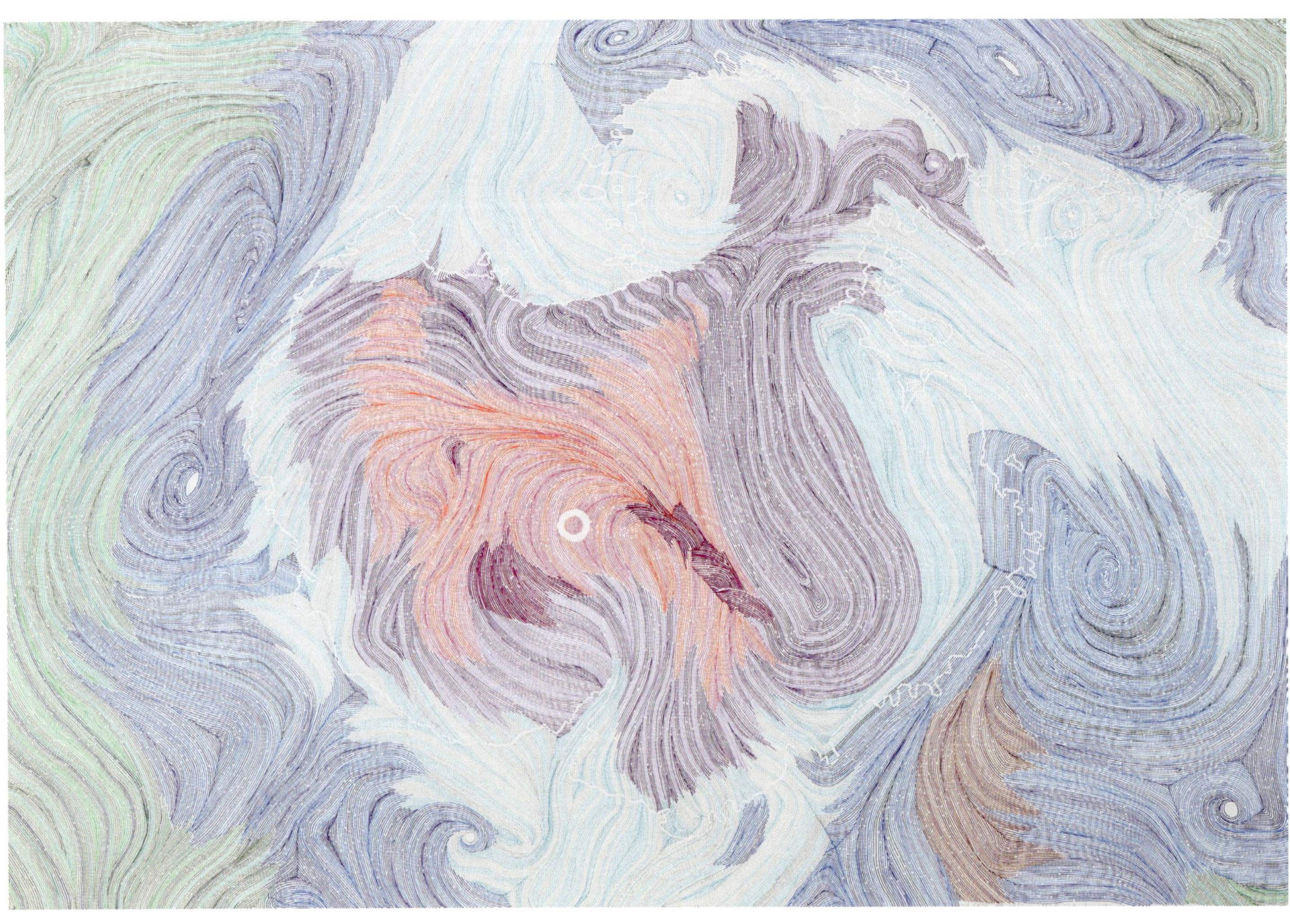

Wind Algorithm 3, 2017

•••

It is relevant to consider Colleen as a woman artist at NSCAD, an undergraduate student in the 1980s, a time when the sculpture studio was a boys' club and proclaiming feminism was uncool; she would never have been included among the feminists there, she told me. They were "too rigid, too exclusive." Even in graduate school in New York, "it was so uncool to be a feminist," Colleen recalled.

Take, for instance, punk/grunge artist icon Kim Gordon, whose band Sonic Youth was in residence at NSCAD for ten days in August 1984.[7] When Gordon and Chuck D pronounce the bridge, about fearing a female planet, with defiant detachment in Sonic Youth's 1990 hit "Kool Thing" (a callback to Public Enemy's title track "Fear of a Black Planet," released the same year), they were riffing off Gordon's awkward interview with rapper LL Cool J for the September 1989 issue of *SPIN* magazine.[8] Faced with his misogyny and the reality of their differing socio-economic situations, Gordon responded sarcastically in the lyrics of "Kool Thing," asking what will be done for her; will we girls be liberated from oppression (of the white, male, corporate kind)? She was making fun of feminism. Even later, when it was evident that the fight against oppression undertaken by angry women in the arts was precisely at the heart of third-wave feminism, it was still hard to associate, according to Gordon: "I'm kind of a sloppy feminist. Any ideology makes me a little nervous because there's some point where it doesn't allow for the complexity of things. I think feminism is really interesting historically. It is a term for me that does belong in the '70s."[9] Colleen similarly remarked, "I'm not a card-carrying feminist," as though there were a card or a prescribed rite of entry.

While Gordon acknowledged in the same interview that the riot grrrl movement resulted from grassroots gusto, she almost chastises feminism as "women who are talking about the male[-dominated] society to girls who just want to have a band." Both Colleen and Gordon are saying more than they mean: each is telling us, inadvertently, about the reality of working as a woman while showcasing the complexity of their lived realities. Colleen, maybe a girl who just wanted to make sculptures, takes that invisible boot off her neck and funnels it. She doesn't "hate men," she told me. What she does hate is oppression.

Many of Colleen's works persist in spotlighting oppression thematically. Less what the works are "about," the ways that many of her objects call to mind systems of oppression suggest a feminist underpinning. For bell hooks (1952–2021), African

American scholar, writer, and activist, "feminism is a movement to end sexism, sexist exploitation, and oppression."[10] The same year Sonic Youth played the NSCAD cafeteria, bell hooks offered her definition of feminism in *Feminist Theory: From Margin to Center*, hoping to alleviate the uneasiness people felt in claiming association with the term.

In Colleen's *Patience* (1992–1995, p. 20), also referred to as *Padded Cell*, the confinement or restriction of mentally ill patients recalls thoughts of institutionalized women and the history of hysteria. All the pills from the 1990s and 2000–09, large or small, similarly invoke the burden of mental illness and the almost literal shackles (as alluded to in her silver, wearable *Charm Bracelets*) of pharmaceutical treatment. In *Exposé* (2011, p. 73), *Bear Girl* (2003, p. 72) and *Donkey Girl* (2003, pp. 71, 72), despite art historical references (such as odalisques or standing nudes), it is the pin-up poses that we see first: women as sexualized and objectified. Sculptures that depict cloth-covered women's figures, for example, *Shrouded Figure* (2005), *Triad* (2005, p. 70), *Undercover* (2011, pp. 74–75), or any of the camouflaged works that obscure women's bodies, for instance, *Grand Prix* (2004, p. 74) or *Tight End* (2004, p. 75), recall the treatment of women in burkas, whether by choice or by force. A long-standing interest in Islam underlies Colleen's shrouded women works, but she acknowledges that the documentary film *Beneath the Veil* by British journalist Saira Shah, which aired on CNN in the fall of 2001 and won a Peabody Award that year, was a catalyst. It documents the public execution of three women in burkas for perceived crimes against the Taliban's version of Muslim law. Seeing it aired after 9/11, Colleen was "compelled" to make something about these women. Are these works a part of hooks's movement? They must be. Only a callous sluggard could hold on to sexist thought and action when faced with such uncomfortable truths.

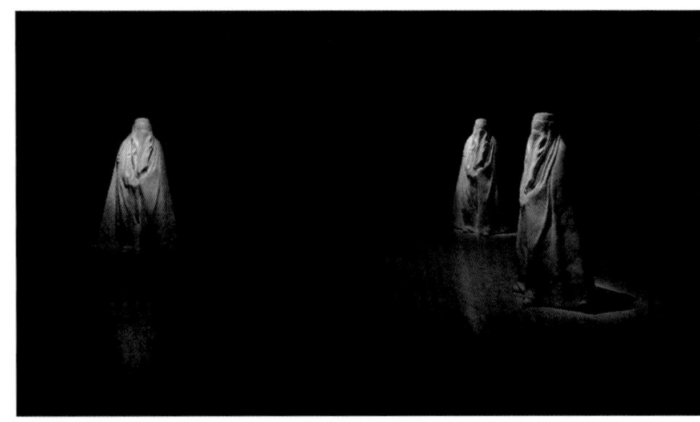

Triad, 2005

Kim Gordon just wants to play in a band. Colleen Wolstenholme just wants to make sculpture. Muslim women might want to smoke cigarettes. Some of the oppressive conditions shaping Colleen's artistic output have not only to do with gender privilege but also with the economic privilege that follows from it. Colleen's pharmaceutical charms, for example, may have continued to circulate in both the art world and public consciousness had the artist not lost her copyright suit against art-market superstar Damien Hirst (whose own pill charms, too closely resembling hers, she claims, were plagiarized). More of her large-scale sculptures

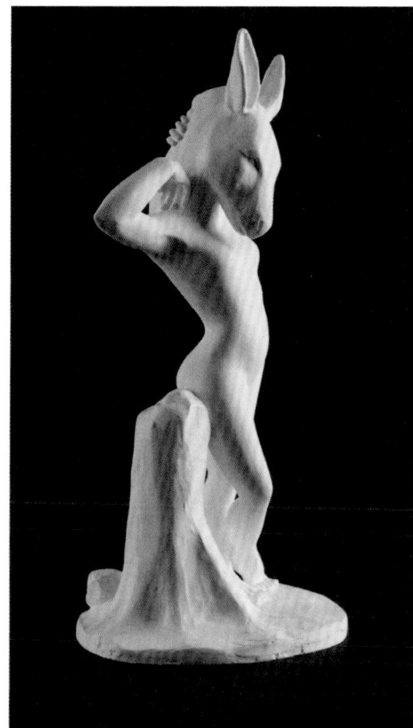

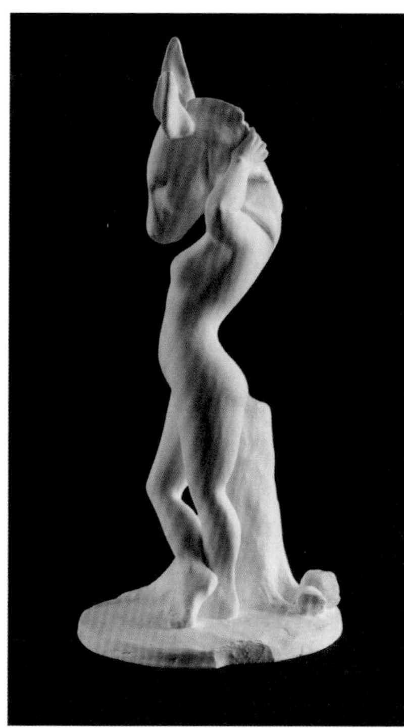

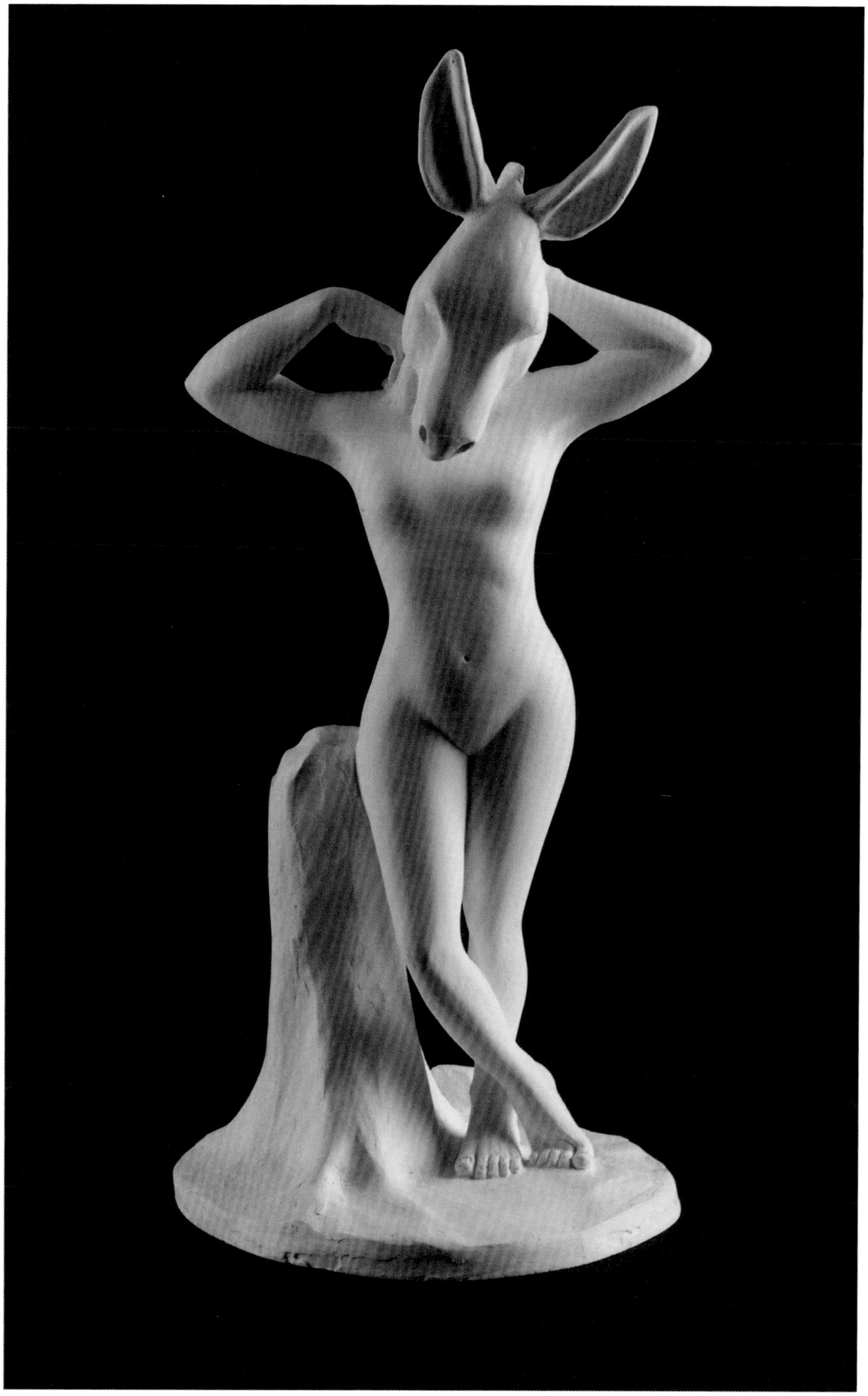

Three views of *Donkey Girl*, 2003

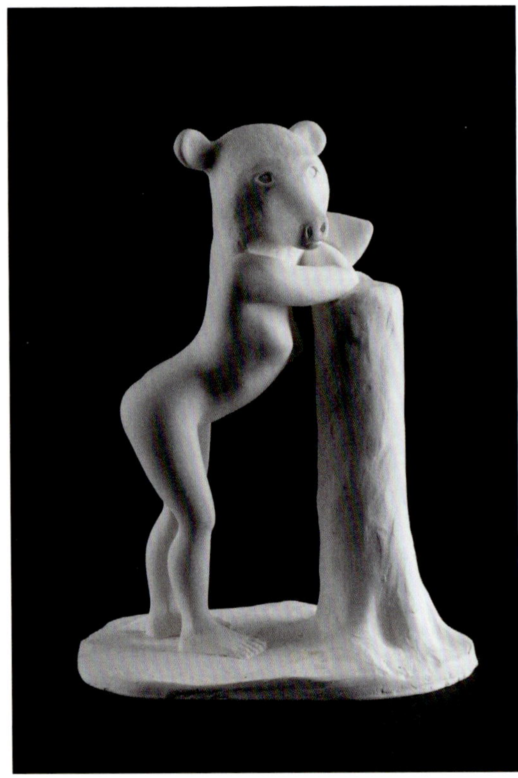

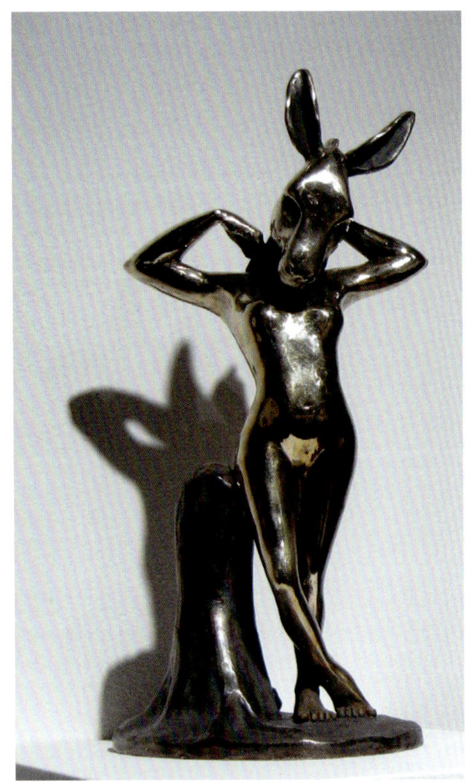

(left to right)
Bear Girl, 2003

Donkey Girl, 2023

would be cast in bronze if funding for sculptors were more readily available. Some aspects of fabrication and technical problem-solving would likely be outsourced. For instance, the construction of screens for an immersive rear-projection *Sea Snow* video installation could be contracted out, since making the display surface is not essential to the work's concept. Technical assistance could resolve glitches in *Hexagraphy* (2018, p. 54–55) – an installation she acknowledges functions more as a concept than an object – ensuring it more fully enacts the intended brain/world relationship. With material and technical support, *Sugar and Spice* (2007, p. 43) could have been an architectural dome. These are economic problems.

That economic burdens shape the course of Colleen's practice as much as a relation to gender-based oppression might make sense through the lens of intersectionality, a defining feature of third-wave feminism. Anti-essentialism – the idea that things, including gender, identity, or objects, do not possess fixed or inherent qualities defining their true nature – runs as a throughline in both the feminist movement and Colleen's thought. References to feminist scholars who reject essentialism, including Karen Barad, Rosi Braidotti, Judith Butler, Donna Haraway, bell hooks, Julia Kristeva, and Genevieve Lloyd, are included in Colleen's

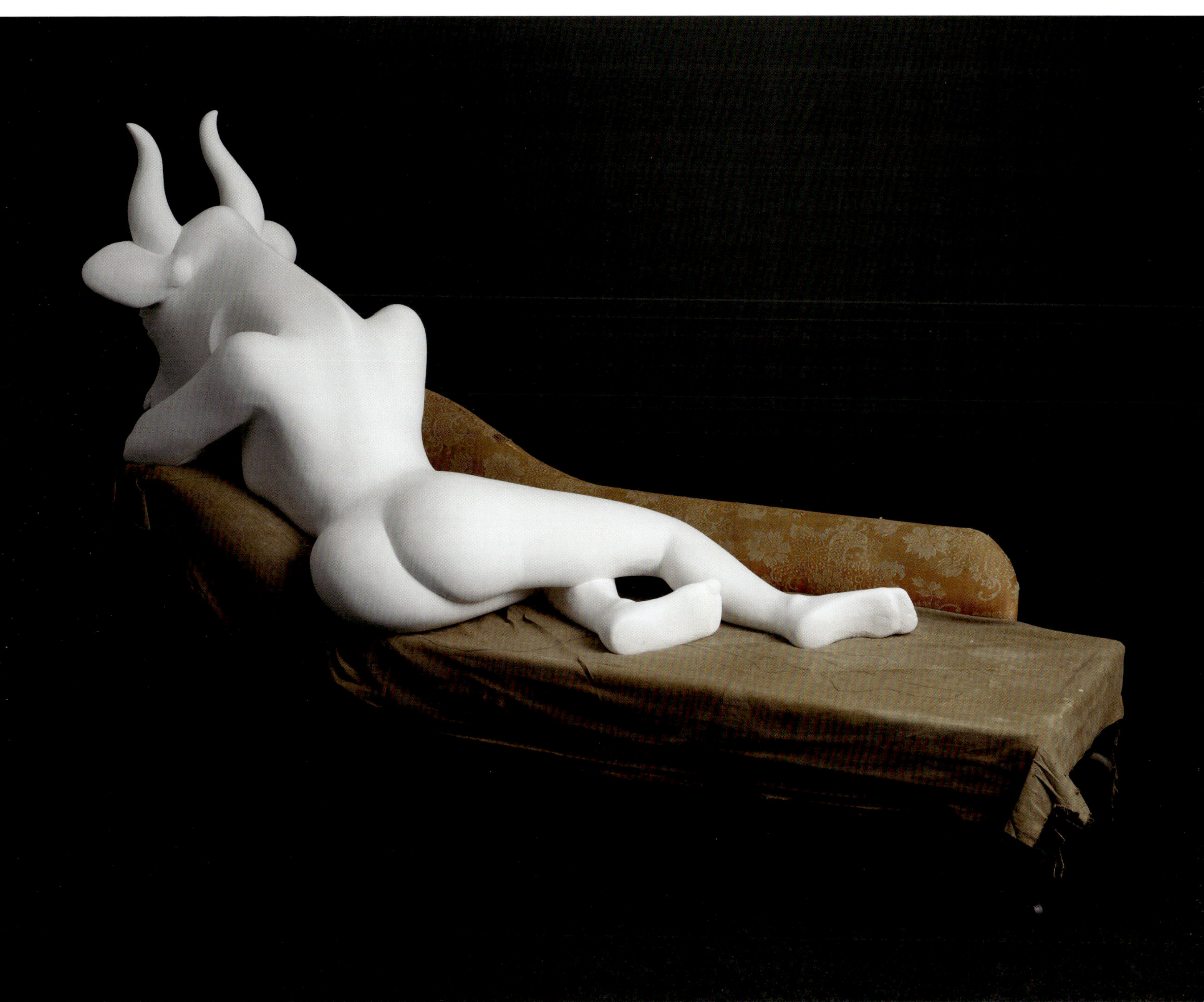

Exposé, 2010

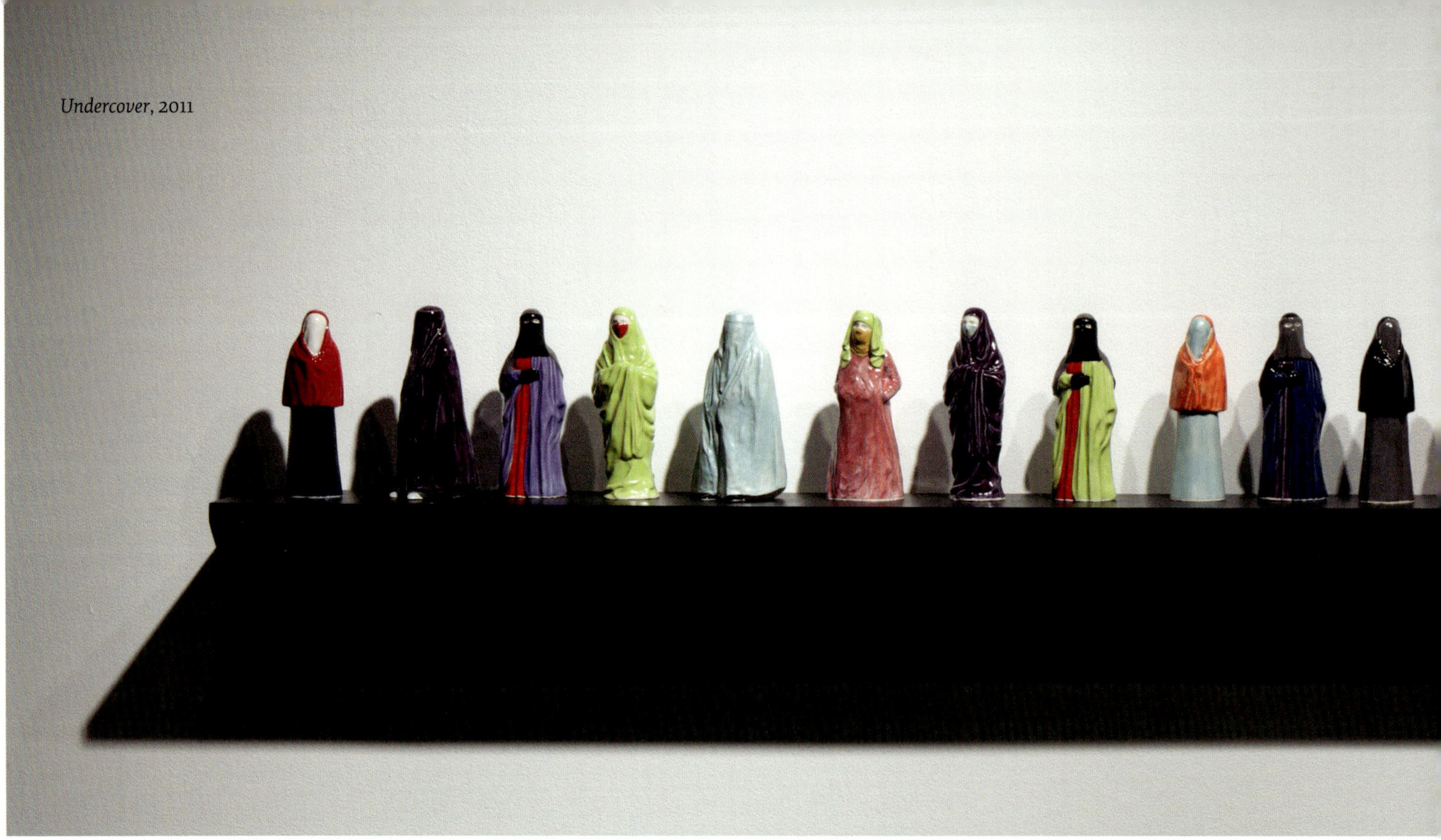

Undercover, 2011

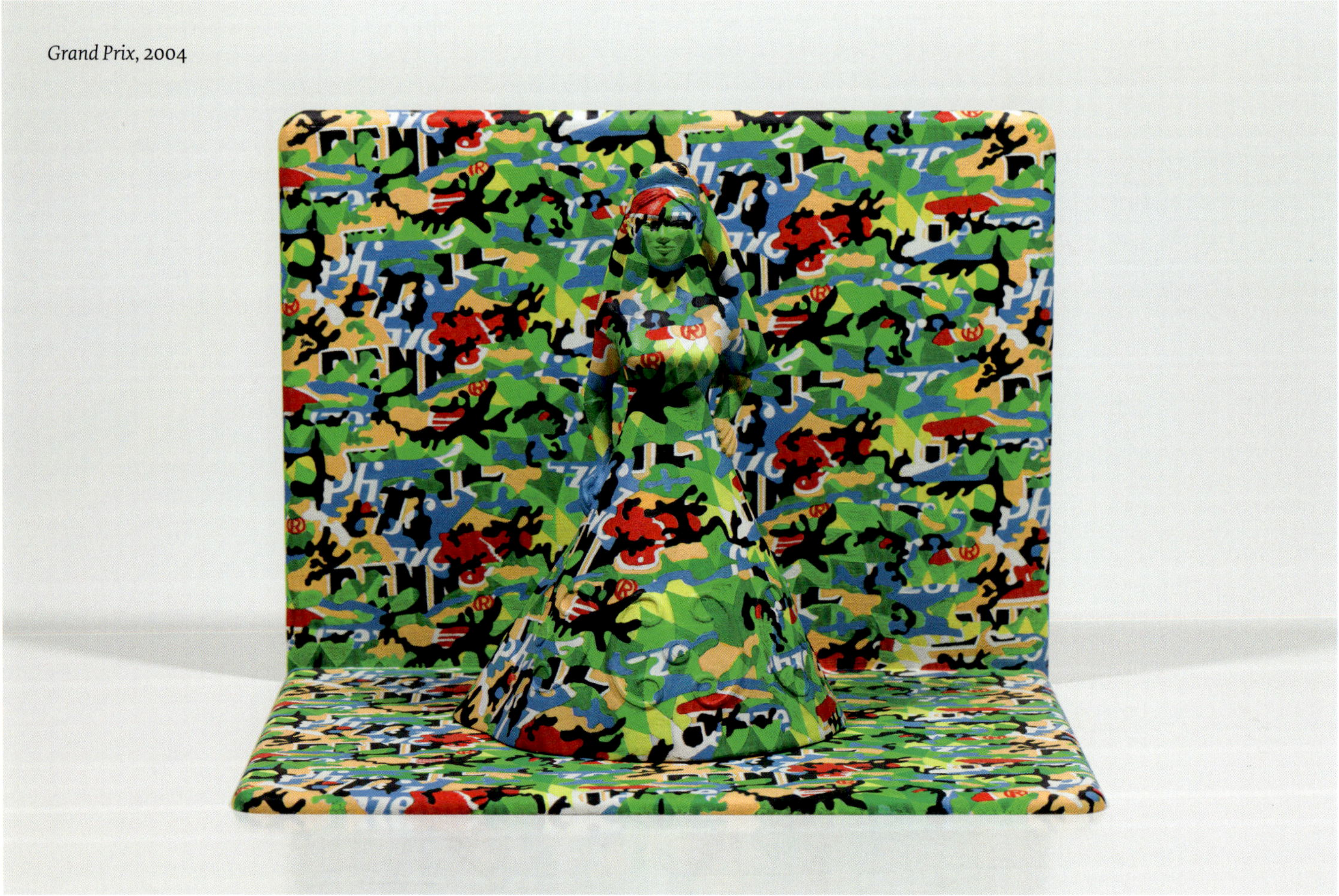

Grand Prix, 2004

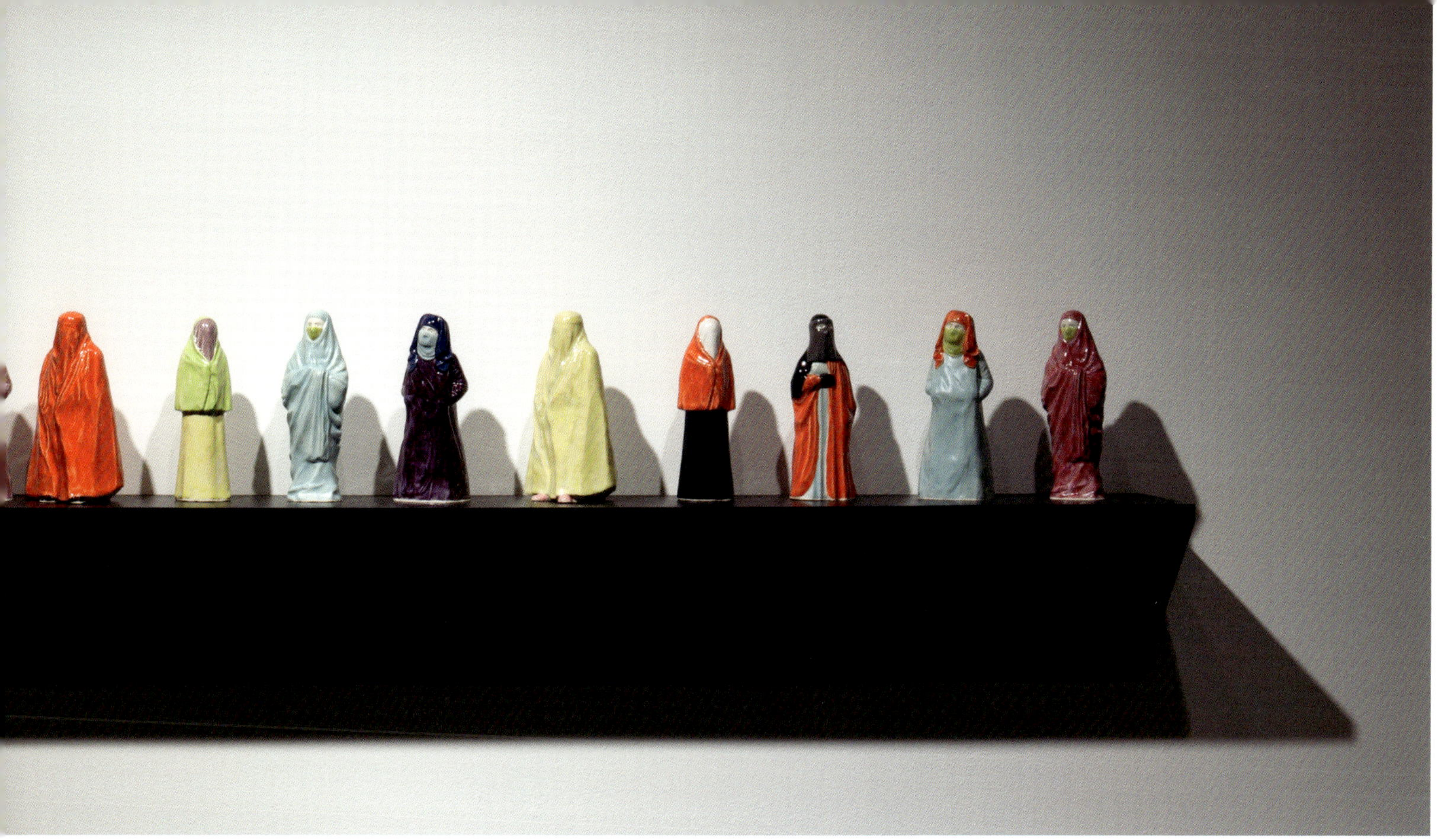

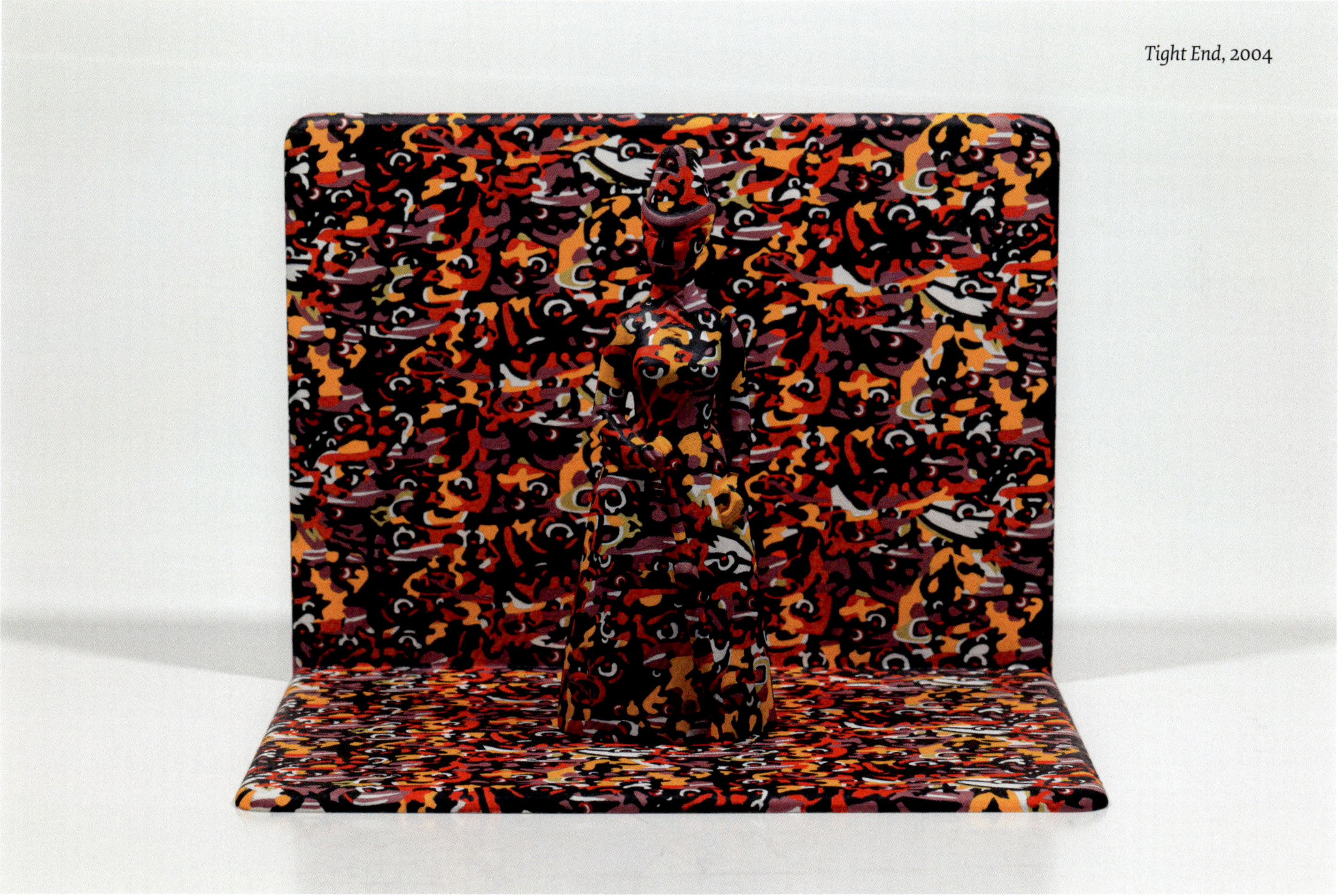

Tight End, 2004

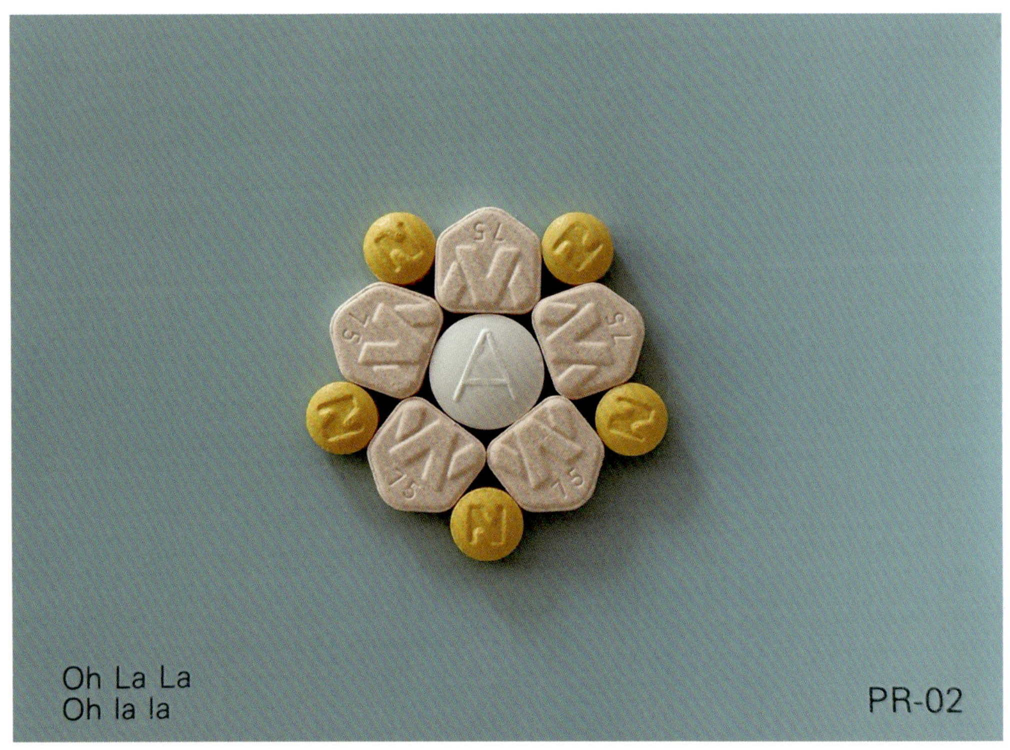

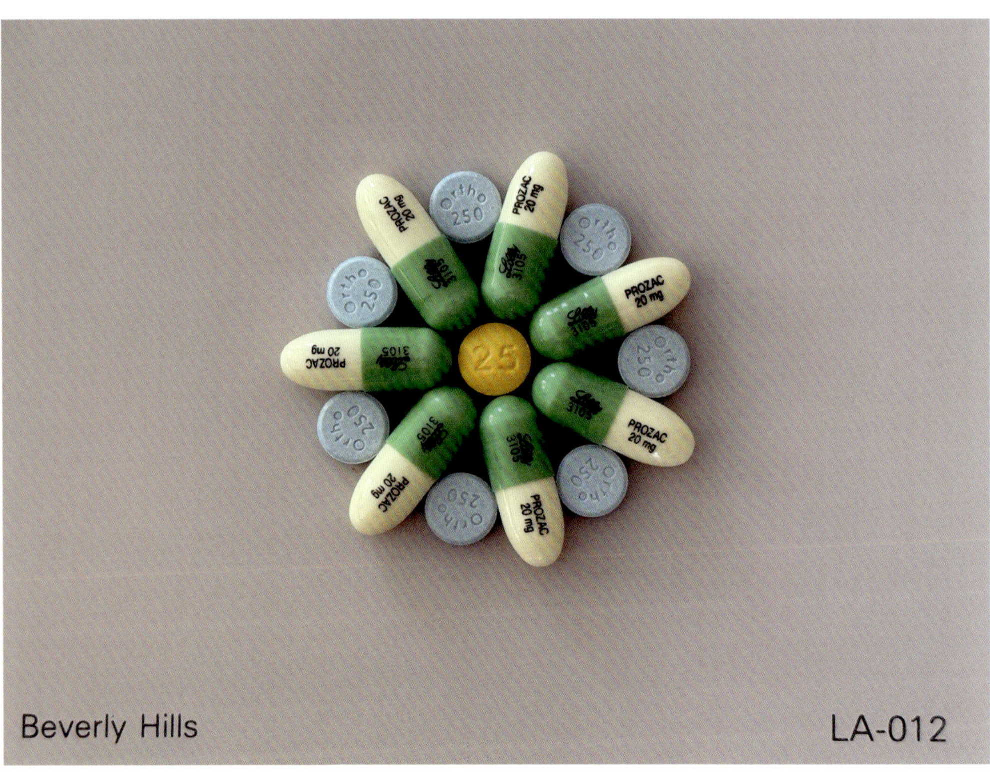

(top to bottom)
Pill Mandala (Oh La La), 2026

Pill Mandala (Beverly Hills), 2026

academic work. Her PhD dissertation, "Apropos Obsolescence" (2018), takes up new materialist philosophy in exploring contingency and decentring of humanity, drawing on Braidotti among feminist vitalists. Moreover, there is a legible aesthetic of decentralized networks in Colleen's artworks. Scanning for patterns, visualmodels of distributed interconnection appear throughout and as early as 1999, in her photographed *Pill Mandalas* (2026, p. 76).[11]

Non-hierarchical structures persist in the works made in the 2000s: in the honeycomb paintings *Om Am Hum* and *You and Me* (2002, p. 34); in the network of tiny photos and logos composing *... they often tend to resemble plants* (2004, p. 40); in works that deploy camouflage such as *Slap Shot* (2004) and *Camouflesh* (2005, pp. 37–39, 96); and — most notably — in *Original* (2005–06, p. 4), the tessellated reworking of Gustave Courbet's *L'Origine du Monde*. Regarding the patterned bones in *Sugar and Spice*, Colleen told me her influence was Persian tilework, as seen in decorative arts at museums in New York. Her time in New York introduced her to concepts that underline these structures, too. A boyfriend interested in philosophy started Colleen on a path of intrigue into "very deep thoughts: Derrida and French stuff." She noted, "I read *A Thousand Plateaus*," Deleuze and Guattari's text introducing the rhizome — a non-hierarchical model of knowledge and connection where any point can link to any other, with no fixed beginning or end — that came out in English in 1987, the year Colleen moved to the big city.[12]

Rhizomatic patterns and topology in general appear as formal interests for Colleen throughout the 2010s. In *Neuraesthezia* (2011, pp. 44, 45, 46–47) cellular relationships — the networks of neurons that constitute a nervous system — are conveyed through a web of tiny, found-image medallions. Drawings *Cell* (2012), *Netmap Red* (2012), and *Grid Cells* (2013) make this interest explicit in the artist's use of minute, connected threads of ink to create a net-like texture. The unevenly patterned ink drawing *Topology* (2013) and the welded steel hexagons of *Hexagonal Matrix* (2015, p. 78) and *Spatial Anomaly* (2018, p. 79), as well as the honeycomb surface of *Matrix Indices* (2018), anticipate the vast, distributed entities that are seen in Colleen's projects to date. It feels relevant to consider these patterns and networks as frameworks — forests of larger perspectives that would otherwise be obscured if we focus too much on the trees: discrete artworks. Deleuze and Guattari's concept of the rhizome (and Colleen's illustration of it) offers a robust framework for feminist thought, as it prioritizes multiplicity, lateral connectivity, and non-hierarchical structures. Third-wave feminism drew on similar principles, rejecting essentialist

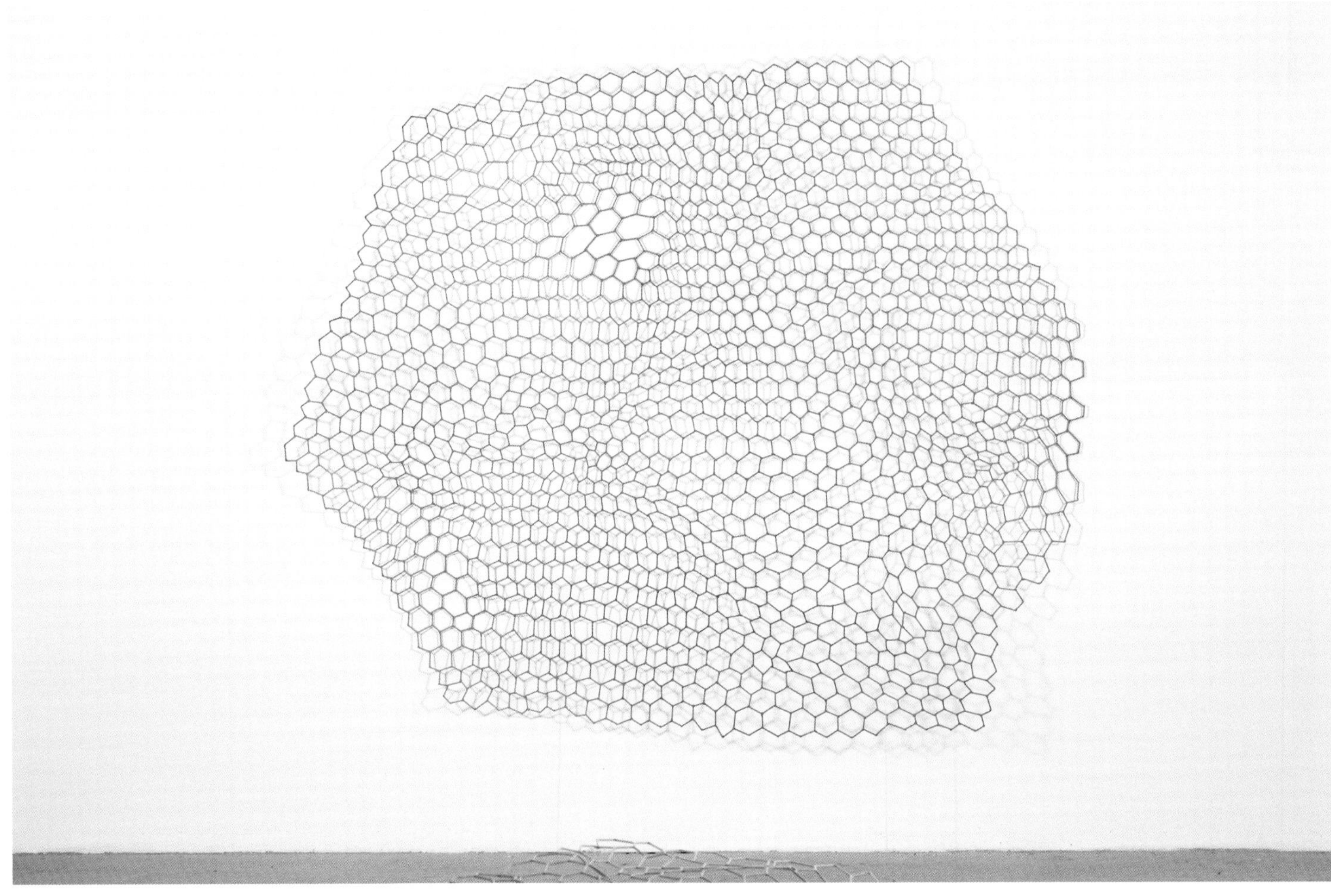

Hexagonal Matrix, 2015

notions of "woman" in favour of plural, intersectional subjectivities that emerged in shifting networks of identity, culture, and activism.

American feminist theorist and historian of science Donna Haraway's cyborg and later "string figure" metaphors resonate with the rhizome, proposing hybrid, non-linear assemblages across species, technologies, and environments.[13] The creation of a string figure, as in a game of cat's cradle, requires collaboration, more than one participant. A string figure for Haraway is the result of shifting patterns in a web of relations. Similarly, Italian-born feminist and posthumanist philosopher Rosi Braidotti's notion of the nomadic subject is directly indebted to rhizomatic thinking, positioning the feminist subject as mobile, relational, and constituted through becoming rather than fixed identity.[14] A nomadic subject describes a way of being that resists fixed identity and embraces continual

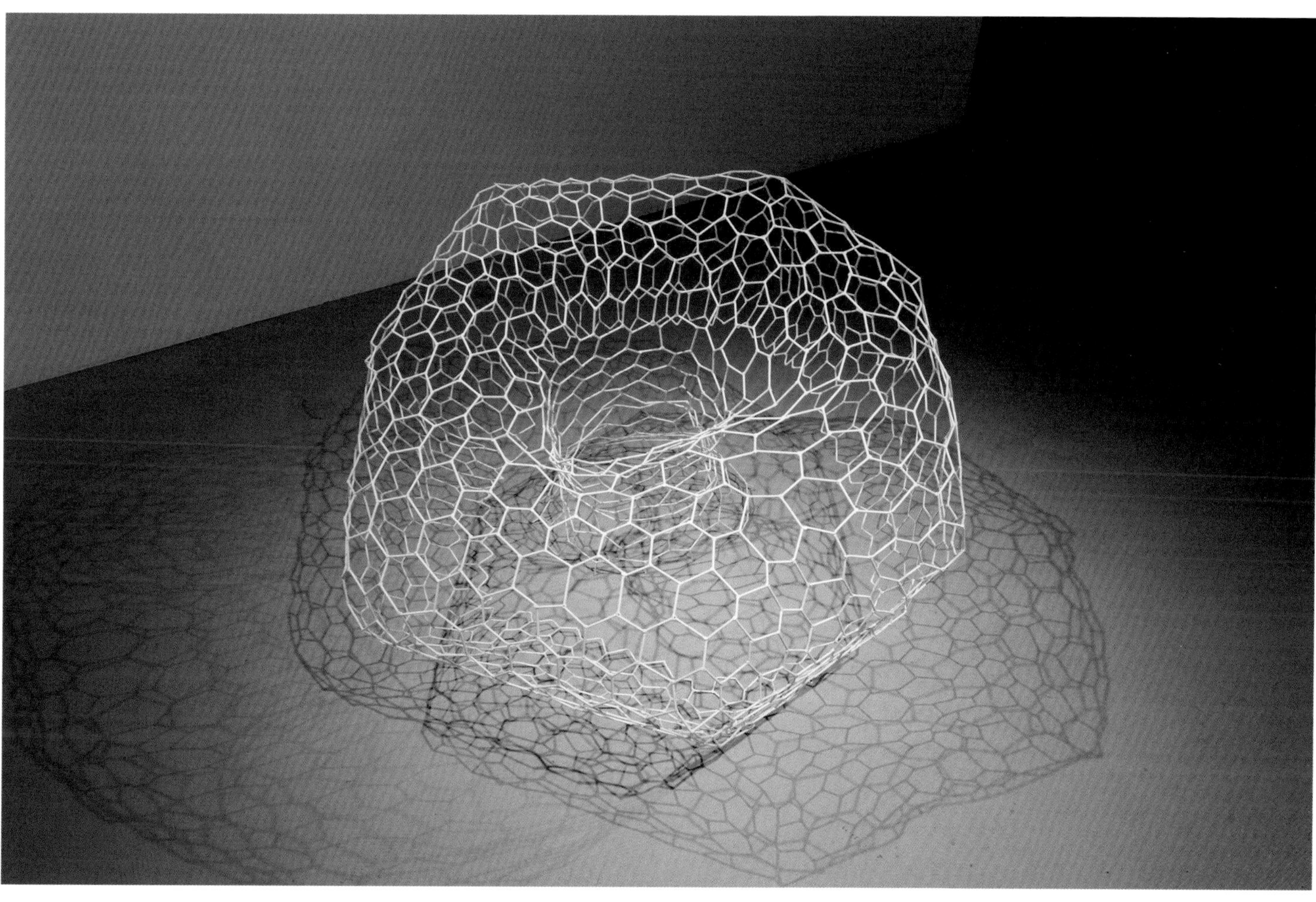

Spatial Anomaly, 2018

transformation – a way for thinking of the self as always becoming and never final. Braidotti employs Deleuze and Guattari's concept of becoming, the idea that identities are contingent processes of transformation.

Haraway and Braidotti, like their anti-essentialist peer Judith Butler, are often considered post-wave feminists. Butler, who argued that gender is constructed contingently, critiqued progressive notions of history.[15] We could situate Colleen there, outside the wave model. Across waves and outside them, there is feminist agreement on the nature of subjective knowledge as situated. Second-wave feminist founder Simone de Beauvoir's perspective enabled us to view women artists not as neutral makers but as gendered, situated subjects who inscribe their lived experiences into their work.[16] Haraway's work on situated knowledges called for a practice of feminist objectivity that privileges "webbed connections" among ways of seeing (and science projects in particular). "Feminists have to insist on a better account of the world," she notes.[17]

To that end, it makes sense that Colleen's curiosity about the nature of relationships, her work in webs, in what is contingent, and in that which – on the way through "becoming" – is not concrete, would translate into an interest in object-oriented ontology. Braidotti's materialist feminism as the main framework upon which Colleen thinks about and makes works was taken over by object-oriented ontology (OOO), which is a branch of speculative realism anticipated by Martin Heidegger, Bruno Latour, and fleshed out by Graham Harman in the mid- to late 2000s. By arguing that objects are real and autonomous and that they have a reality independent of human understanding, use, or perception, OOO challenges anthropocentric thinking. OOO treats works of art as objects among objects, not requiring a subject observer to determine their reality, but rather an entity having a reality beyond interpretation.

In 2019 Harman outlined "a model in which every element of an artwork generates its own discrete background."[18] For artists defining the parameters of their work in a post-participatory era, the making, the thing, the experience of the made thing, and the relationship of artist to audience are all up for consideration. In *Art and Object*, Harman outlined the expanded field: "For the object-oriented thinker, anything – including events and performances – can count as an object as long as it meets two simple criteria: (a) irreducibility downward to its components, and (b) irreducibility upward to its effects."[19] Just like the patterns, the forest, and the trees, "it's more than meets the eye."

Timothy Morton's application of OOO introduces hyperobjects, entities so vast in scale that they exceed ordinary human perception (e.g., weather, capitalism, space).[20] Where Braidotti's nomadic subject navigates networks of relationships, Morton's hyperobjects are the networks that shape and are navigated within. This concept permeates Colleen's late and recent works. "The fate of humanity is a hyperobject," Colleen reminds me in conversation. So is the future of the bottom of the ocean. From earlier projects on deep thought (if not deep thoughts), we can see Colleen interrogating the deep: that which is always present, never fully graspable. Deep sea, for instance, is a hyperobject that occupied much of Colleen's output in the COVID era.

From spring 2021 to fall of 2022, Colleen's mother – her biggest fan and artistic champion – was in a nursing home receiving end-of-life care. Together, they sat and watched documentary footage of deep-sea exploration on YouTube. Interest in the idea of the unknowable, and the way scientists once described the ocean depths as something beyond human understanding, kept her watching. The concept of becoming, of moving and transforming continuously, kept her attending to a painting project: by her mother's bedside, she painted watercolours of sea-floor creatures. "It gives me some necessity to move, to not just sit in front of a TV." After her mother died in October 2022, Colleen started painting the deep sea in acrylic and oil. Paintings such as the triptychs *Into the Deep Blue Sea* (2023, pp. 49–50, 84–86) feature once unknowable beings.

The projects that follow from Colleen are symbolic of the deep. Deep-space paintings of supernovae, illuminated sea kelp hanging sculptures, and a sea snow video installation convey both the sense of things so vast or far away that they are challenging to comprehend and the possibility that things we think we know may be wrong. Advancements in deep-sea exploration allow access to new species and new knowledge. Dark oxygen (oxygen produced without sunlight or photosynthesis), for example, was first observed in 2013, and now it enlightens us to reveal what we thought was true about oxygen production was incorrect. If sea-floor minerals can have electrical potential, perhaps an OOO is useful: possibly (a) objects do have agency, and (b) relationships between materials are real and active even if not perceived by human observers.

Arguably, OOO is a challenging line of thinking to get behind, especially from a feminist perspective. Where OOO decentres artistic intention and viewer perception, it also sets aside social and historical context. If Braidotti's subject is ethical and posthuman, OOO's subject is dissolved entirely into a single ontological plane. For feminist critics, this lens erases political agency. Reclamation of objecthood as a site of power requires an object-oriented feminism, one that rethinks relations between systems, objects, and humans (without dichotomies). Fortunately, that project is under way.

Building on the trajectories of Deleuze and Guattari's rhizome, Braidotti's nomadic subject, and Haraway's string figure, Katherine Behar's *Object-Oriented Feminism* (2016) explicitly extends rhizomatic logics into the domain of objects and material systems, insisting that feminist analysis accounts not only for human multiplicities but also for the agency of non-human actors.[21] Together these thinkers demonstrate how the rhizome has migrated into feminist philosophy, moving from third-wave commitments to multiplicity and intersectionality toward posthuman and object-oriented feminisms that map feminism itself as a living, non-hierarchical network.

Akin to Haraway's tentacular thinking, both anti-anthropocentric and embracing the primacy of object relations, an object-oriented feminism can be symbolized by Colleen's biologically complex and multidirectionally moving squid, ctenophore, and jellyfish.[22] Recent paintings such as *Helmet Jellyfish* (2023, p. 87), *Diplulmaris Antarctica* (2023, p. 89), or *Solmissus Jelly* (2024, p. 88) depict literally tentacular creatures. They give us visual cues to things that are linked by multiple strands of connection, to things that move in fluid, non-linear ways, and to entities (whether living or graphic) that are easily entangled. The deep-blue near-black backgrounds indicate these creatures' native deep sea, which like a dark, deep space evokes the unknown — the possible and the contingent — and ultimately the room for becoming that an ever-evolving feminism requires.

Landing at a point in Colleen's artmaking career where feminist theory aligns with the nuanced and multifaceted tenor of her projects, I can see that feminism is present. As a feminist observer, I view Colleen's artworks as valuable catalysts for thinking through my own questions about agency and the objecthood of art. Perhaps an object-oriented feminism is precisely the lens necessary to continue that line of inquiry in contemporary art criticism. If situating Colleen's work in the context of other feminist artworks, reading it through a feminist lens, and naming her feminism in relation to others' is useful, it is because it substantiates our own places in the network of materials, makers, and viewers. My complex position as viewer/reader is relieved and my own curiosity validated when we allow for Colleen's interest in non-human entities, and entities of potentially unknowable scales, to be read as being as much about subjectivity, oppression, and power dynamics as about material or essential natures.

NOTES

1 Carol Hanisch, "The Personal Is Political," in *Notes from the Second Year: Women's Liberation*, ed. Shulamith Firestone and Anne Koedt (Radical Feminism, 1970), 76–78.

2 Kira Cochrane, "The Fourth Wave of Feminism: Meet the Rebel Women," *The Guardian*, December 10, 2013, https://www.theguardian.com/world/2013/dec/10/fourth-wave-feminism-rebel-women.

3 A project well covered in Heather Davis, ed., *Desire Change: Contemporary Feminist Art in Canada* (McGill-Queen's University Press and MAWA, 2017).

4 I use Colleen's first name deliberately. As an explicitly feminist text, my essay is best served by acknowledging that I am not objective. Colleen is someone I know and have often talked to about her art.

5 Some biographical and anecdotal insight was available to me through a studio visit with the artist in Fredericton, NB, August 26, 2025.

6 "Meaning is not located in the intentionality of the artist nor in the subjective response of the viewer but in the intersubjective exchange between them." From Amelia Jones, *Body Art/Performing the Subject* (University of Minnesota Press, 1998), 12. For more on feminist phenomenology see Sara Ahmed, *Queer Phenomenology: Orientations, Objects, Others* (Duke University Press, 2006).

7 Sonic Youth's performance in the NSCAD cafeteria on August 9, 1984, despite being sparsely attended, is now anecdotally considered the height of NSCAD's cool.

8 The interview, titled "Meaty Beaty Big and Bouncy," appeared in *SPIN* magazine, September 1989.

9 Barbara O'Dair, "Kim Gordon: The Godmother of Grunge on Feminism in Rock," *Rolling Stone*, no. 773, November 13, 1997, https://www.rollingstone.com/music/music-news/kim-gordon-the-godmother-of-grunge-on-feminism-in-rock-184535/.

10 bell hooks, *Feminism is for Everybody: Passionate Politics* (South End Press, 2000), viii.

11 Even the three-dimensional pills call to mind the patterned nature, albeit more linear, of a prescription dosing. Colleen's jewellery booth on the Lilith Fair tour in the late 1990s was a catalyst for mental health confessionals, as women cast aside the stigma associated with antidepressants and regaled their pharmacological regimes.

12 Gilles Deleuze and Félix Guattari, *A Thousand Plateaus: Capitalism and Schizophrenia*, trans. Brian Massumi (University of Minnesota Press, 1987).

13 Donna Haraway, "A Cyborg Manifesto: Science, Technology, and Socialist-Feminism in the 1980s," *Socialist Review* 80 (1985): 65–108; and Donna J. Haraway, *Staying with the Trouble: Making Kin in the Chthulucene* (Duke University Press, 2016).

14 Rosi Braidotti, *Nomadic Subjects: Embodiment and Sexual Difference in Contemporary Feminist Theory* (Columbia University Press, 1994/2011).

15 Judith Butler, *Undoing Gender* (Routledge, 2004), 4.

16 Simone de Beauvoir, *The Second Sex*, 1949, trans. Constance Borde and Sheila Malovany-Chevallier (Vintage Books, 2010).

17 Donna Haraway "Situated Knowledges: The Science Question in Feminism and the Privilege of Partial Perspective," *Feminist Studies* 14, no. 3, (1988): 575–99, 579.

18 Graham Harman, *Art and Objects* (Polity Press, 2019), x.

19 Harman, *Art and Objects*, 2.

20 Timothy Morton, *The Ecological Thought* (Harvard University Press, 2010); and Timothy Morton, *Hyperobjects: Philosophy and Ecology after the End of the World* (University of Minnesota Press, 2013).

21 Katherine Behar, ed. *Object-Oriented Feminism* (University of Minnesota Press, 2016).

22 Haraway, *Staying with the Trouble*.

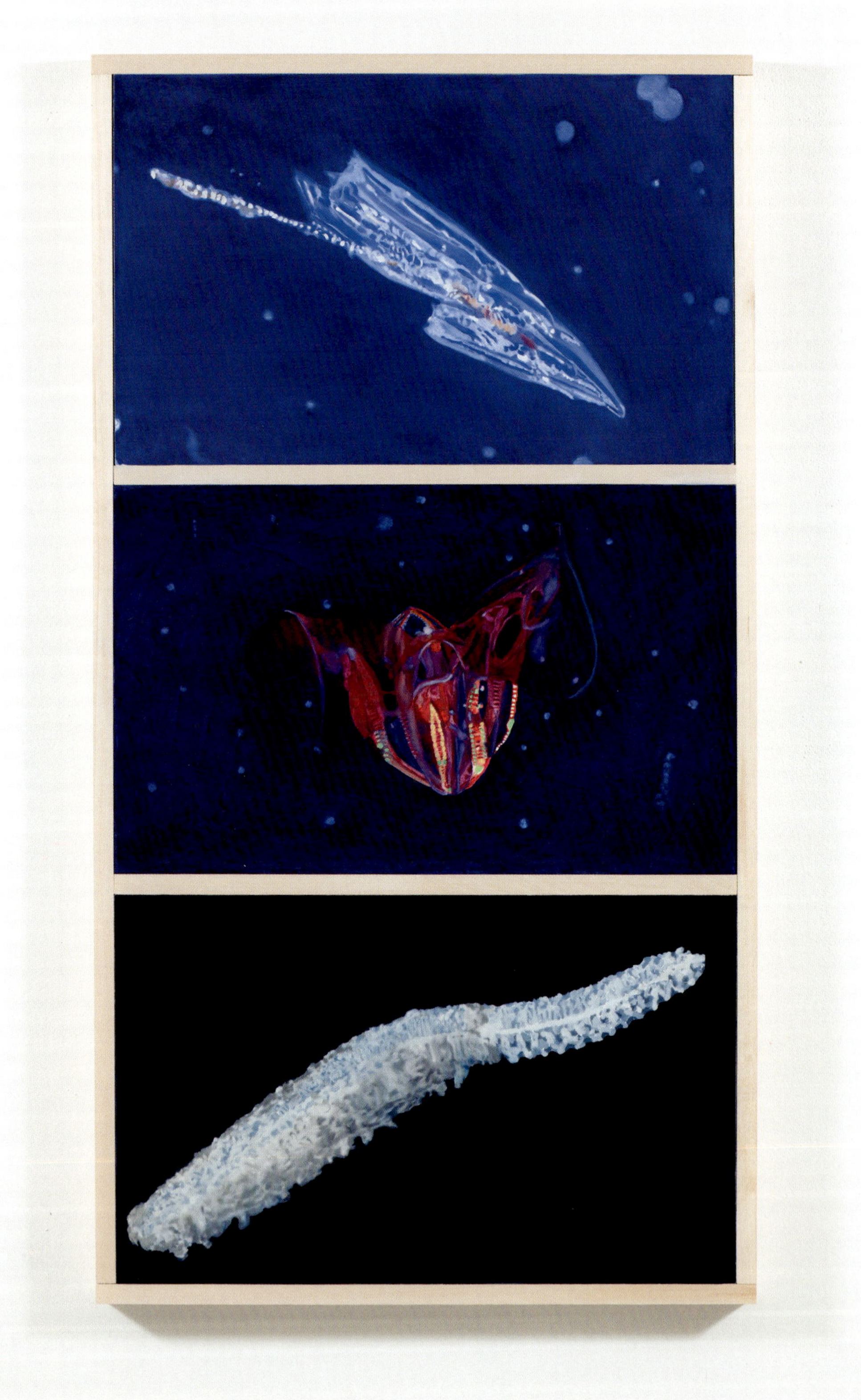

Into the Deep Blue Sea: Triptych 3 (Siphonophore 3, Bloody-Belly Jelly 2, Siphonophore), 2023

Into the Deep Blue Sea: Triptych 4 (Tethys Vagina, Jelly 3, Yellow Ctenophore), 2023

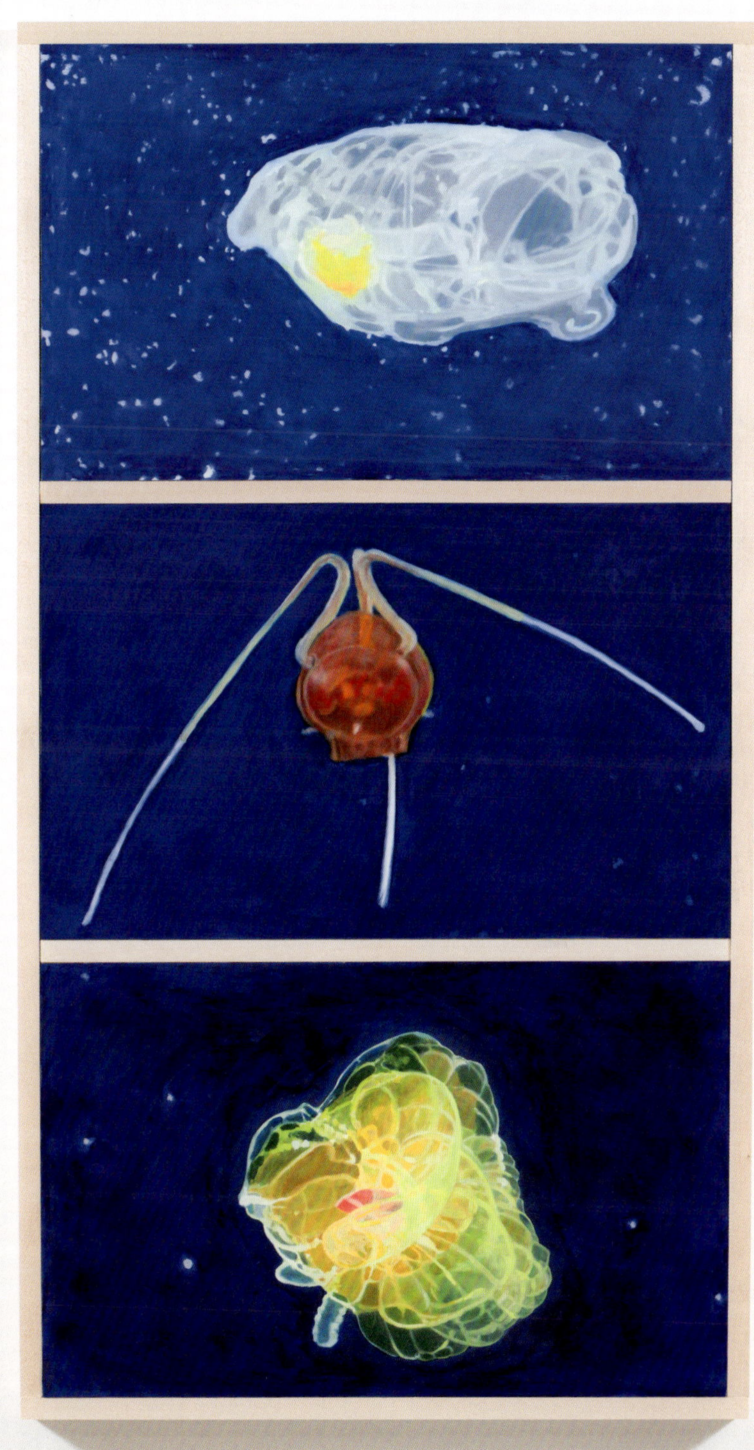

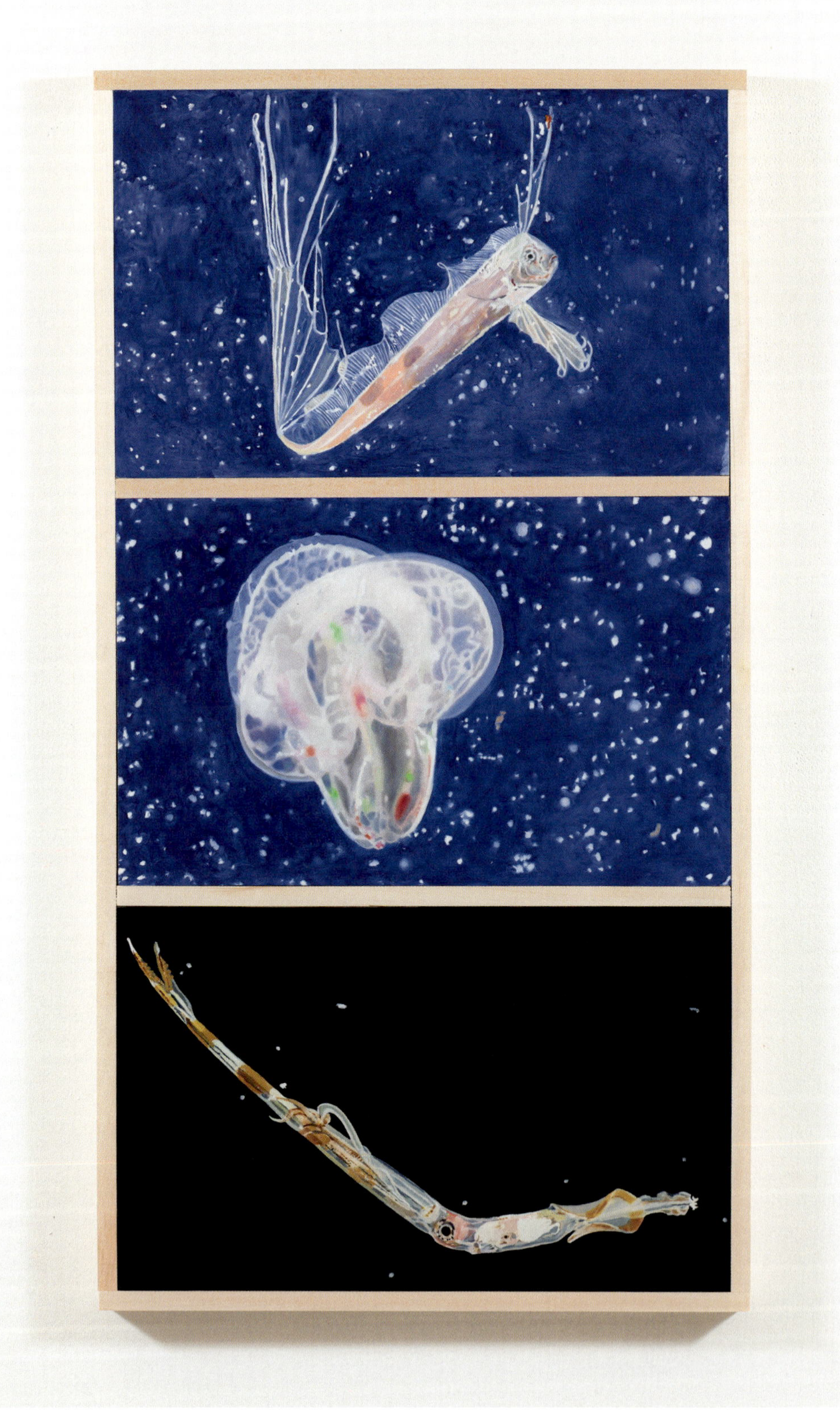

Into the Deep Blue Sea: Triptych 5 (Ribbon Fish, Pink Ctenophore, Striped Squid), 2023

(opposite)
Helmet Jellyfish, 2023

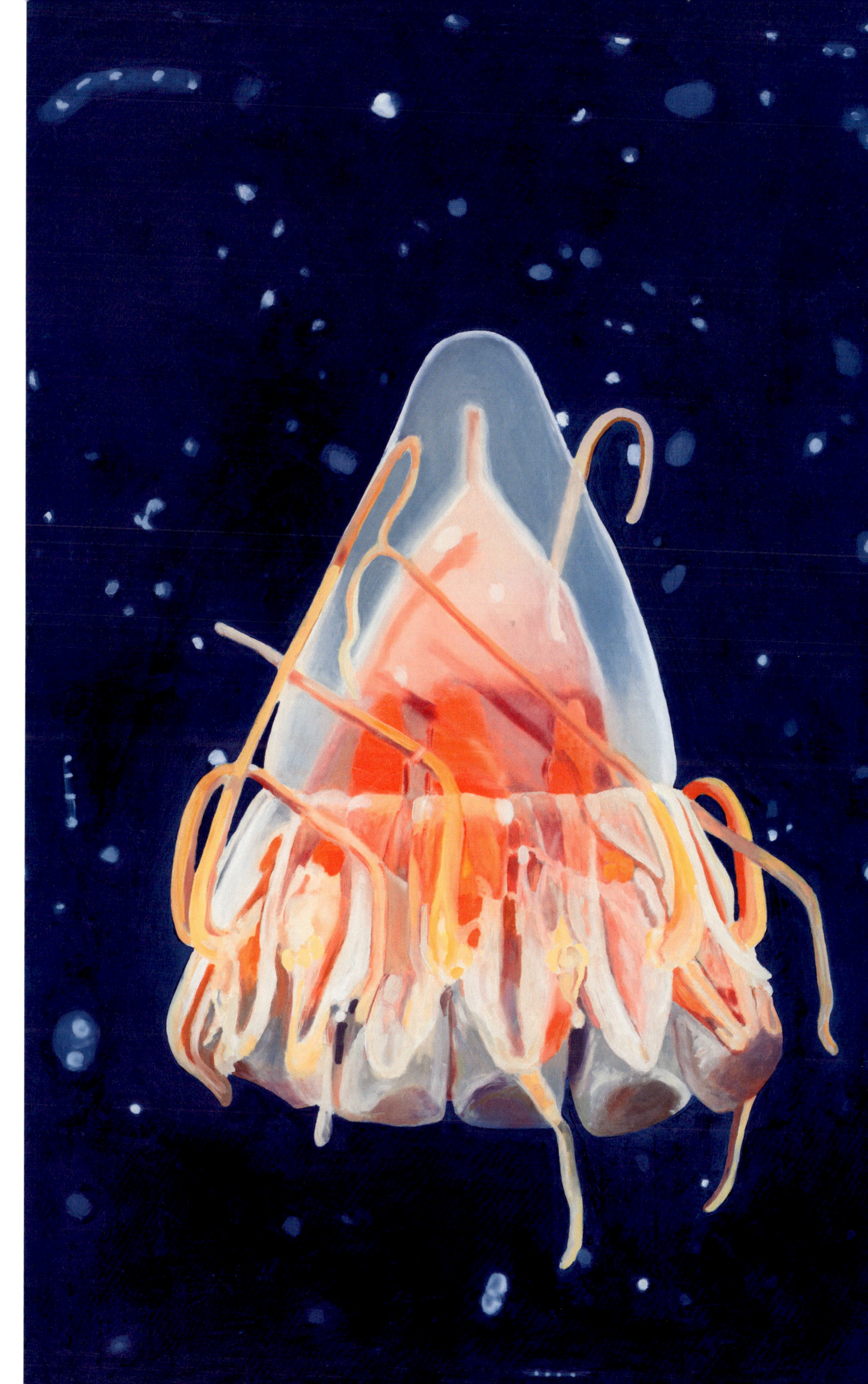

(clockwise from top right)
Bathyphysa Siphonophore, 2024

Barreleye Fish, 2024

Glass Squid 2, 2024

Solmissus Jelly, 2024

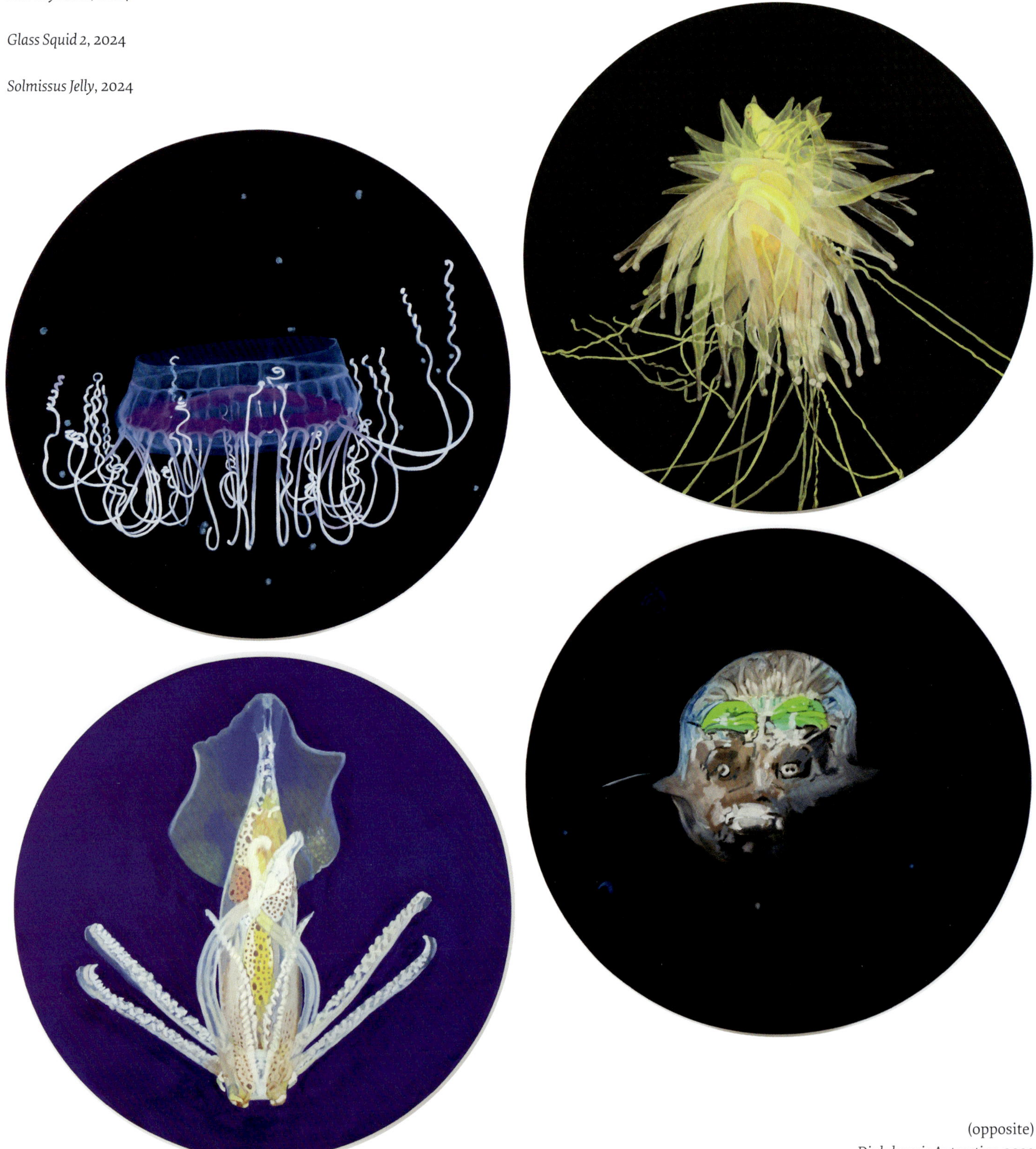

(opposite)
Diplulmaris Antarctica, 2023

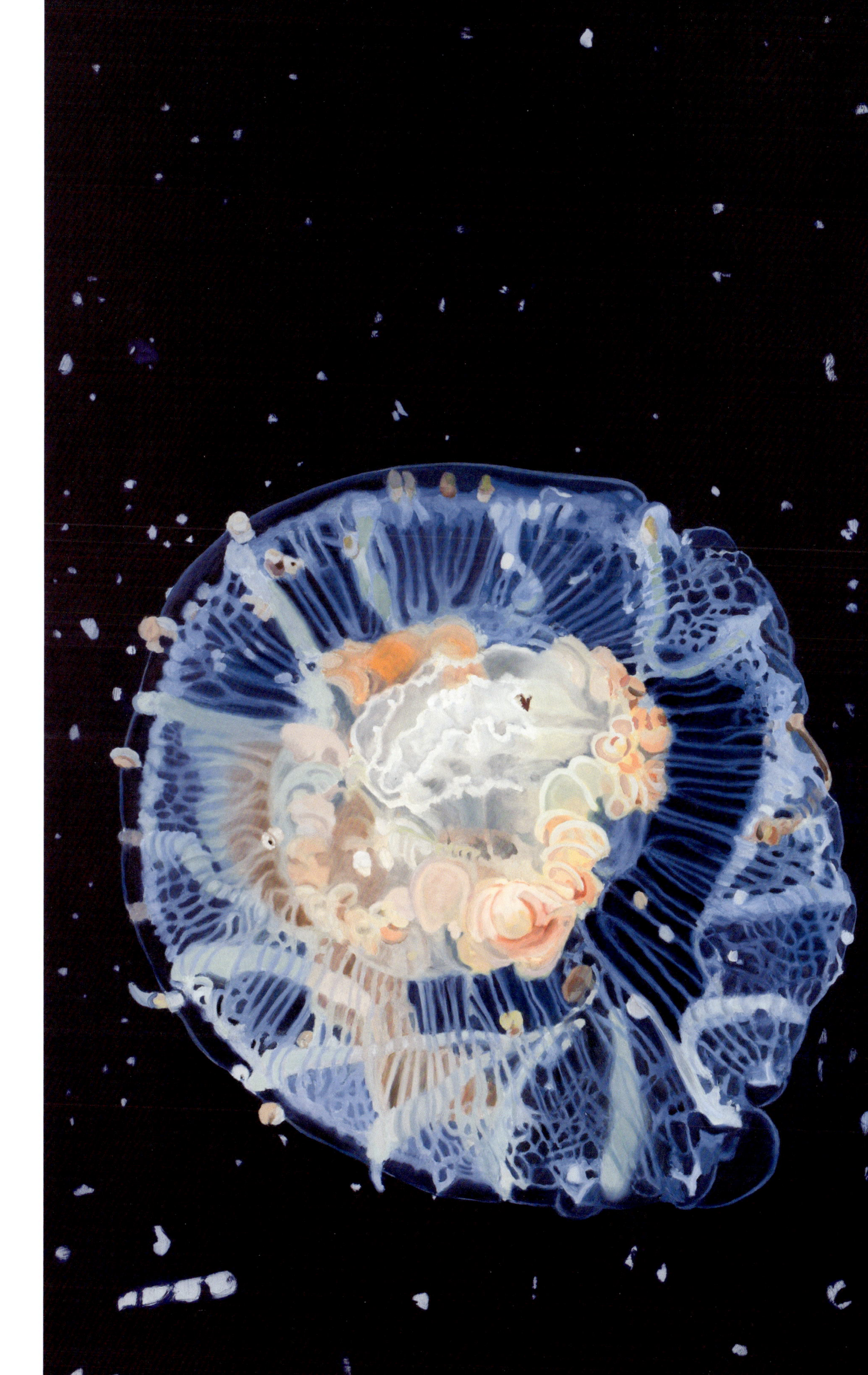

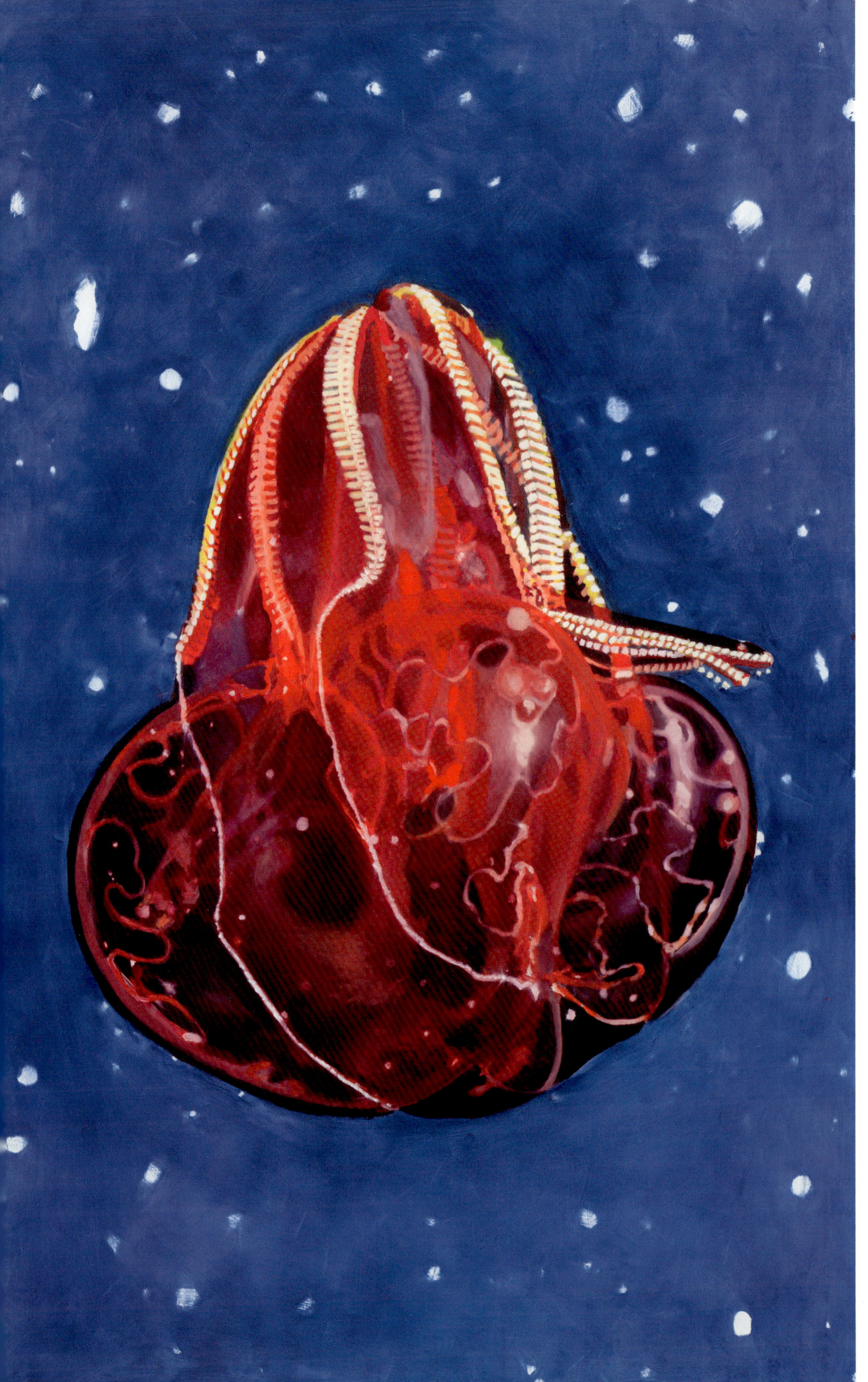

Bloody -Belly Comb Jelly, 2023

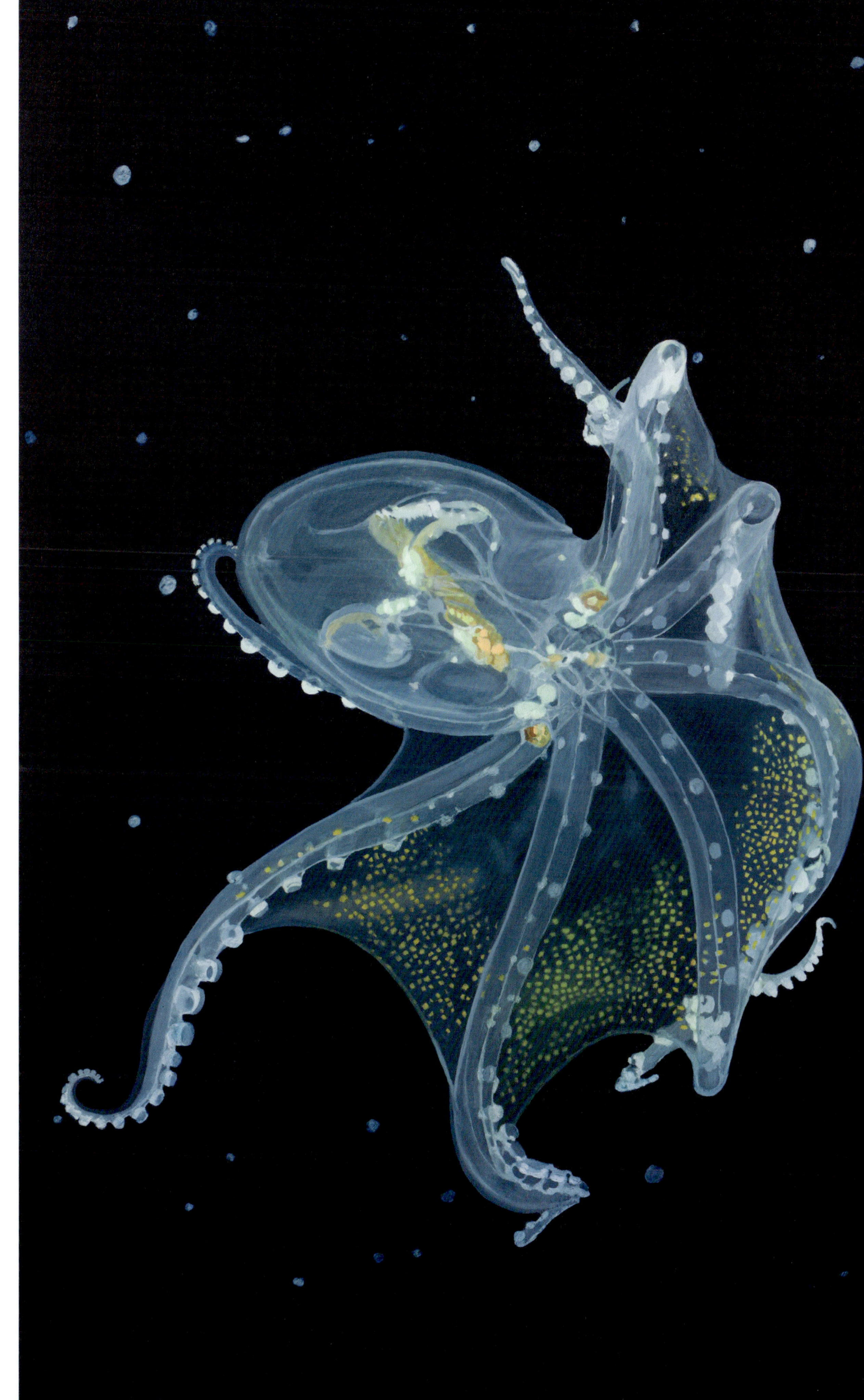

Glass Octopus, 2023

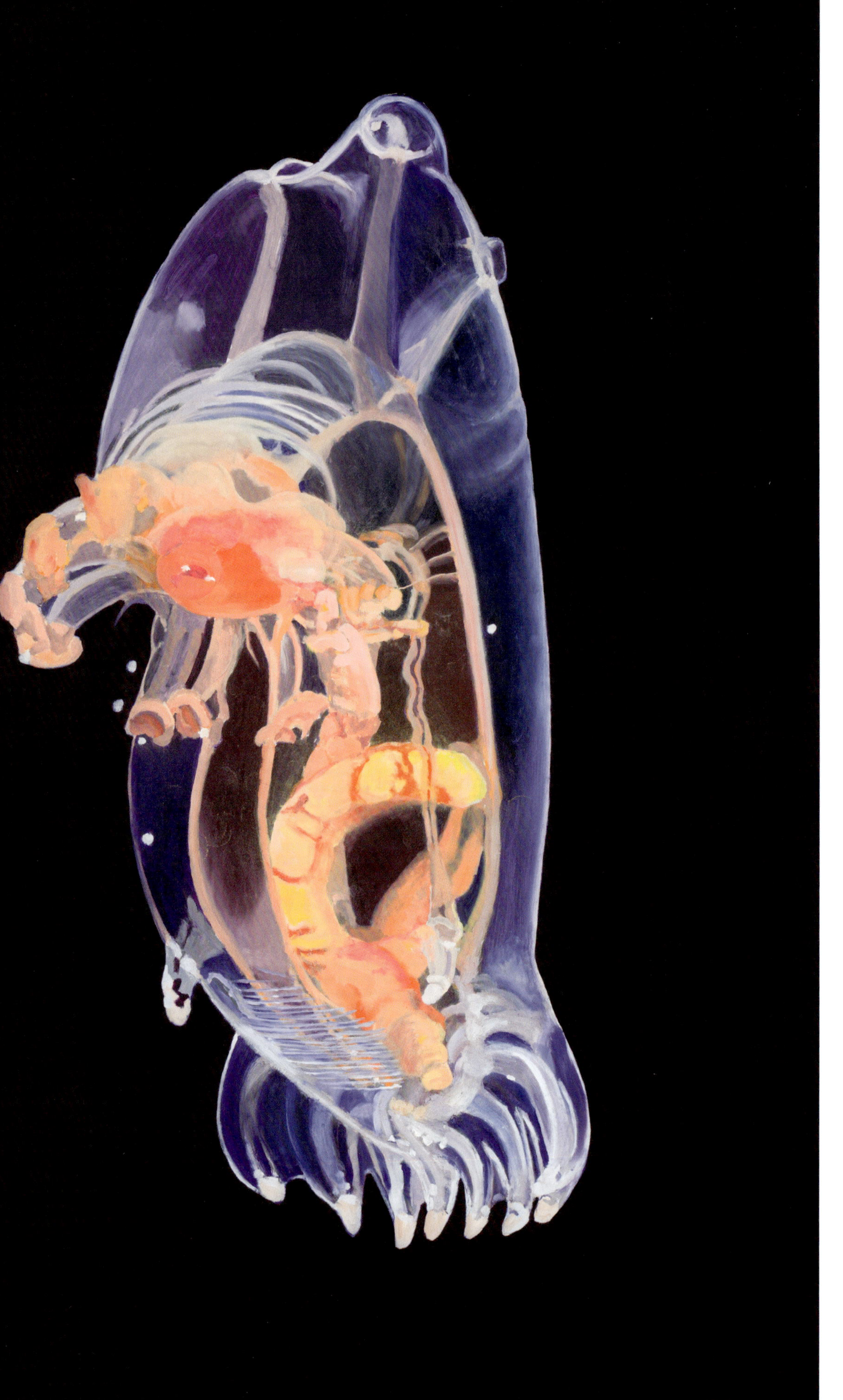

(opposite)
Holothurian, 2023

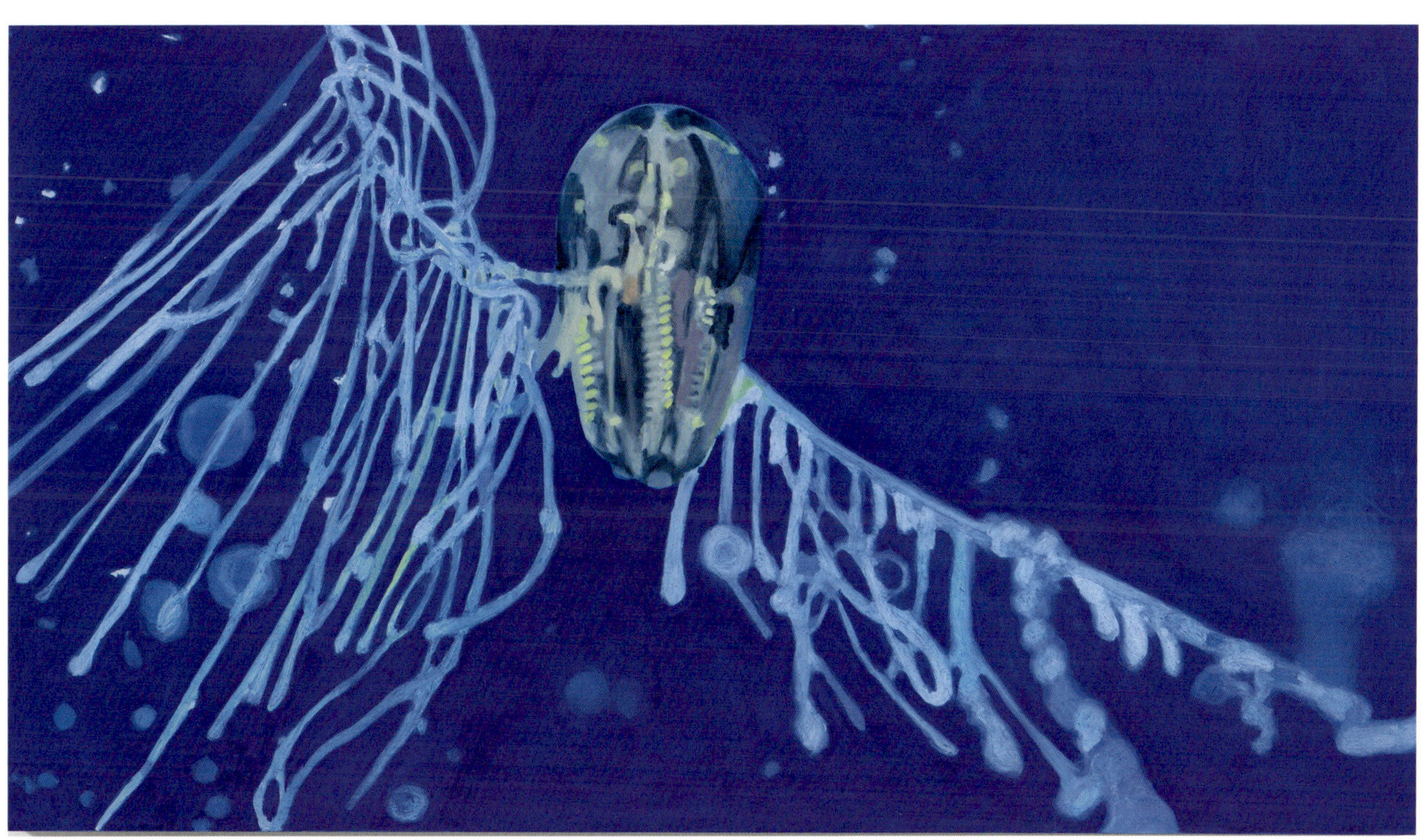

(above)
Bentic Ctenophore, 2023

(overleaf)
Lobate Ctenophore, 2023

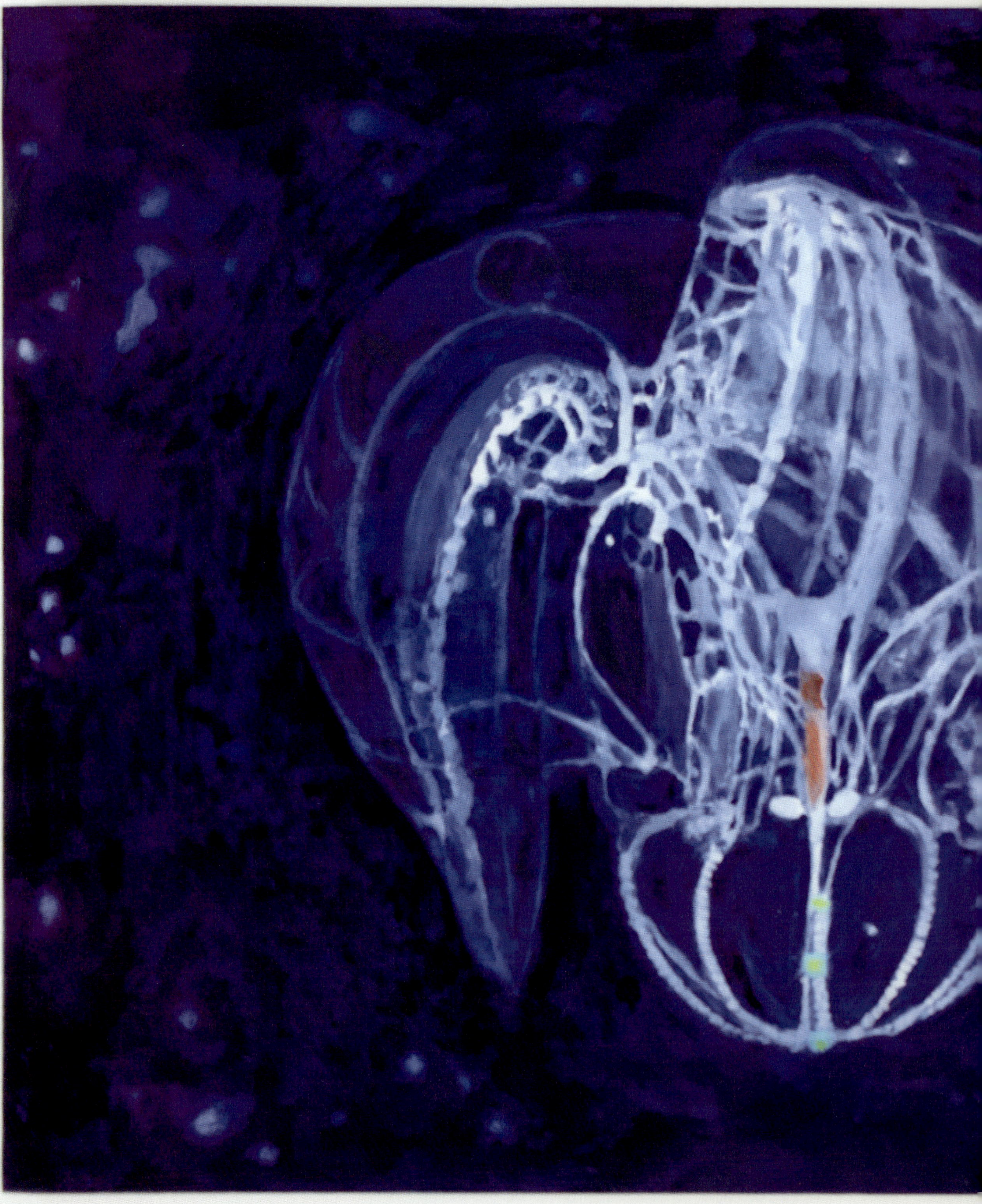

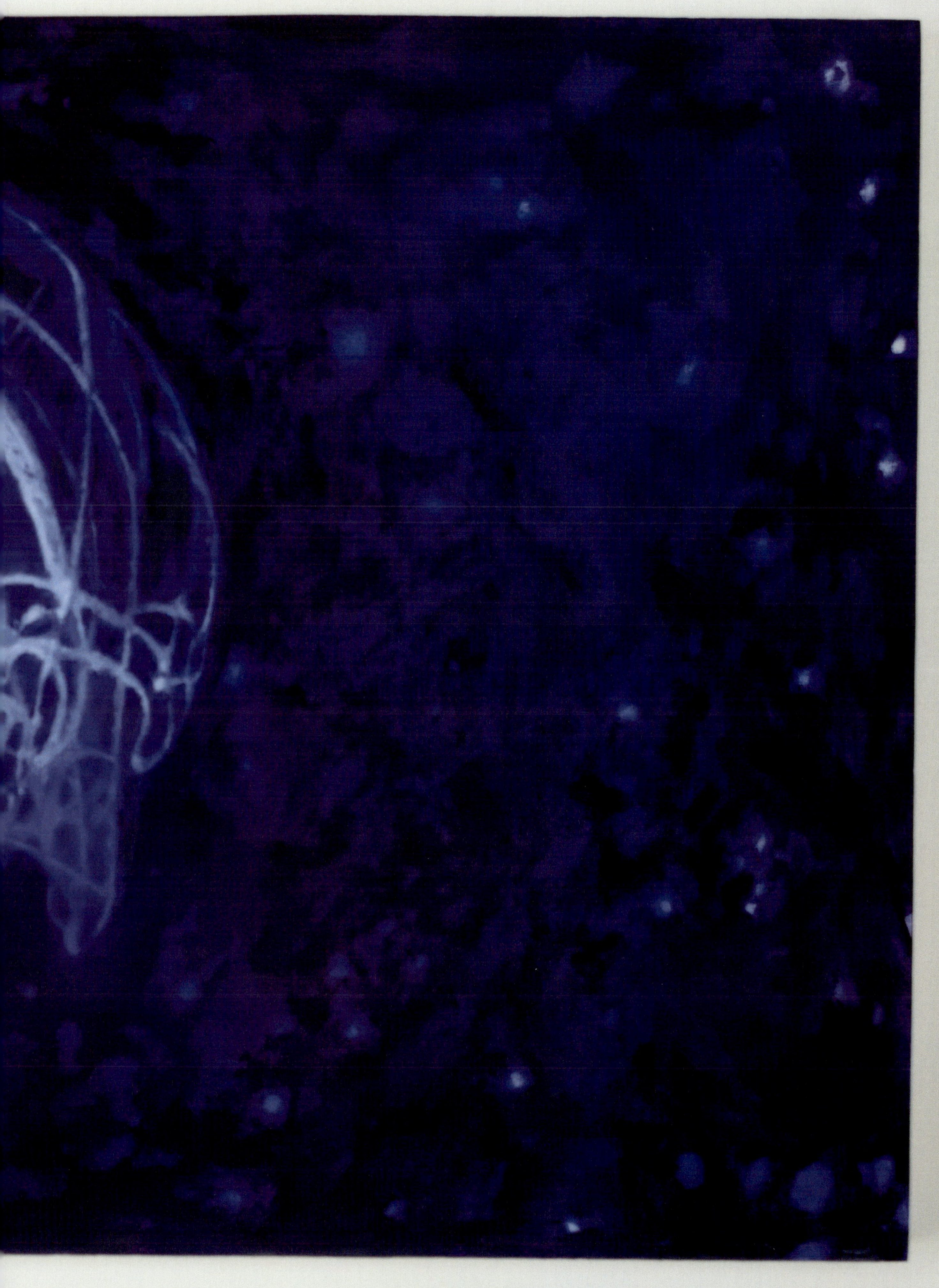

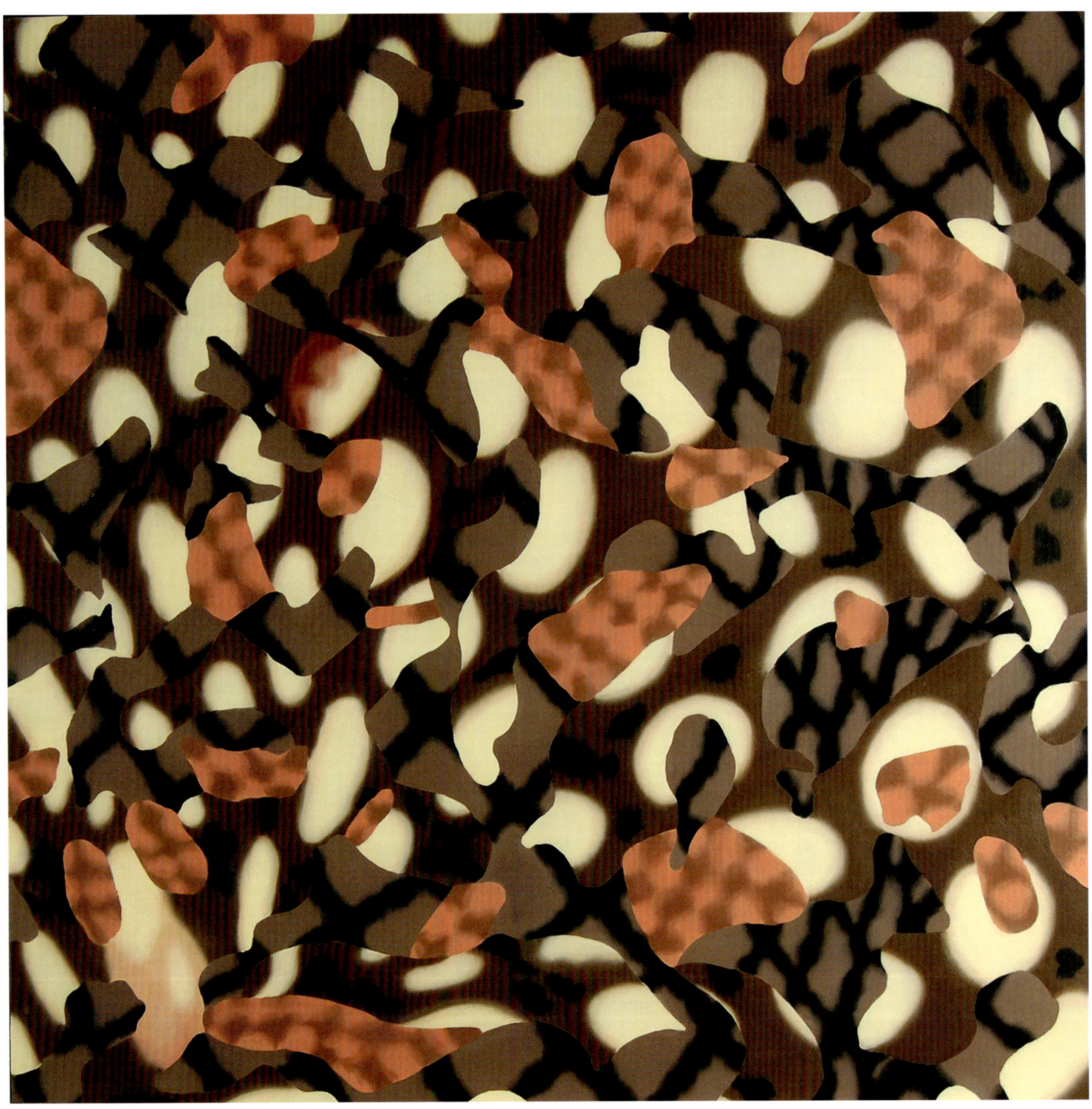

Camouflesh Finland, 2005

Acknowledgements

The artist acknowledges Sue Wolstenholme, Gillian McCain, Sarah McLachlan; Rhéal Olivier Lanthier and François St-Jacques, co-directors, and Michael Patten, operations manager of Art Mûr, Montréal; Robin Peck, Iris Wu, National Oceanic and Atmospheric Administration, and the Monterey Bay Aquarium Research Institute; Ray Cronin and the Beaverbrook Art Gallery; and Sarah Moore Fillmore and the Art Gallery of Nova Scotia.

The Beaverbrook Art Gallery acknowledges the ongoing support of the Province of New Brunswick, the Government of Canada, the Canada Council for the Arts, the City of Fredericton, and our members.

The Art Gallery of Nova Scotia acknowledges the significant and ongoing support of the Canada Council for the Arts and the Government of Nova Scotia.

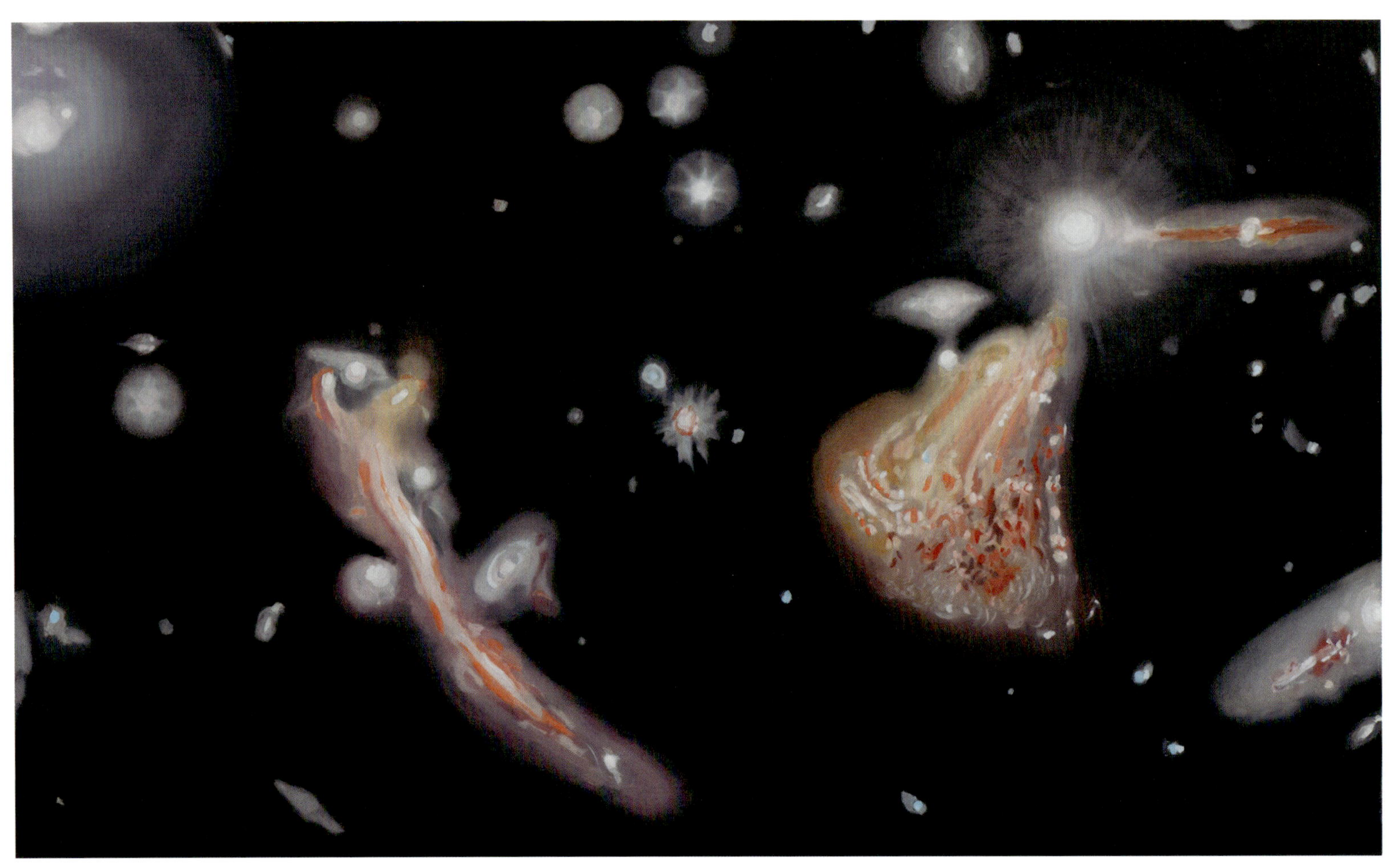

Deep Space 1, 2023

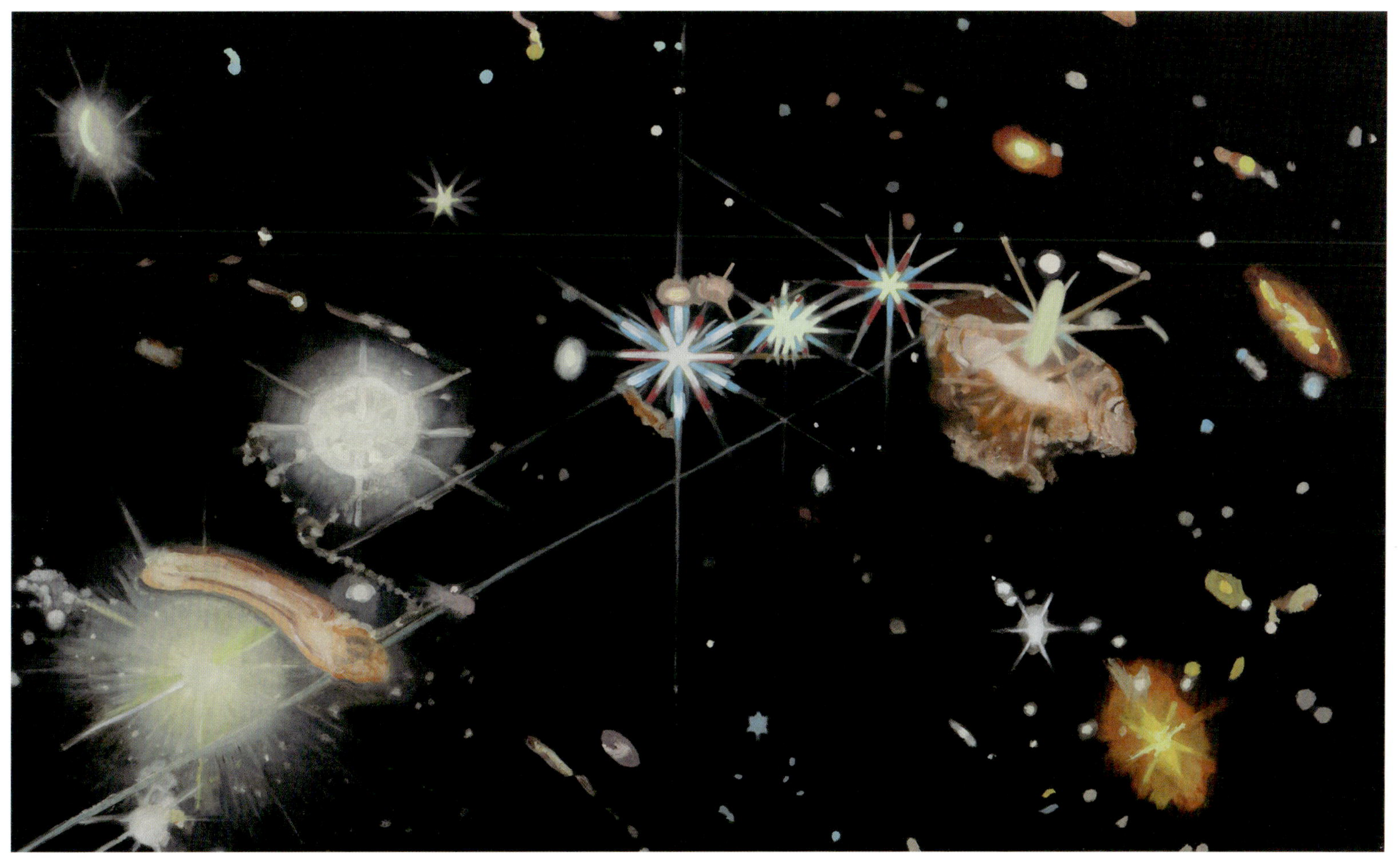

Deep Space 2, 2024

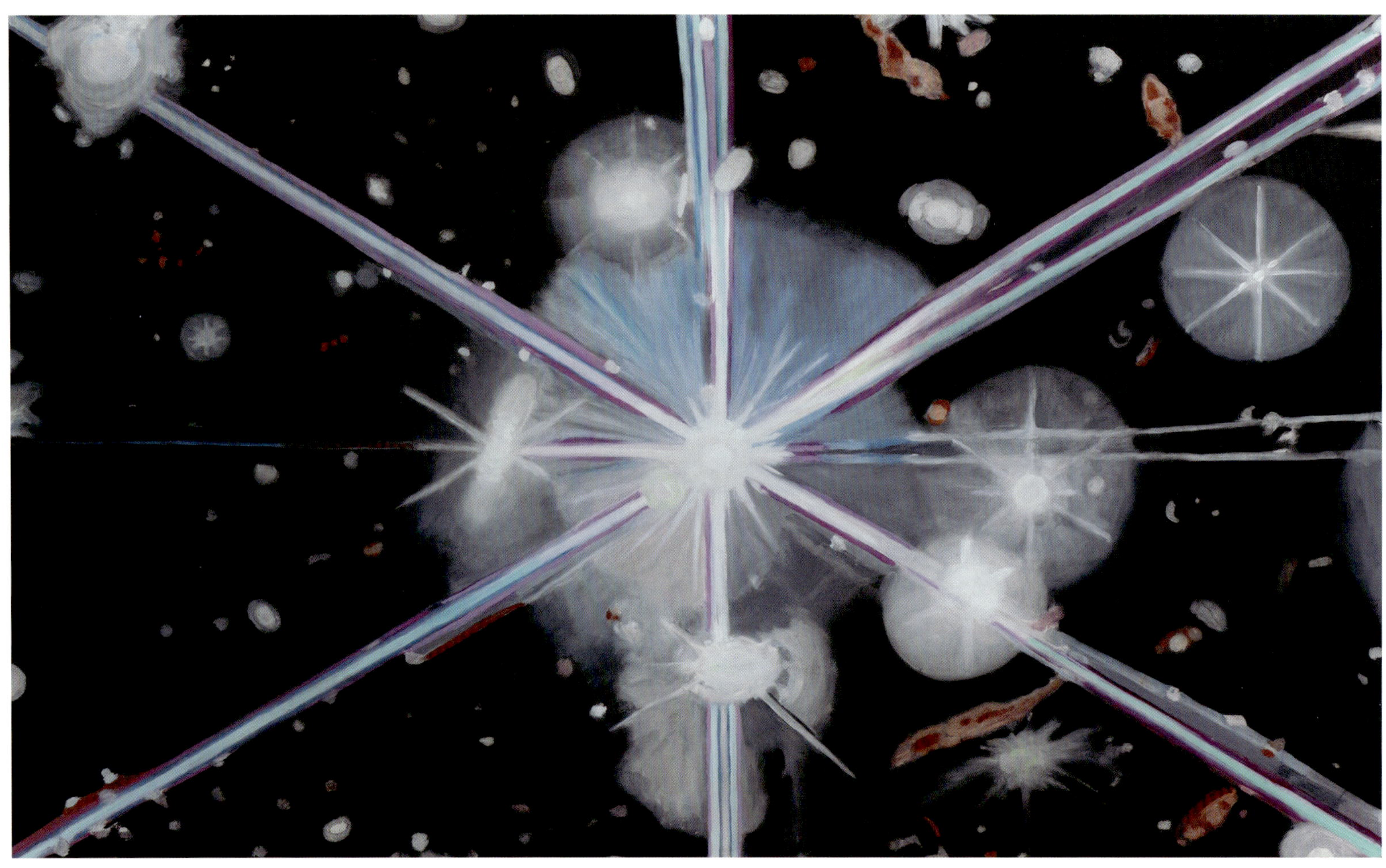

Abell 2744, 2023

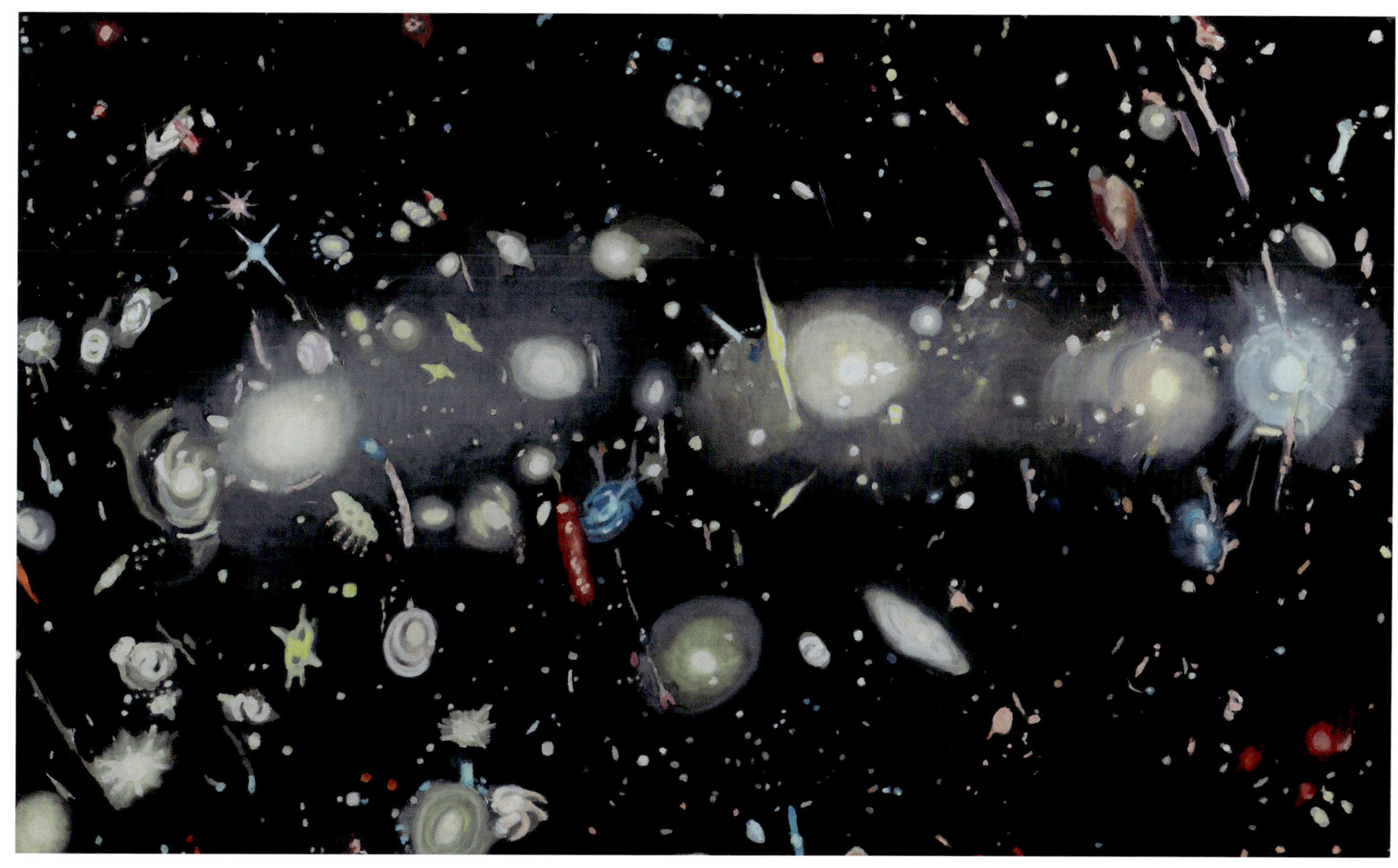

MACSO416, 2023

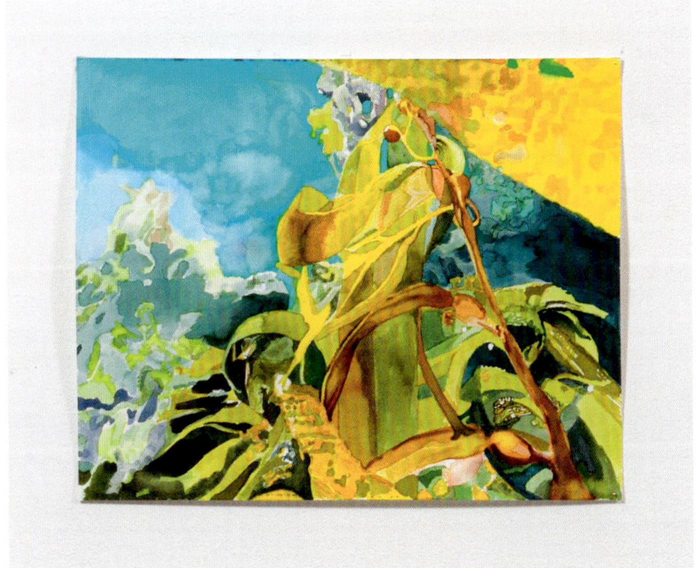

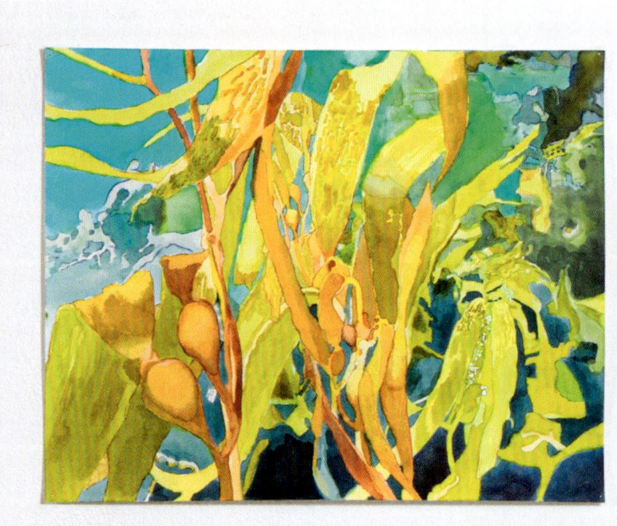

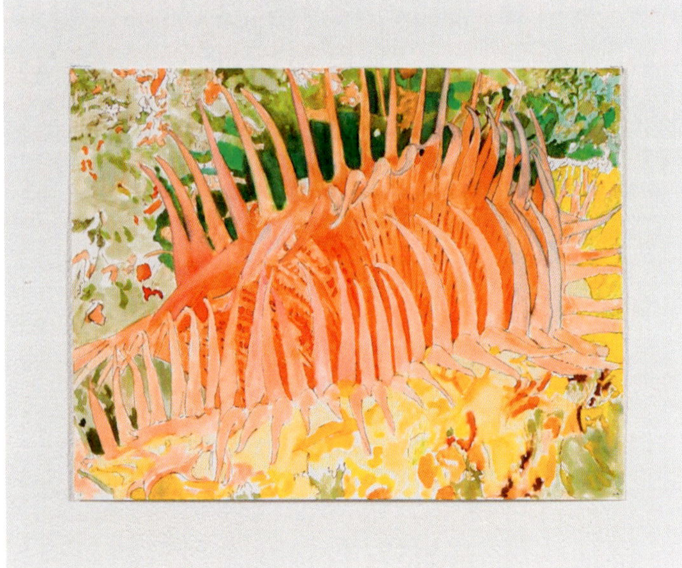

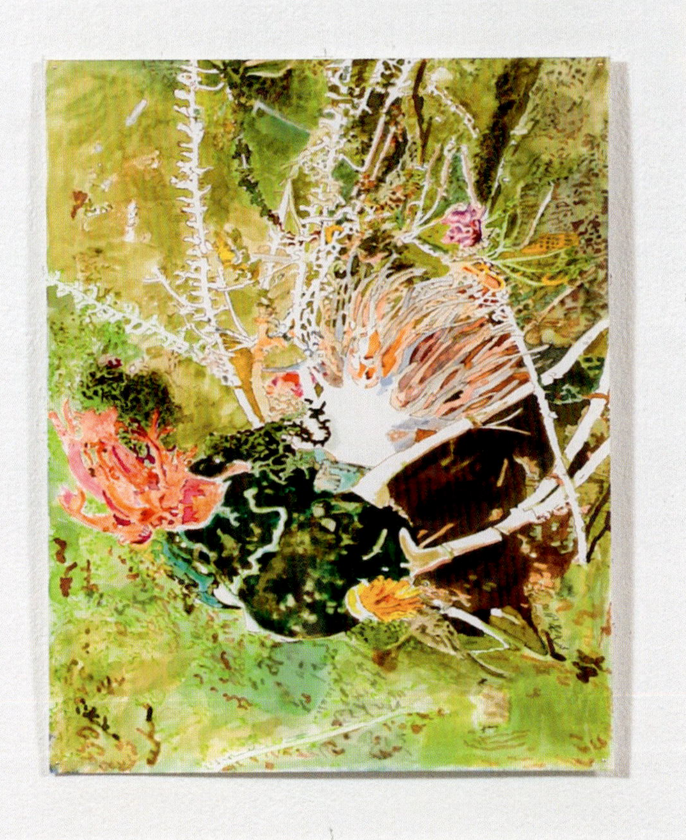

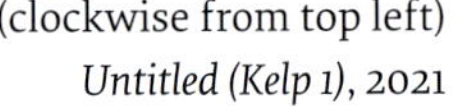

(clockwise from top left)
Untitled (Kelp 1), 2021

Untitled (Kelp 2), 2021

Untitled (Sea Floor 3), 2021

Untitled (Sea Floor 2), 2021

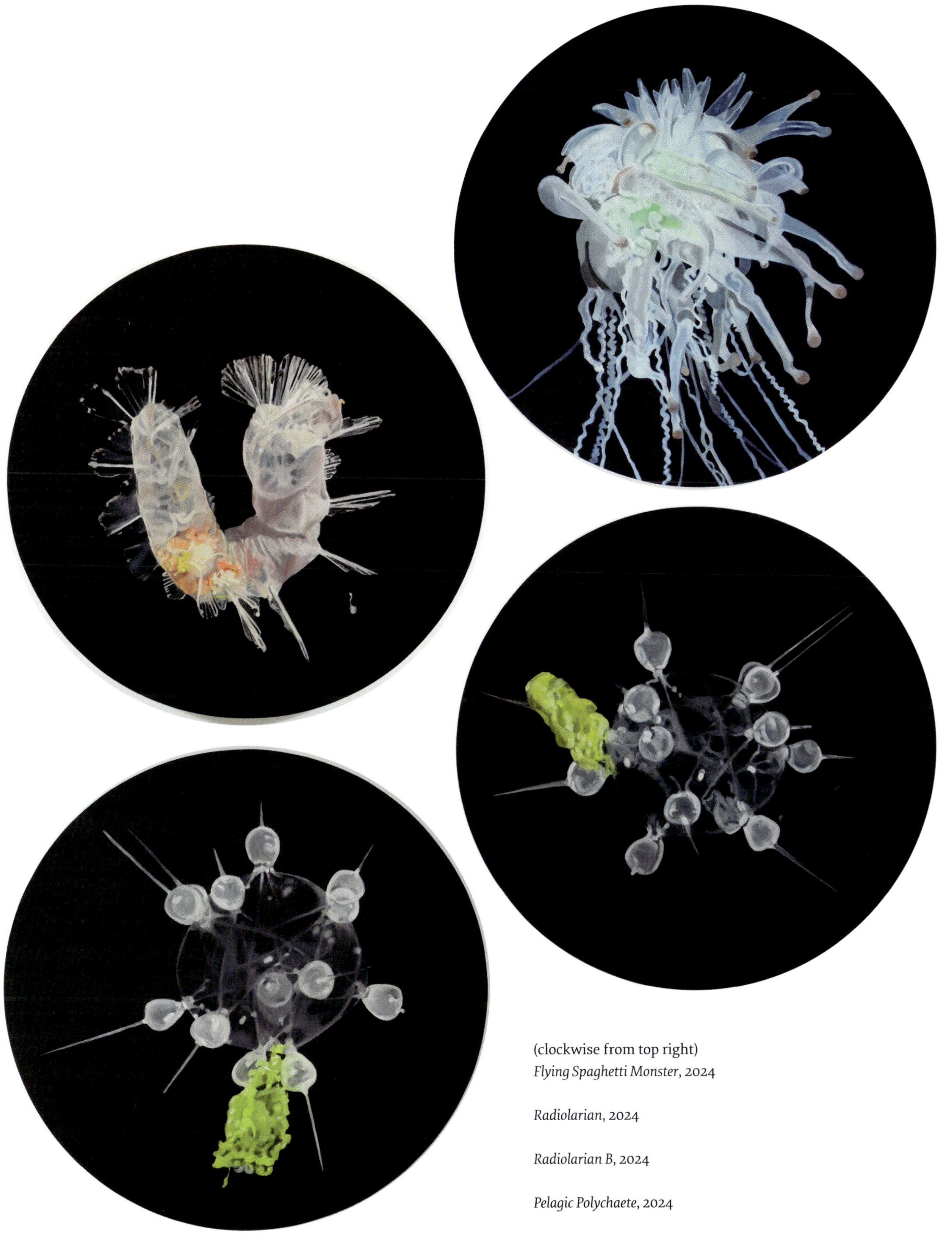

(clockwise from top right)
Flying Spaghetti Monster, 2024

Radiolarian, 2024

Radiolarian B, 2024

Pelagic Polychaete, 2024

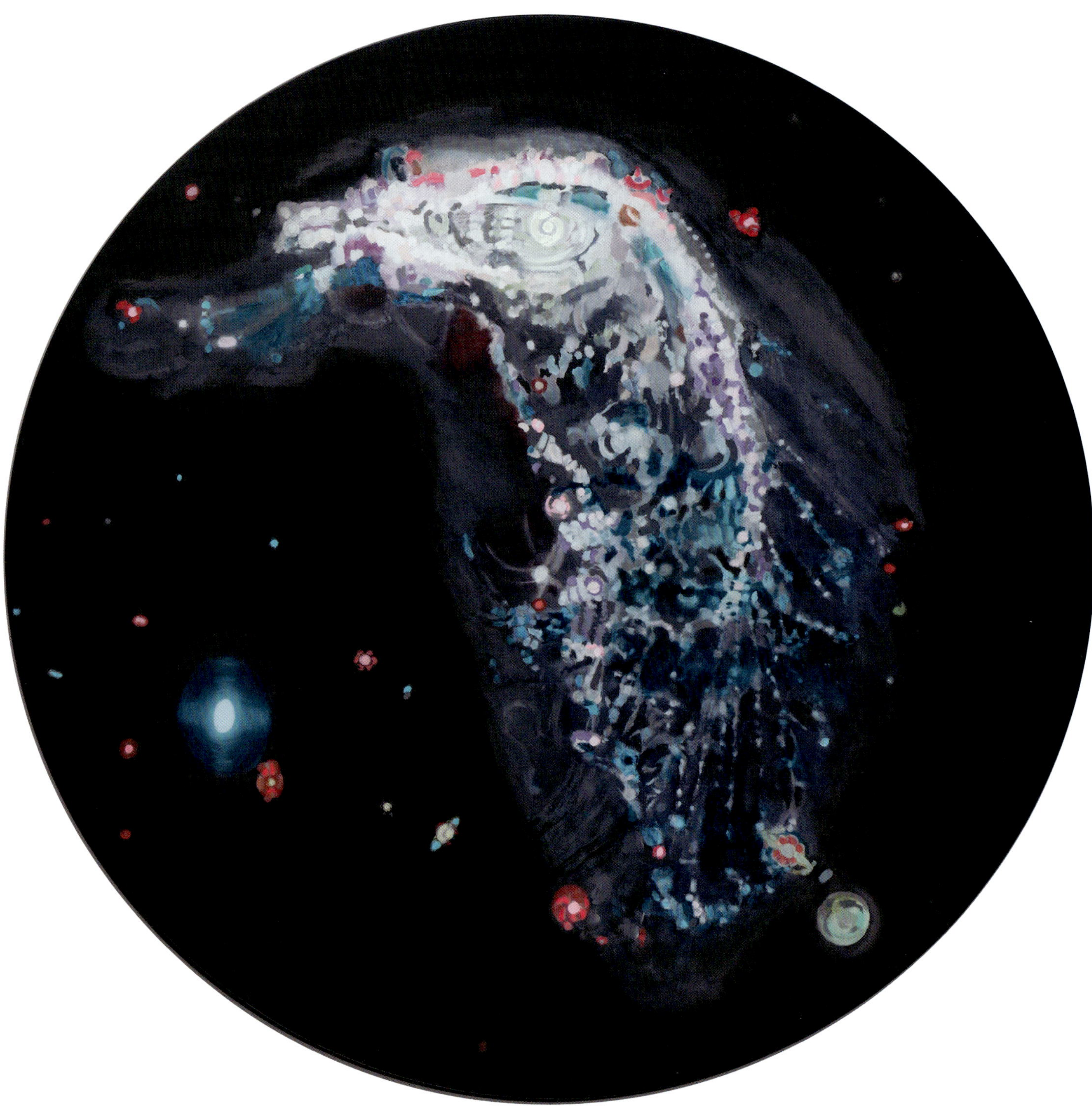

The Penguin and the Egg, 2025

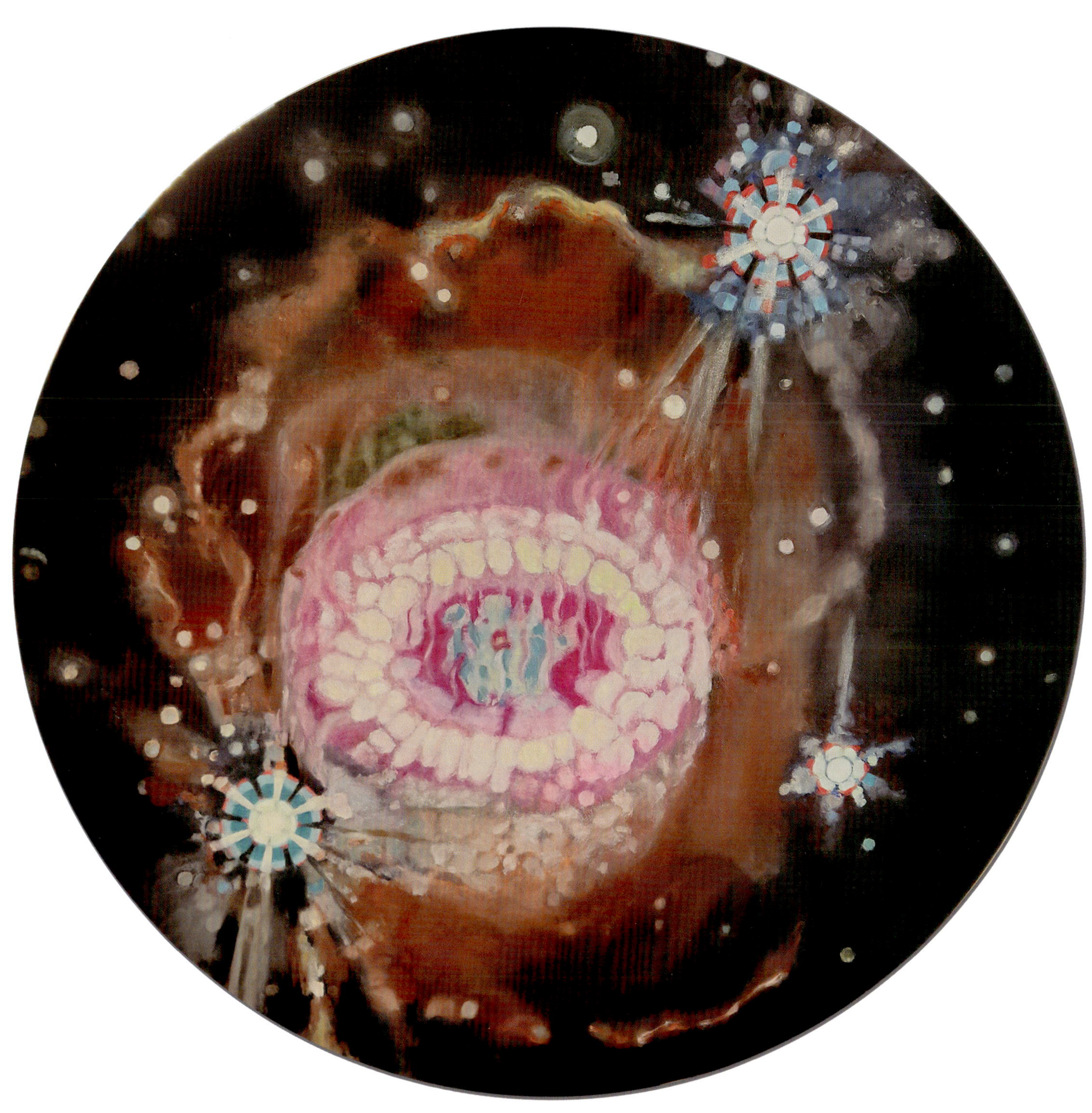

SN1987A, 2025

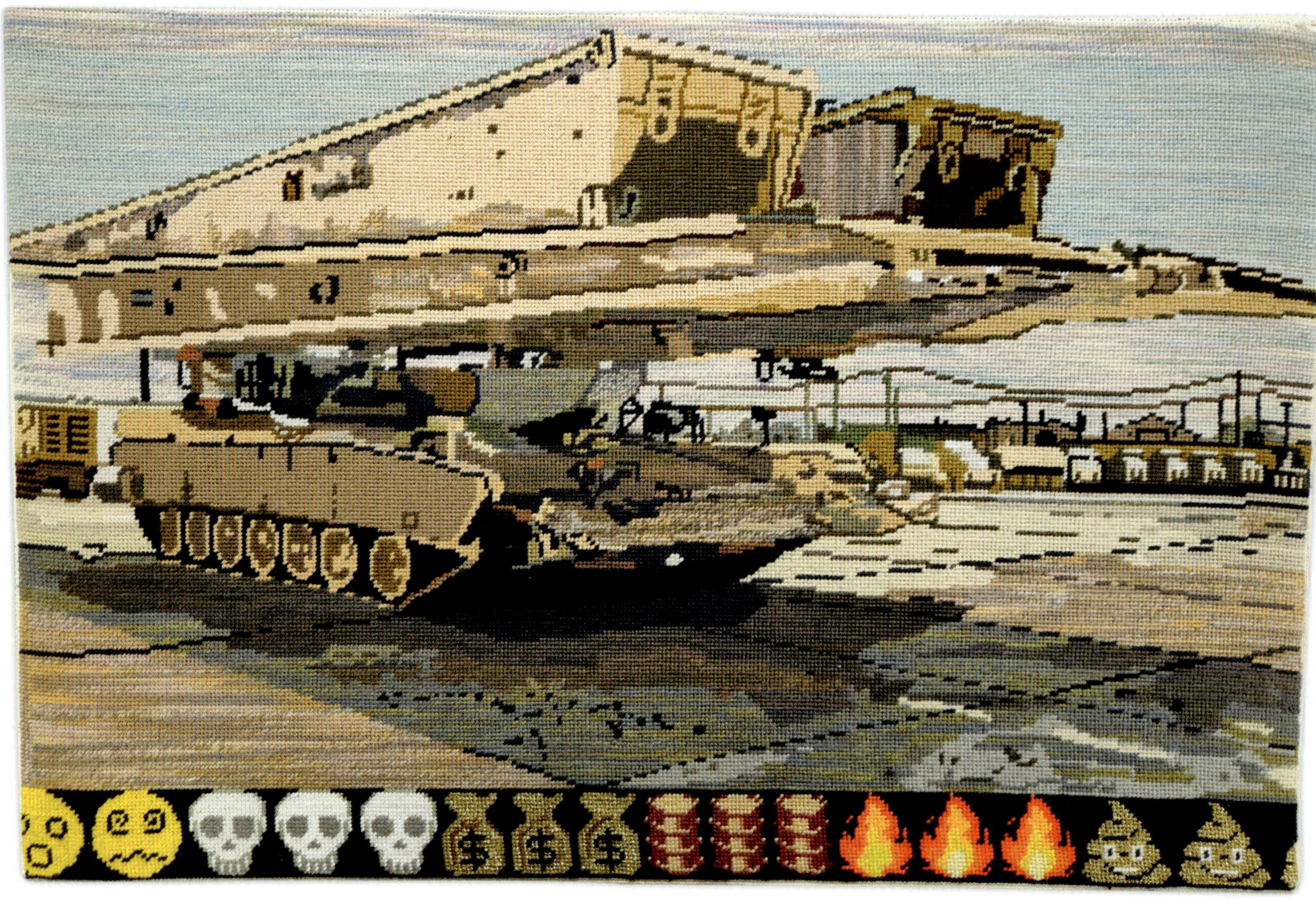

Wolverine Heavy Assault Bridge, 2010–26

Chronology

Compiled by IRIS WU

1963 Born in Antigonish, NS
1965 Moved to Moncton, NB
1967 Moved to Toronto, ON
1968 Wolstenholme's parents separated
1969 Wolstenholme and her mother moved to Halifax, NS
1970 Attended St. Thomas Aquinas School
1972 Attended a "free school," the Eastern Coast Community School
1973 and 1975 Travelled to Europe
1979 Attended Queen Elizabeth High School
1981 Graduated from high school
1982 Started undergraduate studies at the Nova Scotia College of Art and Design (NSCAD), Halifax, NS
1986 Graduated from NSCAD as a fine arts major (concentrating on sculpture)
1987 Participated in NSCAD's New York Studio program
Worked for Andy Warhol's printer, Seymour Berlin, New York, NY
1989 Returned to Halifax, NS, and re-enrolled at NSCAD
Completed a craft major in jewellery in two semesters
1990 Started graduate studies in jewellery at the State University of New York (SUNY) at New Paltz, NY
Participated in *The Medium is Metal: The Essence is Water*, Metal Arts Guild of Canada, travelling exhibition
Exhibited *Amphora* at Galerie Jocelyne Gobeil, Montréal, QC

1991 Adjunct faculty (one term), Metals Department, SUNY at New Paltz, NY
Exhibited at *Talentborse Handwerk*, Internationale Handwerksmesse, Munich, Germany
Exhibited in *The Faculty Selects*, College Art Gallery, SUNY, The College at New Paltz, NY

1992 Exhibited in *The Persistence of Denial*, College Art Gallery, SUNY, The College at New Paltz, NY
Exhibited in *The Armory Show*, Dutchess County Arts Council, Poughkeepsie, NY

1993 Moved back to New York, NY

1994 Graduated with a Master of Fine Arts, SUNY at New Paltz, NY
Exhibited in *From the Cabinet of Maxwell M. Fisch*, Max Fisch, Ludlow Street, New York, NY

1995 Returned to Nova Scotia due to health issues

1996 Part-time faculty (three terms), Jewellery Department, NSCAD, Halifax, NS
Mounted the exhibition *Patience* at Anna Leonowens Gallery, NSCAD, Halifax, NS

1997–99 Toured with Lilith Fair, exhibited and sold pill jewellery
Earned a gold record for co-writing “Do What You Have To Do” on Sarah McLachlan’s multi-platinum recording *Surfacing*

1998 Solo exhibition, *Pills*, at grunt gallery, curated by Robin Peck, Vancouver, BC
Moved to Vancouver, BC

1998–99 Board member, grunt gallery, Vancouver, BC

1999 Solo exhibition, *Pharmacopoeia*, Hamilton Artist’s Inc., Hamilton, ON

2000 Moved to Hantsport, NS, and began building studio
Exhibited in *Desire: Greg Forrest, Lauren Schaffer, Colleen Wolstenholme*, curated by Ray Cronin, Confederation Centre Art Gallery, Charlottetown, PE, and St. Mary’s University Art Gallery, Halifax, NS
Exhibited in *The Time Machine: Sculpture in the 20th Century*, curated by Robin Peck, University of Lethbridge Art Gallery, Lethbridge, AB

2001 Exhibited in *Art and Music Memorabilia*, Horse Hospital Gallery, London, UK

2002 Nominated for Sobey Art Award, national shortlist
Solo exhibition *“AH”* at Saw Gallery, Ottawa, ON
Exhibited in *Surface Tourist*, 15 Cecile Park, Crouch End, London, UK
Exhibited in *Eleven Bulls: 15 Artists*, Project Green, Brooklyn, NY
Exhibited in *Gill / Wolstenholme*, curated by Ray Cronin, AGNS, Halifax, NS

2002–03 Exhibited in *Sobey Art Award: 2002 Shortlist Exhibition*, AGNS, Halifax, NS, and Museum of Contemporary Canadian Art, Toronto, ON

2003 Exhibited in *Container*, curated by Stephen Holmes, Real Art Ways, Hartford, CT

2004 Peer juror, Canada Council, Visual Arts, grants to individuals

Exhibited in *Vision: Marion McCain Atlantic Art Exhibition*, curated by Tom Smart, Beaverbrook Art Gallery, Fredericton, NB

Exhibited in *Placebo: Helen Cho, Colleen Wolstenholme*, curated by Lorna Brown, Artspeak, Vancouver, BC

Exhibited in *Greg Forrest, Colleen Wolstenholme, Jonathan Forrest*, curated by Isa Spalding, Encomium Contemporary Art, Toronto, ON

2004–06 Non-Residency MFA Studio instructor, Maine College of Art & Design, Portland, ME

2005 Part-time faculty, Visual Art, Department of Fine Art, St. Thomas University, Fredericton, NB

Exhibited in *Appearances: New Work from Nova Scotia*, AGNS, Halifax, NS

Exhibited in *The Watcher*, curated by Isa Spalding, Encomium Contemporary Art, Toronto, ON

Exhibited in *Intercession*, Encomium Contemporary Art, Toronto, ON

Exhibited in *Constitution*, curated by Lynn Acoose, Godfrey Dean Art Gallery, Yorkton, SK

2006 Part-time faculty (one term), Department of Sculpture, NSCAD, Halifax, NS

Solo exhibition, *Iconophobia*, curated by Ivan Jurakic, Cambridge Art Galleries, Cambridge, ON

2007 Exhibited in *ICON*, curated by Alexandra Keim, Art Gallery of Calgary, AB

Exhibited in *A Divided Room*, curated by Pan Wendt, Confederation Centre Art Gallery, Charlottetown, PE, and Robert McLaughlin Gallery, Oshawa, ON

Exhibited in *Pictured: Image and Object in Canadian Sculpture*, curated by Ray Cronin, AGNS, Halifax, NS

2008–12 Board member and board president, Khyber Arts Society, Halifax, NS

2008 Exhibited in *When the Mood Strikes Us*, curated by J.J. Kegan McFadden, Platform Gallery, Winnipeg, MB

Exhibited in *Arena: The Art of Hockey*, curated by Ray Cronin, AGNS, Halifax, NS; Art Gallery of Alberta, Edmonton, AB; Just for Laughs Museum, Montréal, QC; and Museum of Contemporary Canadian Art, Toronto, ON

2009 Exhibited in *Heartland*, curated by Jeffrey Spalding, Toronto International Art Fair, Toronto, ON

2010 Part-time faculty (three terms), Steinhardt School, Department of Art and Art Professions, New York University, New York, NY
January/February: Solo exhibition, *Aniconia*, Art Mûr, Montréal, QC
Exhibited in *It Is What It Is*, curated by Josée Drouin-Brisebois, National Gallery of Canada, Ottawa, ON

2011 Exhibited in *Memento Mori / Bone Again*, Art Mûr, Montréal, QC
Exhibited in *Represent!*, Art Mûr, Montréal, QC
Exhibited in *Synaesthesiac*, curated by Ivan Jurakic, University of Waterloo Art Gallery, Waterloo, ON
Exhibited in *Pharmakon*, curated by Marcel O'Gorman, Critical Media Lab, Kitchener, ON
Exhibited in *Synaptic Connections: Art and The Brain*, curated by Dale Sheppard, AGNS, Halifax, NS
Exhibited in *Please Lie to Me*, curated by Rhéal Olivier Lanthier, Art Mûr, Montréal, QC
Death of Wolstenholme's father

2012–14 Teaching assistant, Drawing and Sculpture, York University, Toronto, ON

2012 Moved to Toronto, ON
Studied toward a PhD at York University Toronto, ON
Exhibited in *Skin: The Seduction of Surface*, curated by Sarah Fillmore, AGNS, Halifax, NS

2013 Instructor (summer intensive), St. Thomas University, Fredericton, NB
Solo exhibition, *Shifty Packets*, Art Mûr, Montréal, QC
Exhibited in *Porcelain: Breaking Tradition*, curated by Rhéal Olivier Lanthier, Art Mûr, Montréal, QC

2014 Exhibited in *Cold Pop*, curated by Pan Wendt, Confederation Centre for the Arts, Charlottetown, PE
Exhibited in *Installations of Selected Works from the Permanent Collection*, National Gallery of Canada, Ottawa, ON

2015 Peer juror, Canada Council, Visual Arts, grants to individuals
Exhibited in *Terroir: A Nova Scotia Retrospective*, curated by Sarah Fillmore and David Diviney, AGNS, Halifax, NS

2016 Solo exhibition, *Hyperobjects*, Art Mûr, Montréal, QC

2018 Solo exhibition, *Apropos Obsolescence,* Art Mûr, Montréal, QC

2019 Received PhD Visual Art, York University, Toronto, ON
Assistant professor, Visual Art, Department of Fine Art, St. Thomas University, Fredericton, NB
Exhibited in *Data Aesthetics*, curated by Gentiane Bélanger, Foreman Gallery, Bishop's University, Sherbrooke, QC

2020 Exhibited in *Spheres, Skulls, and Other Icons of the Interior,* curated by Pan Wendt, Confederation Centre Art Gallery, Charlottetown, PE

2021 Exhibited in *Terra Nova*, curated by Rhéal Olivier Lanthier and François St-Jacques, Art Mûr, Montréal, QC
Exhibited in *Tyranny*, curated by David Diviney, AGNS, Halifax, NS
Death of Wolstenholme's mother

2024 Solo exhibition, *Into the Deep Blue Sea*, Art Mûr, Montréal, QC
Granted tenure at St. Thomas University, Fredericton, NB

2025 Exhibited in *Across the Ages: Masterpieces from the Beaverbrook Legacy*, curated by John Leroux, Beaverbrook Art Gallery, Fredericton, NB

SELECTED PUBLIC COLLECTIONS

Art Gallery of Nova Scotia
Beaverbrook Art Gallery
Cambridge Art Galleries
Confederation Centre Art Gallery
Montreal Museum of Fine Arts
National Gallery of Canada

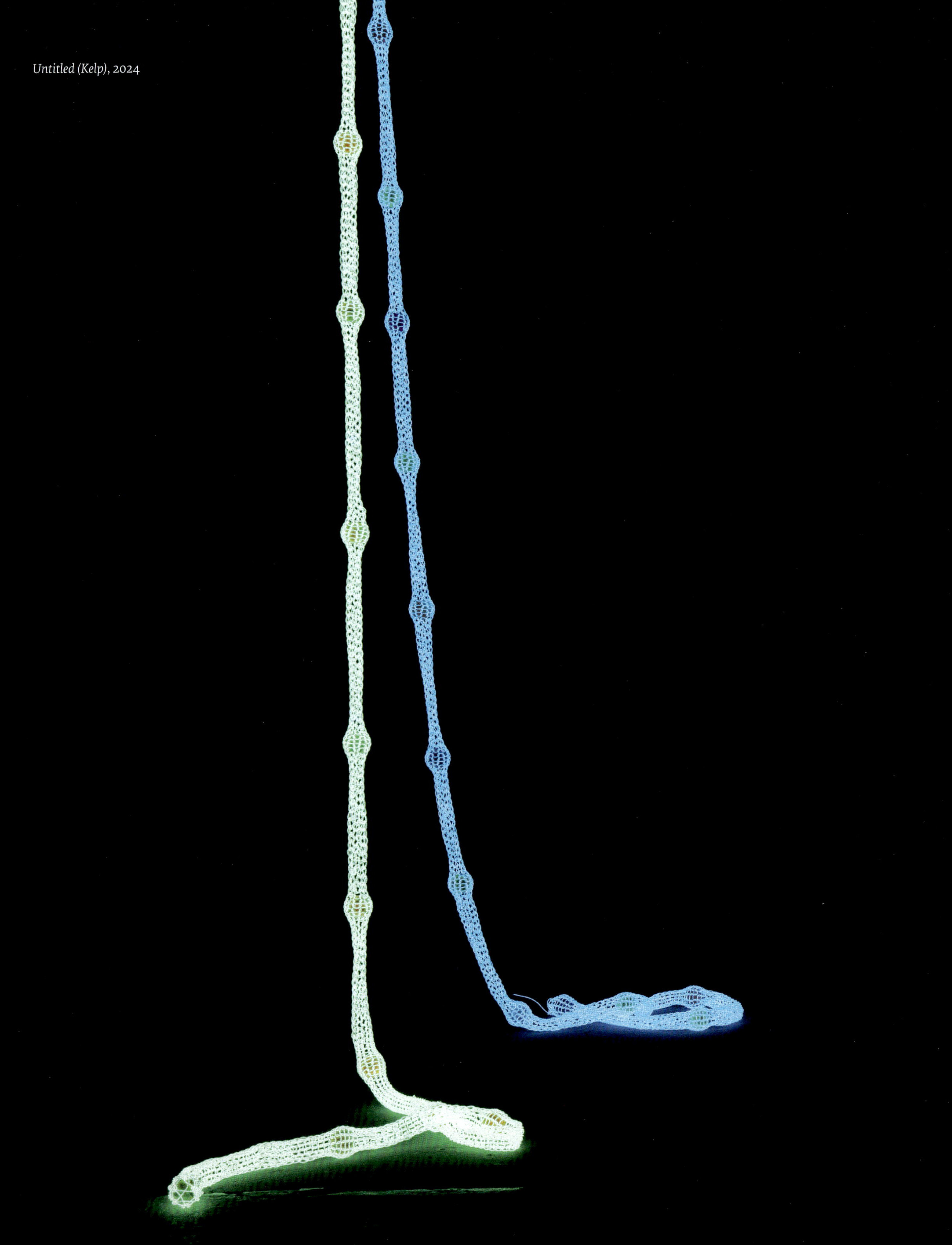

Untitled (Kelp), 2024

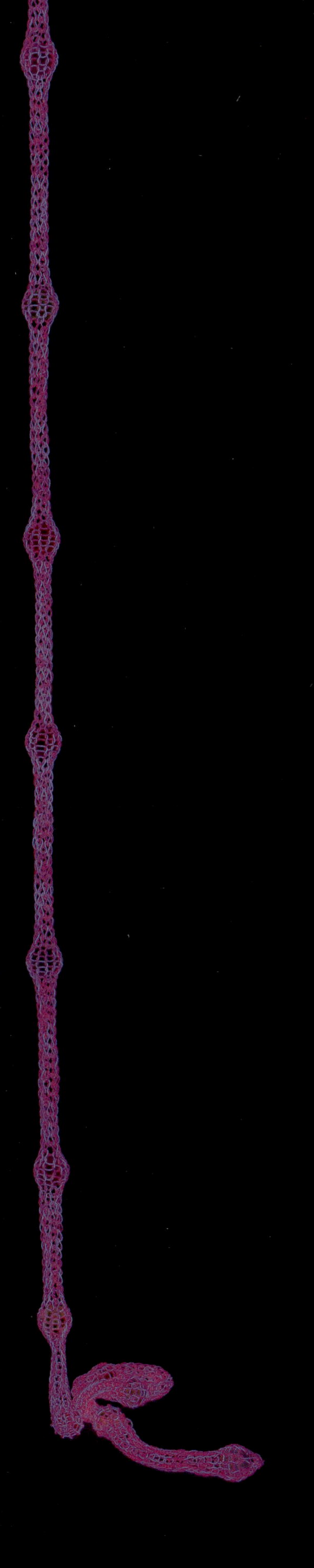

Contributors

Ray Cronin is the Director of Exhibitions, Collections, and Curatorial Initiatives at the Beaverbrook Art Gallery. Between 2001 and 2015 he worked at the Art Gallery of Nova Scotia as both curator and Director/CEO. He has curated numerous nationally touring exhibitions, including *Graeme Patterson: Woodrow*, *Arena: The Art of Hockey*, and *Nancy Edell: Selected Works 1980–2004*. He is the founding curator of the Sobey Art Award. Cronin has written on visual arts for magazines and newspapers for three decades and has contributed essays to over sixty catalogues and books on Canadian art. He is the sole author of fifteen books, including *Halifax Art & Artists: An Illustrated History* (Art Canada Institute), *Colleen Wolstenholme: Complications* (Gaspereau Press), and *Nova Scotia Folk Art: An Illustrated Guide* (Nimbus Publishing). In 2025 he was named a Fellow of the New Brunswick College of Craft and Design. He lives in Fredericton, New Brunswick.

Laura J. Ritchie (she/her) is an independent curator and art consultant, she is a Fellow of the Getty Leadership Institute, a member of the Wallace McCain Institute, and a Mount Allison and Western University alumna. Former Director of MSVU Art Gallery in Halifax, Laura has worked in collections, exhibitions, and administration with the Beaverbrook Art Gallery, New Brunswick Museum, New Brunswick Crafts Council, New Brunswick Arts Board, Museum London, Tom Thomson Memorial Art Gallery, the Commonwealth Association of Museums, Art Gallery of Alberta, and Kelowna Art Gallery. Laura recently co-curated the touring exhibition and edited the publication *Sarah Maloney's Pleasure Ground: A Feminist Take on the Natural World*.

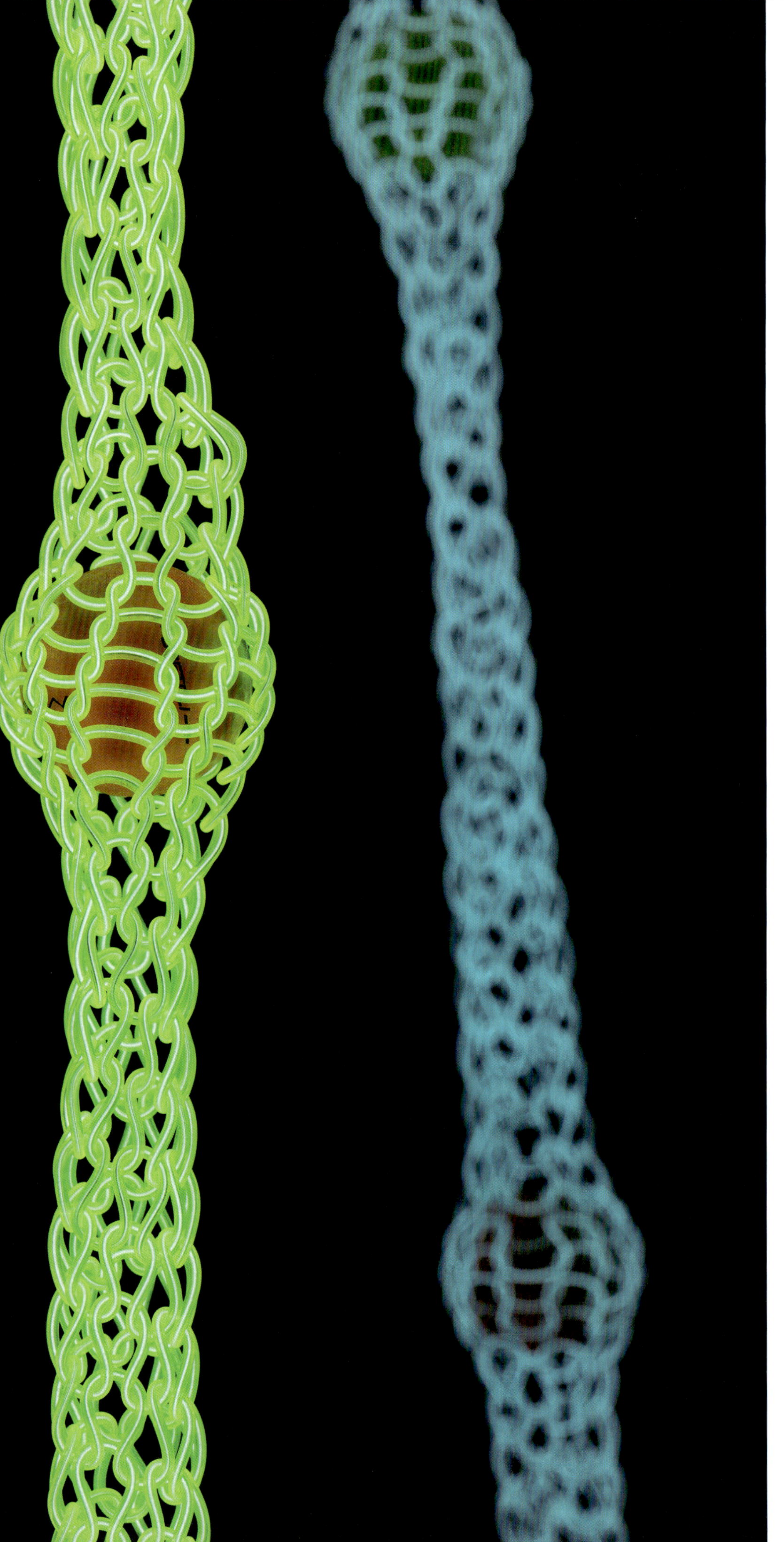

List of Works

All works are from the collection of the artist unless otherwise indicated.
* indicates a work not featured in the exhibition

The Bride Stripped Bare by Herself, Even, 1992 (p. 19)
mixed media
163.8 × 36.8 × 30.5 cm

Pud', 1992 (p. 10)
mixed media
106.7 × 28 × 20.1 cm

Patience, 1992–95 (p. 20)
mixed media
263.0 × 118.5 × 128.5 cm
Gift of the artist, Hantsport, NS, 2003
Collection of the Art Gallery of Nova Scotia
2003.44

Phenobarbital Pillow, 1995 (p. 23)
copper and embroidery cotton
31 × 41 × 13 cm

Prozac Pillow, 1995 (p. 22)
copper and embroidery cotton
31 × 41 × 13 cm
Collection of Gillian McCain, New York

Dexedrine, 1997 (p. 31)
carved plaster
12.5 × 65.5 × 64.0 cm
Gift of the artist, Vancouver, BC, 2001
Collection of the Art Gallery of Nova Scotia
2001.179

Dilaudid, 1997
bronze
22.9 × 45.7 cm diam.

Dilaudid, 1997 (p. 65)
carved plaster
22. 9 × 45.7 cm diam.

Leritine, 1997 (p. 26)
carved plaster
17.78 x 53.34 cm diam.

Paxil, 1997
carved plaster
22.9 × 68.6 × 40.7 cm
Purchased with funds provided by the Canada Council for the Arts Acquisition Assistance Program and the Art Sales and Rental Society, Halifax, Nova Scotia, 2001
Collection of the Art Gallery of Nova Scotia
2001.129

Paxil II, 1997 (p. 30)
carved plaster
22.9 × 68.6 × 40.7 cm

Valium, 1997 (p. 9)
carved plaster
67.8 × 67.5 × 18.0 cm
Purchase in exchange, 2004, with funds provided by the Canada Council for the Arts Acquisition Assistance Program and the Art Sales and Rental Society, Halifax, Nova Scotia, 2001
Collection of the Art Gallery of Nova Scotia
2004.365

Xanax, 2mg, 1997
bronze
26.0 × 89.0 × 18.0 cm
Purchased with funds from the Jane Shaw Law Bequest, 2011
Collection of the Art Gallery of Nova Scotia
2011.17

Xanax, 2mg, 1997 (pp. 62–63)
carved plaster
26.0 × 89.0 × 18.0 cm

Untitled (Kelp) (detail), 2024

Amitriptyline, 1999 (p. 64)
carved plaster
17.8 × 53.4 cm diam.

Drug Company Logos, 1999 (p. 58)
six units, needlepoint
12 x 18 cm each
Collection of Cambridge Art Galleries
A *Frosst*
B *Knoll*
C *Roche*
D *SmithKline*
E *Upjohn*
F *Wyeth*

BuSpar, 2001 (p. 28)
carved plaster
50.8 × 30.5 × 22.9 cm

**BuSpar Column*, 2001 (p. 29)
bronze
243 × 27 × 19 cm
Collection of the Montreal Museum of Fine Arts
Gift of Andrew Danyliw

Spill, 2001 (p. 27)
plaster
24 plaster pills (3 *Amitriptyline* 24.0 × 42.0 × 42.0 cm each;
21 *BuSpar* 21.0 × 31.0 × 52.0 cm each)
Gift of the artist, 2019
Collection of Confederation Centre Art Gallery, Charlottetown, PE
CAG 2019.11 a-x

Why, 2001 (p. 33)
acrylic on board
58.4 × 53.3 cm

Ya, 2001 (p. 32)
acrylic on board
91.5 × 91.5 cm

**SeXY* (diptych), 2002 (p. 34)
acrylic on oil blackboard paint
111.8 × 111.8 cm each

**You and Me*, 2002 (p. 34)
acrylic on oil blackboard paint
66 × 48.3 cm

Bear Girl, 2003 (p. 72)
plaster
30.5 × 20.3 × 12.7 cm

Dazzled, 2003 (p. 35)
oil on wood and plaster
30. 5 × 22.9 × 22.9 cm

Donkey Girl, 2003 (p. 72)
bronze
35.6 × 12.7 × 15.3 cm

Donkey Girl, 2003 (p. 71)
plaster
35.6 × 12.7 × 15.3 cm

Grand Prix, 2004 (p. 74)
oil on wood and plaster
30. 5 × 22.9 × 22.9 cm

Line of Scrimmage, 2004 (p. 36)
oil on board
61 × 61 cm

Slapshot, 2004
oil on board
61 × 61 cm

**...they often tend to resemble plants*, 2004 (p. 40)
ink on paper
destroyed

Tight End, 2004 (p. 75)
oil on wood and plaster
30. 5 × 22.9 × 22.9 cm

Victory Lane, 2004
oil on board
61 × 61 cm

Camouflesh Great Britain I, 2005 (p. 38)
oil on board
61.1 × 61.2 cm
Gift of Sue Wolstenholme, Hantsport, NS, 2012
Collection of the Art Gallery of Nova Scotia
2012.145

Camouflesh Great Britain II, 2005 (p. 39)
oil on board
61.1 × 61.2 cm
Gift of Sue Wolstenholme, Hantsport, NS, 2012
Collection of the Art Gallery of Nova Scotia
2012.146

Camouflesh Finland, 2005 (p. 96)
oil on board
61.1 × 61.2 cm
Gift of Sue Wolstenholme, Hantsport, NS, 2012
Collection of the Art Gallery of Nova Scotia
2012.147

Camouflesh USA, 2005 (p. 37)
oil on board
61.1 × 61.2 cm
Gift of Sue Wolstenholme, Hantsport, NS, 2012
Collection of the Art Gallery of Nova Scotia
2012.148

Homesse, 2005 (p. 41)
archival inkjet on paper with polyester bias tape
304.8 × 304.8 cm
Gift of the artist, 2007
Collection of Confederation Centre Art Gallery, Charlottetown, PE
CAG 2007.15.1

Triad, 2005 (p. 70)
Hydrocal plaster, fibreglass mesh, and polished wax
132.1 × 86.4 × 58.4 cm each
Gift of the artist, Hantsport, Nova Scotia, 2012
Collection of the National Gallery of Canada
45637.1-3

Original, 2005–06 (p. 4)
archival inkjet on paper with polyester bias tape
132.1 × 132.1 cm

Sugar and Spice, 2007 (p. 43)
bronze
217.6 × 217.6 × 2.7 cm
Purchased 2009
Collection of the National Gallery of Canada
42915

Abrams Tank, 2010 (p. 60)
embroidery cotton on canvas
40.7 × 45.8 (framed)
Collection of Gillian McCain, New York

Exposé, 2010 (pp. 6, 73)
plaster, wood, PVC pipe, fibrefill, canvas, antique settee
121.9 cm × 81.3 cm × 183 cm
Gift of the artist
Collection of the Beaverbrook Art Gallery

Wolverine Heavy Assault Bridge, 2010-26 (p. 106)
embroidery cotton on canvas
30.5 × 45.8 cm
Collection of Gillian McCain, New York

Neuraesthezia (with Gillian McCain), 2011 (pp. 44, 45, 46–47)
mixed media
Dimensions variable

Undercover, 2011 (pp. 74–75)
ceramic and wood
30.5 × 124.5 × 10.2 cm

Hexagonal Matrix, 2015 (p. 78)
powder-coated steel
213.4 × 182. 9 cm

Wind Algorithm 1, 2017 (p. 66)
ink on paper
77 × 112 cm

Wind Algorithm 2, 2017 (p. 67)
ink on paper
77 × 112 cm

Wind Algorithm 3, 2017 (p. 68)
ink on paper
77 × 112 cm

A Month of the Air I Breathe, 2018 (p. 16)
inkjet on paper
139.7 × 259.1 cm

A Year of the Air I Breathe, 2018 (p. 15)
video
4 minutes

Hexagraphy, 2018 (pp. 52–53, 54–55)
mixed media
152.4 × 213.4 × 25.4

Spatial Anomaly, 2018 (p. 79)
powder-coated steel
99.1 × 94 × 68.6 cm

Untitled (Kelp 1), 2021 (p. 102)
ink on paper
35.6 × 43.2 cm

Untitled (Kelp 2), 2021 (p. 102)
ink on paper
35.6 × 43.2 cm

Untitled (Sea Floor 1), 2021
ink on paper
35.6 × 43.2 cm

Untitled (Sea Floor 2), 2021 (p. 102)
ink on paper
35.6 × 43.2 cm

Untitled (Sea Floor 3), 2021 (p. 102)
ink on paper
43.2 × 35.6 cm

Untitled (Sea Floor 4), 2021
ink on paper
43.2 × 35.6 cm

Untitled (Sea Floor 5), 2021
ink on paper
35.6 × 43.2 cm

Abell 2744, 2023 (p. 100)
oil on board
61 × 99.1 cm

Benthic Ctenophore, 2023 (p. 93)
oil on board
43.2 × 76.2 cm

Bloody-Belly Comb Jelly, 2023 (p. 90)
oil on board
121.9 × 99.1 cm

Deep Space 1, 2023 (p. 98)
oil on board
61 × 99.1 cm

Diplulmaris Antarctica, 2023 (p. 89)
oil on board
121.9 × 99.1 cm

Glass Octopus, 2023 (p. 91)
oil on board
121.9 × 99.1 cm

Helmet Jellyfish, 2023 (p. 87)
oil on board
121.9 × 99.1 cm

Holothurian, 2023 (p. 92)
oil on board
121.9 × 99.1 cm

Into the Deep Blue Sea: Triptych 1 (Piglet Squid, Ctenophore, Jelly), 2023 (p. 49)
oil on board
124.5 × 66.1 cm

Into the Deep Blue Sea: Triptych 2 (Bloody-Belly Jelly, Barreleye Fish, Lobate Ctenophore), 2023 (p. 50)
oil on board
124.5 × 66.1 cm

Into the Deep Blue Sea: Triptych 3 (Siphonophore 3, Bloody-Belly Jelly 2, Siphonophore), 2023 (p. 84)
oil on board
124.5 × 66.1 cm

Into the Deep Blue Sea: Triptych 4 (Tethys Vagina, Jelly 3, Yellow Ctenophore), 2023 (p. 85)
oil on board
124.5 × 66.1 cm

Into the Deep Blue Sea: Triptych 5 (Ribbon Fish, Pink Ctenophore, Striped Squid), 2023 (p. 86)
oil on board
124.5 × 66.1 cm

Lobate Ctenophore, 2023 (pp. 94–95)
oil on board
43.2 × 76.2 cm

MACSO416, 2023 (p. 101)
oil on board
61 × 99.1 cm

Barreleye Fish, 2024 (p. 88)
oil on board
61 cm diam.

Bathyphysa Siphonophore, 2024 (p. 88)
oil on board
61 cm diam.

Deep Space 2, 2024 (p. 99)
oil on board
61 × 99.1 cm

Flying Spaghetti Monster, 2024 (p. 103)
oil on board
61 cm diam.

Glass Squid 2, 2024 (p. 88)
oil on board
61 cm diam.

Pelagic Polychaete, 2024 (p. 103)
oil on board
61 cm diam.

Radiolarian, 2024 (p. 103)
oil on board
61 cm diam.

Radiolarian B, 2024 (p. 103)
oil on board
61 cm diam.

Solmissus Jelly, 2024 (p. 88)
oil on board
61 cm diam.

Untitled (Kelp), 2024 (pp. 56–57, 61, 112, 114)
mixed media, 3 units
457.2 × 7.6 cm each

Clouds, 2025
plaster and mixed media (3 units)
61 cm diam × 16.5;
61 cm diam × 14;
61 cm diam × 7.6

The Penguin and the Egg, 2025 (p. 104, 119)
oil on board
91.5 cm diam.

SN1987A, 2025 (p. 105)
oil on board
91.5 cm diam.

Untitled (Sea Snow Projection), 2025
video
Continuous video projection

Apkalu, 2026
porcelain
40.6 × 15.3 × 19 cm

Holy Cow, 2026
porcelain
58 × 20.3 × 22.8 cm

Oil Futures (Emojis), 2026
embroidery cotton on canvas
26 × 34 cm

Pill Mandala (Beverly Hills), 2026 (p. 76)
inkjet on paper
76.2 × 91.4 cm

Pill Mandala (Marilyn), 2026
inkjet on paper
76.2 × 91.4 cm

Pill Mandala (Oh La La), 2026 (p. 76)
inkjet on paper
76.2 × 91.4 cm

The Penguin and the Egg (detail), 2025

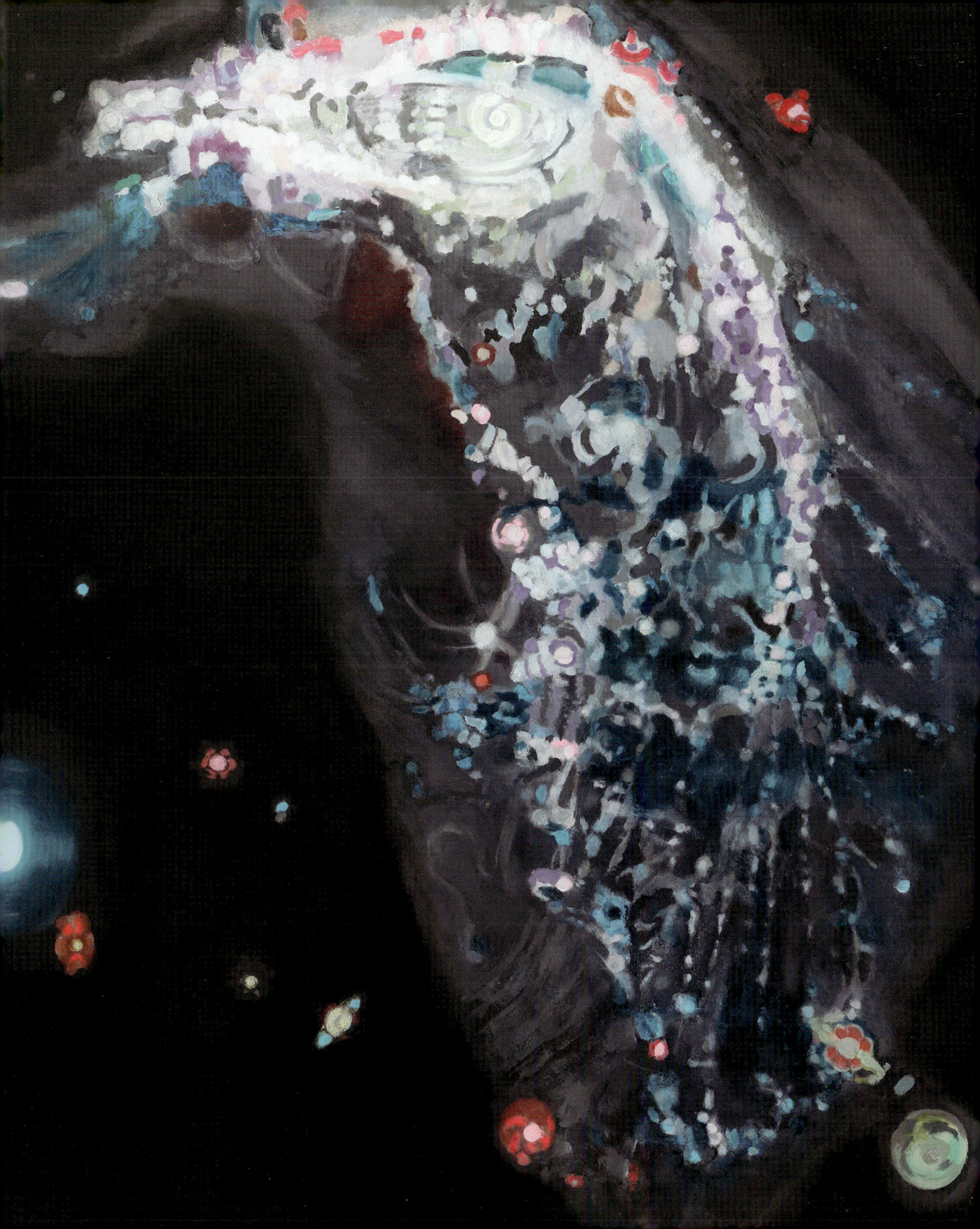

Published in conjunction with the exhibition *Colleen Wolstenholme: Hyperobjectivity* organized by the Beaverbrook Art Gallery, June 20, 2026–November 1, 2026.

Edited by Paula Sarson.
Cover and page design by Julie Scriver.
Cover: Colleen Wolstenholme, *Exposé*, 2010, 121.9 × 81.3 × 183 cm, plaster, wood, PVC pipe, fibrefill, canvas, antique settee. Collection of the Beaverbrook Art Gallery. Gift of the artist.
Back cover: (top) Colleen Wolstenholme, *Leritine*, 1997, carved plaster, 17.78 x 53.34 cm diam. Collection of the artist; (bottom): Colleen Wolstenholme, *Glass Squid 2*, 2024, oil on board, 61 cm diam. Collection of the artist.
Frontispiece: Tasha Kostyuk, unsplash.com.
Printed in Canada by Friesens.
10 9 8 7 6 5 4 3 2 1

Library and Archives Canada Cataloguing in Publication

Title: Colleen Wolstenholme : hyperobjectivity / Ray Cronin and Laura J. Ritchie.
Other titles: Colleen Wolstenholme (2026) | Hyperobjectivity
Names: Container of (work): Wolstenholme, Colleen. Works. Selections. | Cronin, Ray, 1964- writer of added commentary. | Ritchie, Laura, writer of added commentary. | Beaverbrook Art Gallery, host institution, publisher. | Art Gallery of Nova Scotia, publisher.
Description: Catalog of an exhibition held at the Beaverbrook Art Gallery in Fredericton from June 20 to November 1, 2026. | Issued also in French under title : Colleen Wolstenholme : hyperobjectivité. | Includes bibliographical references.
Identifiers: Canadiana 20250311771 | ISBN 9781773104546 (hardcover)
Subjects: LCSH: Wolstenholme, Colleen—Exhibitions. | LCGFT: Exhibition catalogs.
Classification: LCC N6549.W642 A4 2026 | DDC 709.2—dc23

Goose Lane Editions acknowledges the generous support of the Government of Canada, the Canada Council for the Arts, and the Government of New Brunswick.

Goose Lane Editions and the Beaverbrook Art Gallery are located on the unceded territory of the Wəlastəkwiyik whose ancestors along with the Mi'kmaq and Peskotomuhkati Nations signed Peace and Friendship Treaties with the British Crown in the 1700s.

Goose Lane Editions
500 Beaverbrook Court, Suite 330
Fredericton, New Brunswick
CANADA E3B 5X4
gooselane.com

Beaverbrook Art Gallery
703 Queen Street
Fredericton, New Brunswick
CANADA E3B 1C4
beaverbrookartgallery.org

Art Gallery of Nova Scotia
1723 Hollis Street
Halifax, Nova Scotia
CANADA B3J 1V9
agns.ca

Photo Credits:

Michael Alago: 22

Doone Anderson: 60

Art Gallery of Nova Scotia: 20, 31

Beaverbrook Art Gallery: cover, 4, 10, 19, 26, 28, 30, 32, 33, 36, 62–63, 64, 65, 71, 72 (*Bear Girl*), 73, 76, 98, 99, 100, 101, 104, 105, 106, back cover (top)

Cambridge Art Galleries/Scott Lee: 58

Confederation Centre Art Gallery: 27, 41

National Gallery of Canada: 43, 70

Mike Patten: 6, 15, 16, 35, 44, 45, 46, 49, 50, 52–53, 55, 56–57, 61, 66, 67, 68, 72 (*Donkey Girl*), 74, 75, 78, 79, 84, 85, 86, 87, 88, 89 (*Solmissus Jelly*, *Bathyphysa Siphonophore*, *Barreleye Fish*), 90, 91, 92, 93, 102, 103 (*Flying Spaghetti Monster*, *Radiolarian*, *Pelagic Polychaete*), 112, 114, back cover (bottom)

RAW Photography: 9, 37, 38, 39, 96

Colleen Wolstenholme: 23, 29, 34, 40, 89 (*Glass Squid 2*), 94–95, 103 (*Radiolarian B*)